CLASS WARS

CLASS WARS

Money, Schools and Power in Modern Australia

TONY TAYLOR

© Copyright 2018 Tony Taylor
All rights reserved. Apart from any uses permitted by Australia's Copyright Act 1968, no part of this book may be reproduced by any process without prior written permission from the copyright owners. Inquiries should be directed to the publisher.

Monash University Publishing
Matheson Library and Information Services Building
40 Exhibition Walk
Monash University
Clayton, Victoria 3800, Australia
www.publishing.monash.edu

Monash University Publishing brings to the world publications which advance the best traditions of humane and enlightened thought.

Monash University Publishing titles pass through a rigorous process of independent peer review.

ISBN: 978-1-925495-46-1 (paperback)
ISBN: 978-1-925495-48-5 (pdf)
ISBN: 978-1-925495-51-5 (epub)

www.publishing.monash.edu/books/cw-9781925495461.html

Series: Monash Studies in Australian Society

Design: Les Thomas

 A catalogue record for this book is available from the National Library of Australia

Printed in Australia by Griffin Press an Accredited ISO AS/NZS 14001:2004 Environmental Management System printer.

 The paper this book is printed on is certified against the Forest Stewardship Council ® Standards. Griffin Press holds FSC chain of custody certification SGS-COC-005088. FSC promotes environmentally responsible, socially beneficial and economically viable management of the world's forests

CONTENTS

Acknowledgements vii

Preamble ix

Introduction xi

1   The Goulburn Myth, Social Justice and the Menzies Gesture 1962–63 1

2   Snob Value: The Menzies Gesture and Educating for Inequality 31

3   The Gorton Style and Better-Established Schools 45

4   Malcolm Fraser: Let's Pitch It a Little Higher and See How We Get On 61

5   The Whitlam Government: The Chance to Put Their Schemes into Practice 87

6   The Schools Commission: Too Radical, Too Expensive, and Likely to Raise Expectations Too High 109

7   The Schools Commission and the Liberal Way of Progress . . . 129

8   The Hawke-Ryan Years: We Don't Want any Brawls 159

9   Minister Kemp and the Socio-Economic Status System: A Complete Corruption 187

10 Julia Gillard and Irresponsible, Untruthful Fear Campaigns . . . 219

11 Christopher Pyne: Blowing Himself and the Gonski Reforms to Pieces 249

12 Simon Birmingham: Still on a Path to Nowhere? 269

Conclusion 287

Bibliography 301

Index 305

ACKNOWLEDGEMENTS

This project was originally inspired by a request from Monash University Publishing's director Nathan Hollier to write a book on Australia's contentious school funding issue. I owe Nathan for that offer, and for his patience, as the scope of the book went from the original 1996–2017 timeline to a revised timeline of 1962–2017. The book itself is a high-politics study of a major Australian political controversy. In writing about such a difficult and divisive topic I have tried to deal predominantly with motivation and causal relationships behind the political actions that took place after the introduction of direct Commonwealth funding to schools in 1963. The book focuses on New South Wales in the early stages of the narrative since that state had the lengthiest and most direct engagement with Canberra on the issue. I have used newspapers of record (mainly *The Sydney Morning Herald*) as a major source as well as the usual published sources and some unpublished sources. The book has also drawn on the work of, and correspondence with, scholars, writers and activists in the fields of Australian politics and education.

As cited in the footnotes, correspondents included Dean Ashenden, Brian Croke, Van Davy, Jane Kenway, Barry Lamb, Paul Mishura and Jim McMorrow. I thank them for their time and views. I am grateful too for the unstinting assistance provided by library and archival staff at *Catholic Weekly*, my local university campus of Federation University Australia (particularly the wonderful BONUS+ system), the National Library of Australia, Scotch College (Melbourne) and the State Library of Victoria. I am also grateful to the University of Technology Sydney and to Federation University Australia for offering me appointments as adjunct professor. An Australian Research Council Discovery Grant supported several chapters in this book. I owe a debt of thanks also to former colleagues Anna Clark, who read and commented on an early draft, and Sue Collins, whose careful reading of successive drafts, combined with forthright opinion, improved the work considerably. I acknowledge the value of former colleague Sue Leslie's meticulous reading of the penultimate draft and the painstaking work of professional editor Duncan Fardon. I am also grateful for the expert analysis and commentary of Frank Bongiorno and Stuart Macintyre, who read the penultimate version.

I dedicate this work to my wife Scilla and to our children Kate, Sam and Dan, all of whom have benefited in different ways from attending a mix of schools, both government and non-government.

My own schooling was courtesy of the Northern Irish and English parochial systems and of De La Salle College, Pendleton, Manchester.

PREAMBLE

On 2 May 2017, in a surprise policy reversal, Liberal prime minister Malcolm Turnbull publicly announced his government's new plan to introduce a sector-blind and needs-based Commonwealth school funding model. A confident Turnbull was flanked by Simon Birmingham, the Coalition government's education minister, and by David Gonski, the architect of a previous Labor government's failed needs-based funding scheme known as 'the Gonski plan'. Turnbull promised that 'Gonski 2.0' would mark the end of 'the school funding wars', a series of intense and socially divisive conflicts that had beset modern Australian politics for over half a century.

Turnbull's apparent confidence about peace replacing war was misplaced. Australian Labor Party (ALP) education spokesperson Tanya Plibersek called the new plan 'an act of political bastardry'. The Australian Education Union vice president condemned the proposed policy on the grounds that it was non-consultative. The Greens threatened to withhold their support in the Senate unless the government came up with more money. Vocal elements within the powerful Catholic education sector complained bitterly that their schools would lose out. Former prime minister Tony Abbott began a campaign within the Coalition ranks to undermine Turnbull's policy. The wars, which had their origins in a Commonwealth Coalition government decision made in October 1963, were not over yet.

INTRODUCTION

In mid-October 1963 Robert Menzies, leader of the Australian Liberal Party and prime minister in charge of a conservative coalition government elected in 1961, made a not very surprising announcement: there would be an early House of Representatives election in late November. Menzies needed to improve his existing lower house majority of just two MPs, and the narrowness of that majority had led to election speculation in the press as early as June that year.[1] A fortnight after giving notice of his snap election Menzies then made an announcement that was surprising. The prime minister declared that he was about to provide a limited amount of Commonwealth funding for secondary school science facilities and for senior scholarships. The money would be made available for all schools including those of the Catholic Church. This offer of direct state aid to Catholic schools was unprecedented.

The precarious nature of Menzies' majority had mainly been a consequence of electoral anger over the so-called 'Holt Jolt', Treasurer Harold Holt's unprecedented 1961 credit squeeze. The growing popularity of Arthur Calwell too as new leader of a seemingly less divided ALP played a part in Menzies' anxiety. Calwell, an old-school Catholic ALP politician with old-fashioned White Australia views was in charge of a party that had been badly split by the defection of many Catholic members during the 1955 creation of the pro-state-aid Australian Labor Party (Anti-Communist). Two years later the

---

[1] 'The Coming Budget and Possible Early Election', *Sydney Morning Herald*, 25 June 1963.

splitters became the Democratic Labour Party (DLP), a group whose pro-Liberal voting preferences were to be crucial in keeping the ALP out of national office for fifteen years (1957–72).

As for the Catholics in general, Australia's large community of more than two million adherents had a history of self-sufficiency when it came to education funding, a tradition that went back to the 1880s. Over time, this separatist approach had turned out to be self-damaging. By the early 1960s, diocesan Catholic schools were in a precarious financial position and members of the Catholic community were clamouring for financial aid from the states and the Commonwealth. There was however certain to be strong hostility to any such move from conservative Protestant and secular ALP opinion. There was also a potential constitutional obstacle to the Commonwealth's capacity to give direct aid to the Catholics. Ostensibly, Section 116 of the Australian Constitution prevented the Commonwealth Government from funding religious schools, on the grounds that giving Commonwealth money to the Catholics would be regarded as preferential treatment to a religious denomination.

There had been relevant historical precedents. For example, in Ireland, the most Catholic nation of all, the National School system, established in 1831, offered non-denominational education to all school students, majority Catholics and minority Protestants alike. The major denominations were able to operate schools within the National Board's 'moral and literary' curriculum while receiving financial support, as long as religious instruction in each school was separate, voluntary and in accord with parental wishes. In effect this meant that while almost all Board schools were administered by the Catholic Church and catered to mainly Catholic students, Protestant students could be withdrawn for separate religious instruction in

INTRODUCTION

those schools. Despite some attempts by the Church to gain state recognition of what was essentially a state-funded Catholic system with Protestant elements, the Irish national system lasted in Ireland – and in its successor nation the Republic of Ireland – until 1965.

When Northern Ireland, with its Protestant majority and 300-year history of violent sectarian differences, seceded from a newly independent Ireland in 1920, Protestant-run schools were to become state-run 'county schools', and Catholic-run schools were to be voluntarily-run with some state assistance. This arrangement met with opposition or indifference from both denominations. Subsequent attempts to move towards non-denominational state schools were blocked by hardline Protestant opinion, which wanted Bible teaching in all state-funded county schools as well as local (effectively Protestant) control over teaching appointments. Parish-based Catholic schools were to be voluntarily supported with some state assistance. By the 1930s, Northern Ireland had a dual system of better-off, state-supported Protestant county schools and less well-off Catholic voluntary schools, an arrangement which lasted until 1968, the year before the Troubles began – a conflict that was to last until the 1998 Belfast (or Good Friday) Agreement. During that period 1969–98 an estimated 3600 people were killed and 40,000 injured, an outcome of Northern Ireland's long history of sectarian differences and imposed social and political inequality.

While Scotland too was a nation that exhibited strong sectarian differences, it had not, since the eighteenth century at least, suffered from a purposely divisive rule from London. At a time when the introduction of mass elementary education had become a necessary feature of industrialising societies, secular elementary education in Scotland was provided in 1872 by the terms of the Education

(Scotland) Act, which established a network of non-denominational elementary board schools. As was the case in Australia, the Catholic bishops of Scotland opted out of that particular arrangement. They objected to government oversight, an absence of Catholic religious instruction, and possible Church of Scotland (Protestant) evangelising in their parochial schools. In 1918, following almost half a century of under-funded voluntary educational provision for a rapidly expanding Catholic population in the west and central Lowlands, the Scottish bishops accepted state aid and agreed to open their schools to all students and accept state supervision. These state-supported and voluntary-aided schools operated alongside non-denominational board schools, as remains the case today.

England and Wales (the latter governed from Whitehall until 1998) faced similar educational problems to Scotland when it came to religious matters. In 1870, to deal with the growing educational needs of a rapidly industrialising England and Wales, a progressive Liberal government passed the Elementary Education Act. The provisions of that Act led to the funding of universal elementary education to be administered by local non-denominational school boards supervised by Whitehall. These schools were in general shunned by the Catholic community, which continued to work on its separate program of late nineteenth-century school expansion. In 1902, Conservative and Unionist education minister Arthur Balfour brought in an education measure which became known as Balfour's Act, abolishing school boards, creating local education authorities in their place and offering local authority rate aid support to all denominational 'non-provided schools' in an effort to support Anglican schools and offset the secularist tone of Board schools.

INTRODUCTION

The inclusion of Catholic schools in this voluntary aided system caused uproar, particularly among the Nonconformist churches (mainly the Presbyterian, Methodist, Unitarian, Congregationalist and Baptist congregations), powerful opponents of 'Rome on the Rates'. A pro-secularist and progressive Liberal Party also opposed Balfour's measure on different grounds: that it offered state aid to any religious school. Nevertheless, despite a furore which lasted for four years and which contributed to the defeat of the Conservative and Unionist government in 1906, the Balfour Act remained in place as the first piece of legislation in England and Wales that provided state aid to Catholic schools. These state-aid provisions were later modified as a minor part of the progressive 1944 Education Act to increase funding for Anglican and Catholic schools as 'voluntary aided' establishments. At the same time, all school students in state-funded schools were obliged to begin the day with an ecumenical Christian 'collective act of worship', a practice that was to fall in to disuse by the 1970s.

In summary, the state-aid issue was resolved by compromise in England and Wales by 1902, and in Scotland by 1918. In Northern Ireland and Australia, sectarian educational differences were still unresolved in 1963.

This meant that, prior to his November 1963 announcement, Menzies seemed to be blocked both politically and constitutionally from giving the Catholics any Commonwealth assistance. Not that he had given any recent indications of wanting to take such a step. On the contrary, Menzies had publicly rejected the idea on several occasions. In late 1963, however, he bypassed the constitutional hurdle by announcing that he would make available Commonwealth funds worth £9 million per annum for three years for science facilities and scholarships for *all* Australian secondary schools, thus avoiding any hint of preferential treatment.

There was certainly a need for some kind of Commonwealth intervention in school funding, amidst talk of an 'education crisis'.[2] The Catholic school system, which educated just over 20 per cent of all Australian students, was faced by five major issues. The first of these was rapid post-war student population growth of two kinds, Irish-descent students and 'New Australian' migrant students, many of whom came from Catholic Italy. Secondly, while traditionally it had been the Church's religious orders who had provided unsalaried teachers to Australia's Catholic schools, after the war the proportion of salaried lay teachers in Catholic schools had been steadily rising. By 1959, 20 per cent of unsalaried teaching nuns, brothers, or priests in New South Wales had been replaced by salaried teachers. Bearing in mind the age demographic of the religious staff, a rise in salary costs was a problem that was unlikely to go away. Indeed, by 1965 that percentage of salaried teachers rose to 31 per cent and by 1970, 50 per cent.[3] A third problem for a Catholic education sector that had traditionally focused on primary education was the additional cost of providing 'secondary education for all', a post-war slogan that drove secondary school expansion in Australia.

A fourth problem occurred in the major cities, where metropolitan Catholic schools were burdened with small, outdated and decaying inner-city buildings clustered in areas of declining population. To

---

[2] 'Aust. Education "Second Rate," Conference Told', *Sydney Morning Herald*, 22 May 1958, and 'A.L.P. Committee Sees Serious Crisis In Australian Education', *Sydney Morning Herald*, 14 June 1962.

[3] See, K. Canavan, 'The Quiet Revolution in Catholic Schooling in Australia', *Journal of Catholic Education*, 2 (1) p.52. Catholic schools in the other jurisdictions faced the same problem.

INTRODUCTION

compound the issue, some primary schools had declining school numbers while others had overcrowded classrooms, a difficult resource planning issue. The main urban population growth area for Catholics (and others) was in the new suburban fringes of the major cities – a phenomenon that required the building of new schools at heavy cost. Finally, there was the general decay of older school buildings in regional or rural dioceses that had very limited capacity to raise money for renovations. In 1957, for example, Mother Celestine, principal of Our Lady of Mercy Preparatory School in Goulburn, had been told by the registration section of the state education department that if she wanted the school to stay in business then the Catholic authorities would have to build five additional brick lavatory cubicles for her infant boys. The state education department's report stated that the existing three cubicles were in poor condition and inadequate. Mother Celestine and the local Goulburn diocese claimed there was no money for the work and said the state should fund the renovations. A nationally famous dispute ensued, lasting five years.

Government schools were generally better off than their Catholic equivalents but they did have their own problems. Nationally, Australian public education was straining to deal with a rapid post-war rise in population that included the baby-boomer generation and Australia's post-war influx of non-Catholic European migrants.[4] In New South Wales, the majority of the state's government primary schools contained classes of more than forty students, with 10 per cent

---

[4] There had been a 72 per cent increase in New South Wales students since 1944, according to ALP state premier and education minister Robert 'Bob' Heffron, writing in 1959. See 'Big Increase in Enrolments at Public Schools', *Sydney Morning Herald*, 1 January 1959. In New South Wales an additional 20,000 migrant students per annum had needed places 1954–58. See 'N.S.W. Schools Still Need More Teachers', *Sydney Morning Herald*, 9 December, 1959.

of kindergarten classes containing 50 to 60. The growing secondary school sector too had overcrowding, a result of teacher shortages, a rising tide of student numbers and school leavers returning to school after having failed to find work.

In an effort to deal with the state's expanding student population, successive New South Wales governments had poured money into the construction of new schools, quadrupling its loans for school building over 1951–59. In its haste to build new schools, however, the state government neglected the older schools, many of which were dilapidated and unsuited to the demands of mid-twentieth-century educational practice. Not only that, the government had neglected teachers' working conditions. In August 1958 a teacher at a New South Wales Teachers' Federation conference pointed out that New South Wales was the only state in Australia that did not supply lavatory paper to its schools. He explained, 'In our school we [each] pay about 3/6 a term to buy toilet paper – but we do it grudgingly.'[5] The conference passed resolutions demanding that the education department provide separate rooms for classes, staff dining rooms, central heating, convenient toilet facilities and fire-fighting equipment.

On the other side of the social divide, the wealthy and selective New South Wales non-government schools of the 1950s and the 1960s existed in a separate world. Although they received no government aid, they could rely on donations, bequests, fundraising activities and school fees to deal with rising student numbers, with the increasingly expensive requirements of the state's secondary curriculum and even with the increasingly stringent health and sanitary regulations of the

---

[5] '3/6' is three shillings and sixpence, slightly less than one sixth of a pound.

INTRODUCTION

state authorities. In contrast to the Catholic schools, struggling to provide even lavatories, and to government school staff being obliged to provide their own lavatory paper, these elite schools could by private effort and endowment expand and improve their facilities and services.

This was the educational landscape that faced Menzies when he decided to intervene in school education in late 1963: Catholic school systems across the nation in decay, government school systems scarcely coping with increased demographic and curricular demands, and the wealthier independent schools standing aloof and comfortably above it all. Why did Menzies, who had already been contemplating retirement from politics for two years, take on the new and potentially difficult educational challenge of bringing in direct state aid to all schools? After all, government schools were the responsibility of state governments, Catholic diocesan schools were the responsibility of the Church, and the other wealthier non-government schools were largely responsible for themselves.[6]

There is a commonly accepted explanation for the prime minister's decision … Menzies, having in 1962 witnessed sectarian strife over state aid to Catholic schools in Goulburn, became anxious about the financial viability of Catholic education in Australia. Were this system to collapse, a huge fiscal and resource burden would be placed on the states and possibly on the Commonwealth. Accordingly, Menzies established a funding precedent that would help stabilise the finances of Catholic schools and provide an equitable benefit to both independent and government secondary schools. At the same time,

---

[6] There was an exception. Government schools in the Australian Capital Territory were the responsibility of the Commonwealth.

the decision would help his government garner second-preference votes of the predominantly Catholic members of the DLP.[7]

There is, however, a different explanation for these events. To begin with, the Goulburn incident's connection with Menzies turns out to be more myth than reality. The prime minister's decision had a much broader context than has been generally recognised. Moreover, the Menzies promise to deliver a just measure of state aid to all Australian schools was not an even-handed funding initiative. Over time, and by increments, that Menzies reform, outwardly fair but in reality inequitable, was to change into a Coalition funding policy of increasingly preferencing non-government schools.

Menzies' immediate motivation for changing his mind in 1963 was simple. After the war, he had developed a special interest in science education and wanted to improve funding opportunities for science facilities in the mainly Protestant, self-funded independent schools. To do this he was compelled to give the same degree of funding to the Catholic systemic schools to get around the Constitution's Section 116. Such a manoeuvre could, in the short term, attract voting preferences, not that he placed any great weight on that speculative thought.[8] Menzies was much more interested in the long-term prospect of broadening the base of the Liberal Party by attracting supporters from outside the party's traditional middle-class Protestant community.

---

[7] See for example prominent conservative Catholic commentator Miranda Devine's article, 'Latham trips on "them" to reach us', *Sydney Morning Herald*, 16 Sept 2004, and a commemorative feature article by fellow conservative Catholic commentator Gerard Henderson, 'The lessons of Goulburn resonate in schools 50 years later', *Sydney Morning Herald*, 21 August 2012. See also '1963 Election', *George Negus Tonight*, ABC Television, 4 October 2004.

[8] DLP support was also valuable to the Coalition in the Senate from 1955 to 1958, 1961 to 1964 and 1964 to 1967. After 1967 the DLP disappeared from the Senate and its national vote declined sharply from the early 1970s onwards.

INTRODUCTION

Giving money to Catholic schools for restricted and uncontroversial purposes was a start. Menzies was also obliged to give funding to state government schools, again to meet the terms of Section 116, but these schools were largely irrelevant to his strategic thinking.

To put it simply, before his planned retirement in 1966, Menzies was to offer limited, short-term but very useful assistance to mainly Protestant independent schools, many of which were wealthy but some of which were not. He was also offering short-term state aid to struggling Catholic schools for political reasons, and short-term aid to state schools because he had to.[9] In doing so, Menzies gained an immediate but evanescent preference benefit for his government, but more importantly he had begun the process of providing long-term Commonwealth benefits to Australia's elite schools and tying his party more closely to Australia's Catholic community. As for the Catholic schools, Commonwealth assistance with laboratories and scholarships was to prove inadequate. By the late 1970s, the Catholic schools were still in deep financial trouble.

Australia's public education system too remained in trouble during the 1960s, but almost all of its money came from the states. They were the government school bankers and were unlikely to go broke.

This revised interpretation of the Menzies state-aid decision is one theme of this book, a point of view that runs against conventional explanations of the history of state funding for schools. In late 1963 the prime minister was chiefly interested in helping out the kinds of school with which he was familiar as an independent school alumnus and which provided the Liberal Party with a majority of

---

[9] The grants were not indexed and after renewals were terminated, as were the scholarships in 1974 and the capital grants in 1975. The long-term benefits for elite schools came with the recurrent grants system that began operating in 1970.

its politicians and a large number of its voters. Menzies was also interested in attracting Catholic votes for the Liberals despite opposition to state aid from Protestant opinion and from official ALP policy, the former for anti-Catholic sectarian reasons and the latter for secular anti-religious reasons.

As the Commonwealth funding system was to develop, change and expand under a series of Coalition governments, the ratio between state and Commonwealth funding altered. When the new capital funding system was set up in 1964 for implementation in 1965, government schools (approximately 75 per cent of total students) were to receive 75 per cent of Commonwealth funding and the non-government sector was to receive the remaining 25 per cent. By 2014, the fiftieth anniversary of the legislation that provided the first Commonwealth grants, the ratio was reversed, with non-government schools receiving more than 64 per cent of Commonwealth funding for their student population of 35 per cent. This trend has exacerbated sectoral and political differences about education funding that continue to divide Australian political opinion.[10]

These current differences of opinion are just the latest stage in an internecine and partisan conflict over funding schools that goes back more than a century and a half. As ALP elder Graham Freudenberg memorably described, 'the oldest, deepest, most poisonous debate in Australian history (is) about government aid to Church schools. The mystic incantation "state aid" has broken governors, governments, parties, families and friendships throughout our history'.[11]

---

[10] See 'School education: expenditure. Budget Review 2013-14', www.aph.gov.au/About_Parliament/Parliamentary_Departments/ Parliamentary_Library/pubs/rp/BudgetReview201314/SchoolExpend.

[11] G. Freudenberg, *A Certain Grandeur: Gough Whitlam's Life in Politics*, Macmillan Melbourne, 1977 edition, p.24.

INTRODUCTION

Initially to do with the politics of class and Protestant versus Catholic sectarianism (1830–1963), subsequently the conflict became more about secularism versus religion (1945–63) and, later, private versus public sector schooling (1964–2017), with the last of these three affected by the politics of action and retaliation. Freudenberg's most poisonous debate remains an entrenched dispute with no clear winner and no end in sight.

This book is an investigation of how this ideologically-driven contest developed in modern Australia as a series of tactical and strategic political struggles that continue to ill serve the majority of Australia's children. *Class Wars* will attempt to explain the motivations, the actions and the consequences of the policies of the major political figures involved.

As part of this investigation, the important role that social justice (natural and distributive) has played in maintaining this social divide will be examined. Such an assertion about the negative role of social justice may seem contradictory since it is normally associated with the socially cohesive rather than the socially contentious side of politics. Matters will become clearer as the reader discovers that in Australia there are three conflicting views about social justice when it comes to school funding.

The first of these is based on the Liberal Party's development over time of an ideological rationale for Commonwealth and state support for non-government schools. This position is based on a conservative worldview that social justice is a matter of individual freedom to choose a school, and that an exclusive and meritocratic academic culture is preferable to an open entry and egalitarian vision.

The second approach is the progressive social justice perspective of the Labor Party. To mid-twentieth-century Labor supporters, secular public education was a benefit that should be available to all, including the disadvantaged, the disabled and the marginalised. Moreover, public education was a national investment that required a substantial and unstinting contribution from all taxpayers, who had a duty to contribute to a general social benefit.

A third point of view is the Catholic position on social justice. In this case, the argument is that in a democracy – and within the law – a religious denomination has unique and inalienable social rights. One of these rights is the provision, where practicable, of a denominationally-based education. The children of taxpaying Catholics have a right to receive Commonwealth funding for these schools.

The rise in social and political status of Australia's sizeable Catholic community during the period 1963–2017 is explored. This rise that has principally been brought about by the improved educational, social and political status of members of the Catholic community as well as by the Catholic hierarchy's highly politicised involvement in educational politics. As recently as 1963, many Australian Catholics, particularly those of Irish descent, were shut out of the Protestant ascendancy that had run federal politics since 1901. In contrast, by 2017, Australia had witnessed the comings and goings of three Catholic prime ministers (a converted Kevin Rudd, Tony Abbott and a converted Malcolm Turnbull) during a ten-year period. Not only that, Tony Abbott's 2014 Cabinet of nineteen ministers contained eight Catholics. Furthermore, between 2013–17, two Catholic Liberal education ministers were appointed: Christopher Pyne and Simon Birmingham. The rise of this twenty-first-century Catholic elite in Australia, with its close hierarchical ties to the Liberal Party, is due in no small part to its organisational and political response to the state-aid question.

INTRODUCTION

A fifth matter investigated here is the growing realisation by both major political parties, but mainly the Liberal Party, that Australia's working-class/lower middle-class non-Catholic communities could, like the Catholics, be won over to a political point of view, by generous funding arrangements for low-fee denominational schools.

This book also examines the fate of the reports of two major commissions of inquiry: the 1973 Karmel Report and the 2012 Gonski Report. Each was designed to provide a fair and progressive approach to school funding and each was in turn sabotaged by ALP and Liberal partisan politics.

The slow movement of Australia's education system towards a residualised, two-nations schooling model, is discussed. Bearing in mind that socio-economic status plays a major part in educational achievement, the increasingly wide distributive gap that currently exists between non-government schools and disadvantaged government schools has adversely affected the social justice opportunities of many families who have little or no choice about which schools to send their children.[12]

Finally, there is an important point to make about this political conflict over school funding, the 'class wars' of this book's title. Public debates about education tend to be centred around the notion of funding as both a totemic and a functional element on each side of the argument. Yet increased funding is not the single most important element in providing a good education. Other significant factors include quality of teaching and school leadership, level of parental support for child and school, the socio-economic status of parents and the provision of high-quality material resources, as well

---

[12] By 2017, fees in several established non-government schools were edging over the $35,000 per annum barrier.

as an effective and culturally-attuned curriculum and assessment framework.

School funding has gained its symbolic political power because, for many of the politicians who enact the legislation, for those in the media who comment on education, and for many parents anxious about how their children might benefit from schooling, the funding equation is relatively easy to understand: more money means better schools.[13] These more complex objectives are less easily explained and less easily attained.

---

[13] Allowing for a minority of knowledgeable politicians who have a more nuanced view of education, professional media and academic commentators who can see both the wood and the trees in educational debates and parents who have an informed view of the Australian school system. Chris Bonnor and Jane Caro make the point that there is more to a good education than money in their accessible 2102 book *What makes a good school?*. See also educator Alan Duncan's June 2017 Grattan Institute report *Educate Australia Fair* which makes the point that needs-based finding in itself is not enough to alleviate the plight of disadvantaged students who also need evidence-based, targeted improvements such as better pre-school opportunities.

Chapter One

THE GOULBURN MYTH, SOCIAL JUSTICE AND THE MENZIES GESTURE 1962–63

While Menzies was contemplating how to strengthen his political position in 1962, a mid-year burst of sectarian animosity broke out in the small regional New South Wales city of Goulburn. Ostensibly, the dispute between the local Catholic diocese and the New South Wales education and health authorities was over the funding of school lavatories. This local quarrel, however, has since been regarded as having very broad ramifications. Indeed, the Goulburn incident has generally been regarded as a major turning point in Australian educational, social and political history.

The Goulburn dispute had begun in 1957 when the state education department demanded that Mother Celestine, principal of Our Lady of Mercy Preparatory School, build five (later reduced to three) additional lavatory cubicles for her school students. Resistance to the state authorities in the form of the temporary closure of Goulburn's Catholic schools on 13 July 1962 (later inaccurately known as the 'Goulburn School Strike') was led by Goulburn's ambitious and assertive Auxiliary Bishop John Cullinane, who was assisted by his parish deputy Father Francis Keogh. Their case was simple: if the state government insisted on new lavatories for a Catholic school, the state should pay for them. Cullinane and Keogh had the strong support of a lay committee led by local dentist Brian Keating, and had gained the guarded public endorsement of the normally cautious Eris O'Brien, Archbishop of Canberra and Goulburn.

While this was indeed a protest against the refusal of the state's education department to fund the Catholic schools that served a predominantly working-class community of Irish-descent, what happened at Goulburn was also a call for social justice. In this instance the call came from a socially and economically aspirational group with a strong religious and ethnic identity, a group that regarded itself as oppressed and marginalised in a nation dominated by a hostile Protestant majority. Indeed, the term 'social justice' was used throughout the campaign, with the normally composed Francis Keogh at one stage crying out excitedly at a protest meeting, 'It's not too hard to imagine the flag of justice flying over that toilet block'.[1] For the Catholics of Goulburn, demanding justice was an expression of an inherited Irish Catholic historical consciousness that had witnessed and resisted oppression and neglect by the British for almost 500 years.[2] The Irish-Australian Catholics of Goulburn were well schooled in the argument for natural and distributive

---

[1] Cit., 'A "Strike" Changed it all', *Goulburn Post*, 16 July 2012.

[2] Since 1541 when Henry VIII's royal rule was extended to Ireland. A more intense period of persecution of Irish Catholics occurred in the seventeenth century, followed in 1845–52 by what is now called the Great Hunger. In this context Catholic means Christian up to the time of the Reformation and Catholic thereafter. Probably the best and most accessible book on Irish historical consciousness and mythology is R.F. Foster's, *The Irish Story: Telling Tales and Making it up in Ireland*, London, Penguin Press, 2002.

CHAPTER ONE

elements in social justice, as was a predominantly Catholic ALP state government.³

While the origins of 'social justice' lie in mid-nineteenth-century European efforts to deal with the human consequences of the Industrial Revolution, a post-World War II desire for humanistic and progressive social reform was also important. Often associated with radical social democratic forms of politics, social justice was also a preoccupation of the mixed secular and religious reformist social movements of the 1960s and 1970s, with their emphasis on civil rights, individual and social needs, and the avoidance of military and other violence.

The Catholic Church has been associated with repressive and uncaring behaviour towards its congregations and others: from its attitudes and activities during the sixteenth- and seventeenth-century Counter Reformation, to the anti-reform sentiments of the First Vatican Council 1869–70, the symbiotic relationship with fascist regimes 1922–43 (known as 'clerical fascism') and on to the sexual abuse scandals (in at least thirteen nations) of the late twentieth and early twenty-first centuries.⁴ At the same time, the Church has to be viewed as both a single organisation and a collection of semi-autonomous parts. It includes both the radical priests of the Liberation Theology movement in Latin America and the ultraconservative Opus Dei movement. The mid-twentieth-century political interventionist approach of the Catholic Church's

---

3   The Australian Catholic community's aspirational status and its role in political activism at that time has been dealt with in Michael Hogan's excellent *Australian Catholics: The Social Justice Tradition*, North Blackburn, Victoria, Collins Dove, 1993.

4   Nations to date are Argentina, Australia, Austria, Belgium, Canada, Ireland, Norway, Philippines, Poland, Portugal, Tanzania, United Kingdom and the United States.

'Melbourne Line' contrasted with the politically anti-interventionist approach of the 'Sydney Line'.[5]

Social justice had been adopted in modified form as a social desideratum by the twentieth-century Catholic church after the promulgation in 1891 of the pre-emptive papal encyclical *Rerum Novarum* (regarding capital and labour), with its social amelioration, pro-union, pro-private ownership of property, anti-socialist and anti-unrestricted capitalist message.[6] Non-Catholic political philosophers too were becoming interested in a social justice model based on the importance of individual liberty, with concomitant rights and responsibilities, as well as equity in the distribution of economic resources. However, as the twentieth century progressed, it was assertive capitalism, aggressive fascism, dictatorial communism as well as expansionist militarism, instead of a concern for social justice, that became the dominant ideologies that were to shape world events at the expense of liberty and individual rights. In that context, the idea of natural and distributive justice was important to Australia's Irish-Catholic community.

The modern Australian Catholic version of social justice first made its appearance at the beginning of World War II when, from 1940 onwards, Australian and New Zealand Catholic bishops began to issue joint annual statements on 'Social Justice Sunday', the third Sunday in each September. These statements, published as pamphlets, cost three pence each (later six pence) and 100,000 of the social

---

[5] See for example Sandra Fullerton Joireman's edited book, *Church, State, and Citizen: Christian Approaches to Political Engagement*, Oxford, Oxford University Press, 2009, especially Robert B. Shelledy's chapter, 'The Catholic Tradition and the State: Natural Necessary and Nettlesome', pp.15–34.

[6] The phrase *rerum novarum* literally means 'of new things' but a common broader translation has it as 'revolution' or an abrupt change.

CHAPTER ONE

justice essays, which were often quite substantial pieces of writing, were printed and disseminated via the parish network each year to become an important element in the Australian Catholic political and historical consciousness of the 1950s and 1960s.

Initially written by a fervent young lawyer and editor, B.A. 'Bob' Santamaria, the statements were heavily influenced by the consequences of the 1930s Great Depression, by the inhumanity and godlessness of Communist totalitarianism, and by the human cost of war. Targeted in the statements were totalitarian attacks on the freedom of the individual and the evils of unbridled capitalism. Social justice itself included the right to life (from conception onwards) and the right to a Catholic concept of the 'decent family'. Such decency referred to a family operating within a patriarchal system with family members piously educated in Catholic schools, with mothers managing the home and with the men earning a living wage. Catholic social justice also meant the right to own private property (as opposed to relying on collective ownership) and eligibility for unemployment benefits, based on 'social adjustment' in the form of an equitable distribution of 'human possessions'.[7]

The Catholic hierarchy eventually dropped Santamaria as their social justice author in 1954. Political journalist Alan Reid had published a damaging exposé in Sydney's *Sun*, which made it plain that Santamaria was an anti-Communist *eminence grise* behind a network of societies within both the Catholic church and the ALP, a story that contributed to the ALP schism of 1955. Even so, by 1962 the Catholic community of Goulburn would have been well aware of social and

---

[7] See M. Hogan, ed., *Justice Now! Social Justice Statements of the Australian Catholic Bishops First Series: 1940–1966*, Sydney, Department of Government and Public Administration, University of Sydney, 1990.

educational injustices and how they affected their small community. And the bishops were also active in their canonical duty to provide an exclusively Catholic education for Catholic children, where practicable.

The Catholic Church in Australia too was fully aware of the thoroughly comprehensive 1960 United Nations Convention against Discrimination in Education. Article 1, for example, states that:

> For the purposes of this Convention, the term 'discrimination' includes any distinction, exclusion, limitation or preferences which, being based on race, colour, sex, language, religion, political or other opinion, national or social origin, economic condition or birth, has the purpose or effect of nullifying or impairing equality of treatment in education.

Moreover, Article 26.3 deals with parental choice, decreeing that 'Parents have a prior right to choose the kind of education that shall be given to their children'.[8] The United Nations argument was a favourite of Santamaria's who used it, for example, at a 1960 Christian Social Week meeting organised by the Melbourne branch of the Institute for Social Order, a Jesuit social studies organisation.[9]

Catholic opinion that this convention applied to their school students was based on the proposition that they were being discriminated against because the Australian state governments demanded that they attend schools wherever possible, and yet the same states would not fund denominational schools directly.[10] Not that the UNESCO argument would have impressed Menzies. No UNESCO convention

---

[8] United Nations Educational Scientific and Cultural Organization, *Legal Instruments*, http://portal.unesco.org/en/ev.php-URL_ID=12949&URL_DO=DO_TOPIC&URL_SECTION=201.html.

[9] 'Proposal by Santamaria for "Benefits"', *Sydney Morning Herald*, 12 September 1960.

[10] Set apart from the states at this stage were Australian Capital Territory schools, which were directly funded by the Commonwealth.

CHAPTER ONE

was ratified during his post-war terms in office. Such ratification had to wait until 1966 when Harold Holt succeeded Menzies as prime minister.

It needs to be borne in mind as well that social justice and civil rights were the joint causes also being fought for by oppressed black Americans and South Africans in the late 1950s and early 1960s. While there is no direct evidence that the Catholics of Goulburn were inspired by events in Alabama, Mississippi and Sharpeville, the Australian media outlets were constantly carrying shocking images from across the Pacific and the Indian Ocean of supposedly democratic societies in which segregated education was the norm.

Keating, then a dentist, an alderman and a highly regarded deputy mayor of Goulburn, was part of a new post-war generation of educated, aspiring middle class Australian Catholics. The young Keating had volunteered for service with the RAAF during World War II and had been posted as pilot officer to 115 Squadron RAF Bomber Command as aircrew, in an arm of the Allied services that during 1939–45 suffered 47 fatalities out of every 100 aircrew members. During his service, Keating flew thirty missions in Lancaster bombers, was awarded the Distinguished Flying Cross (probably as a periodic award for consistently brave service) and was demobbed in 1945. In answer to an interviewer's question about why he became involved in the Goulburn incident in 1962, protest organiser Brian Keating's reply was revealing:

> The simple answer is that we [had] four [school age] children and that my wife is English, a Lancashire lass, who was used to governments giving significant aid to Catholic schools and was angry that the Australian government offered nothing. So was I. As a returned soldier – ex RAAF Air Crew, who saw active service in the UK, completing a tour with Bomber Command, 30 raids on Germany – I believed that this was a

serious injustice and that our democratic rights were ignored by cowardly [NSW] politicians.[11]

Looking beyond Goulburn, there is no doubt that diocesan Catholic schools at that time were disadvantaged compared with their secular rivals.[12] Overcrowding was an endemic problem of Australian Catholic primary schools. Inspectors' reports noted that in 1951 St Brigid's Primary School in Marrickville had a kindergarten class of 93 students, and in 1953 Balmain Primary School had a kindergarten class of 84 students. In his 2001 interview, Keating explained the problem which had confronted Goulburn: 'All primary schools in the state were poorly equipped … no auxiliaries. No real libraries, no tuck-shops, no assembly hall, little sporting space and very little [*sic*] sporting facilities'.[13] And in the early 1960s the Catholic school system in New South Wales was about to face fresh financial pressures as the demand for secondary school education rose and the state government introduced a new and expensive upper-secondary reform school program: the Wyndham Scheme.

Named after the progressive New South Wales Director of Education Harold Wyndham (1946–68) the scheme was based on the idea of a universal broad-based comprehensive secondary education for all in the first four years of secondary schooling, with an additional provision of two years of upper secondary schooling as a prelude to a Higher School Certificate examination system. Wyndham was

---

[11] J. Luttrell, 'Recalling the Goulburn 'Strike': An Interview with Brian Keating', *Australasian Catholic Record*, vol. 89 no. 3, 2012, p.351. Periodic DFCs for accumulated acts of bravery were often awarded without individual citations.

[12] Catholic systemic schools were run by dioceses. A smaller number of non-diocesan schools were run by religious orders and they varied in their financial status from relatively wealthy to threadbare.

[13] J. Luttrell, 'Recalling the Goulburn Strike', p.351.

CHAPTER ONE

knighted in 1969 for his services to education. His scheme is still regarded as a landmark event in Australian education history.

With the urging of Cullinane, and under the leadership of Keating and his lay committee, Goulburn Catholics in July 1962 closed their schools.[14] Most of their 2000 students were sent off to be taught in the already overstretched government system. This precipitate action placed both the Catholic Church and the ALP state government of premier Robert Heffron in a bind. Prior to 1962, Australia's most senior Catholic clergyman, Sydney-based Cardinal Norman Gilroy, had been restrained rather than radical in his approach to state aid and to political action, part of the so-called 'Sydney Line'. As for Heffron, while sympathetic to the cause of school improvement and supportive of mainstream Catholicism, he was unable to act, for three reasons. First, it would look as if a newly re-elected ALP government was caving in to the Catholics. Second, the national ALP had already expressly banned state aid. Third, the state government was heavily committed to the Wyndham reforms and could not postpone them just because Catholic schools were poorly resourced.

Heffron, a Catholic turned Anglican, was on a midwinter holiday in Cairns during the Goulburn protest, which had by now become the object of nationwide media attention and the focus of strong support from DLP figures. The premier astutely left the handling of the crisis to his education minister Ern Wetherell, who prevaricated, hoping the Goulburn impasse would resolve itself. It eventually did.

---

[14] Cullinane's features appeared as a thumbnail photograph captioned, 'Not me, the laymen', which headed a major feature article, 'The Goulburn Lock-Out' in Sydney's influential weekly news magazine *The Bulletin*. The article, published on 21 July 1963, was written by journalist Peter Kelly and it outlined the course of events that had led to the shutdown, stressing the embarrassment caused to Gilroy and Heffron.

The organisers of the Goulburn closures came to the bitter realisation that their actions had gone too far and were actually damaging the Catholic cause. The Catholic schools of Goulburn reopened on 27 July 1962. After another clash with the Sydney hierarchy, the ebullient Cullinane, now tainted by the Goulburn incident's association with the DLP, was transferred to the Melbourne diocese in 1967, where he remained until his early retirement in 1974.

The Goulburn closures had at least one positive outcome for the Australian Catholic community. The town's organisers helped set up a national education association, the Australian Parents' Council (APC), to act as a pressure group. But the vocal support of the DLP for the Goulburn closures and the perceived close connections between the DLP and the APC, only increased the Sydney archdiocesan resistance to changing its gradualist policies on state aid. Sydney's long term prognosis at the time was that the granting of comprehensive state aid for Catholic schools by any State or national ALP government in the near future would be an unlikely event. ALP politicians at whatever level, it was thought, would be reluctant to go against the party's national executive, which was then dominated by Western Australia's hardline anti-state aider Francis Edward 'Joe' Chamberlain, and by the union-dominated and utterly doctrinaire Victorian Left ALP faction known as the 'Junta'. State Coalition governments too would be equally reluctant to give (Protestant) taxpayers' money to schools.

If Goulburn was on Menzies' horizon in 1962, it was only as an object lesson in what could go badly wrong if there was a revival of ugly sectarian debates about schooling. On that issue, Menzies had been keeping in touch with events in Goulburn through his local Catholic confidant Archbishop Eris O'Brien. The prime minister

CHAPTER ONE

remained reluctant to provide Commonwealth funding for Catholic schools even though there were signs that mainstream opinion was shifting. *The Bulletin*, led by the formidable and independently-minded Peter Hastings, carried an editorial on 21 July 1962 headlined 'The Collapse of Australian Education?'. The unnamed author discussed teacher shortages in Victoria, a dearth which, it was argued, had led to the recruitment of unqualified and incompetent teachers, falling standards everywhere and poor teacher training courses. *The Bulletin* concluded Commonwealth intervention was necessary.[15]

Following the turbulent educational, religious and political events in Goulburn, a state-aid hiatus ensued in New South Wales. In Canberra on 6 November 1962 Menzies repeated his government's position in tabling a White Paper, 'The Commonwealth and Education', in the House of Representatives. The prime minister was firm. Notwithstanding the Commonwealth's 1961–62 direct expenditure of £33 million (and growing) on ACT schools, universities, training, and international education projects, he continued to point out that education was a matter that fell within the states' areas of responsibility and he believed state governments were better placed to assess and provide for local needs.

It was Sydney's Cardinal Gilroy who, in September 1962, inadvertently provided Menzies with the solution to achieving consensus on the issue by publicly advocating giving state aid to *all* non-government schools, rather than just to Catholic schools. This was not a new idea but it was a novel suggestion coming from

---

[15] For more on Hastings see Gavin Souter, 'Hastings, Peter Dunstan (1920–1990)', *Australian Dictionary of Biography*, Canberra, National Centre of Biography, Australian National University, http://adb.anu.edu.au/biography/hastings-peter-dunstan-12607/text22709 (2007), accessed 3 October 2016.

Australia's leading Catholic and it was a move away from the Church's special-pleading stance towards a more inclusive view. On the face of it, Gilroy's suggestion overcame the stumbling block of Section 116 of the Australian Constitution. If Menzies were to accept the Gilroy solution and offer state aid to all denominational schools, the prime minister could avoid that particular constitutional hurdle and have the perfect wedge with which to put pressure on an ALP still suffering from the consequences of the 1955 split. As for those secularist and Protestant voters who might dislike allocating Commonwealth tax revenue to Catholic schools, they could be appeased by the Protestant schools' shares of the handout, and conservative Protestants would still vote for the Liberal-Country Party anyway.

Even so, in early 1963, it was a risky step to take and would not go down well in Liberal branches at the state level, nor in a Menzies government where the only Catholic member of Cabinet during the post-war period had been Liberal Senator (Michael) Neil O'Sullivan.[16] Beyond Cabinet, John Cramer, a junior minister (1956–63) and a prominent Catholic Liberal, was half-jokingly referred to by his colleagues as 'the Papist'.

Ironically, the ALP too provided Menzies with a blueprint for possible wedging tactics over the state-aid issue. According to historian Ross Fitzgerald:

> When covering the [March] 1963 NSW ALP conference, [*Daily Telegraph* political journalist] Alan Reid had been impressed by a policy document that proposed state aid for libraries and science blocks. It was not adopted, but Reid did not forget it. He mentioned the document to Menzies, who asked for a copy.[17]

---

[16]   In Cabinet 1956-58.

[17]   Ross Fitzgerald and Stephen Holt, *Alan "The Red Fox" Reid, Pressman Par Excellence*, Sydney, New South, 2010, pp.160-161.

CHAPTER ONE

At a time of national public and political anxiety about Australia's scientific capability, the science education scheme seemed more generally acceptable than the fraught and expensive option of per capita school funding or any kind of long term grant for recurring expenses.[18]

This science block idea of the ALP's played into Menzies' hands. The prime minister had been a firm believer in increasing the quality of Australia's universities and, in the late 1950s and early 1960s, he was also a frequent public advocate for increasing Australia's scientific and technological capability at both university and school level. In higher education and research, Menzies had in 1945 advocated using Section 96 (Commonwealth financial assistance to any state on the terms and conditions that it sees fit), though at that stage he was in opposition. When in government, he did use it to fund university reforms in 1951–57. In 1956 he had set up the Murray Committee to investigate the state of Australia's universities, with the committee's report arguing for increased Commonwealth spending on higher education. The government then established the Australian Universities Commission in 1959 and substantially raised the funding for the Commonwealth Scientific and Industrial Research Office (CSIRO).

Menzies gradually came to realise that, with some help, he might be able to step in at the federal level by using the Gilroy solution to take his government where Calwell and the national executive of the ALP could not go. If Commonwealth Government intervention in education could be finessed to avoid political division between Catholics and Protestants, there might be a marginal (but crucial)

---

[18] See 'The Sorry State of Science in Schools', *Sydney Morning Herald*, 23 January 1962.

electoral advantage to be gained through a very limited and cross-denominational Commonwealth intervention. The benefit to the Coalition would then come in the form of increased Catholic preferences marshalled by a grateful DLP.

The prime minister's change of view about state aid was directly inspired by the noticeable success of the 1958–63 Industrial Fund for the Advancement of Scientific Education in Schools, chaired by Sydney Church of England Grammar School headmaster Leonard Charles (L. C.) Robson. This initiative raised more than £1,266,000, but for non-government Headmasters' Conference (HMC) schools only.[19] Menzies was a great supporter of the fund and had himself opened the second stage of the Sydney Church of England Grammar School's new advanced and deluxe science wing in April 1963, funding for which had been split between the Old Boys' association (£120,000) and the Industrial Fund (£20,000). By 1963, however, ongoing support for the fund had been hit by the 'Holt Jolt', with Robson and others putting pressure on Menzies for Commonwealth funding to replace declining private subscriptions. Menzies acknowledged in his 1970 memoir the influence this fund had on his science education decision.[20]

Later that year the ALP was yet again busy tearing itself apart, this time over defence policy, following Menzies' 1962 government's lease of a base at Exmouth in Western Australia to the United States Navy. The base was to be a communications link in the deployment of United States strategic missiles, including the nuclear-armed submarine-launched ballistic missile Polaris. In May 1962, Menzies

---

[19] Robson had been influential in founding the HMC (along British lines) in 1931.
[20] Robert Gordon Menzies, *The Measure of All the Years: Prime Minister of Australia, 1939–41 and 1949–66*, London, Cassell, 1970, p.95.

CHAPTER ONE

had quietly announced the early stages of the negotiation and in November 1962, just before the Christmas break, the prime minister declared that the proposed lease would be open to debate in the House of Representatives, a debate he knew would further divide the ALP factions.

The response of the ALP's anti-nuclear Left was apoplectic and a special Federal Conference was convened in Canberra on 20 March 1963 to debate the matter. The Conference, after much wrangling, actually reached a compromise position, arguing for Australian involvement in any United States decision-making process about going to war. However, this meeting gave rise to the legendary occasion when political journalist Alan Reid made good use of five *Daily Telegraph* photographs that captured images of an apparently subservient Calwell and his equally powerless deputy Gough Whitlam waiting outside the Kingston Hotel to hear what the '36 faceless men' of the national executive had decided about the proposed naval base.[21]

From a Coalition point of view, the television and newsreel images and accompanying stories were a godsend. Here was a telling depiction of the leader and deputy leader of the national ALP waiting to hear their fate at the hands of party officials. The damage to Calwell's leadership of the ALP and to the ALP cause was considerable. Menzies (as well as Liberal leaders in later years) made much of this apparently anti-democratic relationship between what were appointed ALP officials and elected ALP members of the federal parliament.

---

[21] Actually, there were 35 men and one woman, Phyllis Benjamin from Tasmania, an elected ALP member for Hobart in the Legislative Council (upper house).

Adding difficulty to difficulty for the ALP, a by-now ailing Archbishop Mannix publicly spoke out against it. Irish-born Mannix, Melbourne's long-serving archbishop (1916–63) and a controversial prelate with the public demeanour of an affronted prophet, never held back when he felt his intervention was needed in political matters, be they the 1916–17 anti-conscription debates, Irish nationalism or state aid.

Shortly before the ALP national conference in July, Mannix publicly declared that Catholic schools had 'nothing to hope for from the ALP'.[22] The archbishop even drew Calwell and his deputy leader Gough Whitlam into the UK's sordid Profumo scandal, when he argued that the two ALP leaders should, because of '[recent] shocking revelations of the low standard of private morals of some public men, support Catholic schools rather than "weaken" them'.[23]

While Mannix had once been, according to ALP speechwriter Graham Freudenberg, 'the man he [Calwell] most loved and admired' the two had fallen out in the 1950s over the ALP split.[24] Now Australia's best-known Catholic cleric was publicly undermining the ALP at a difficult political juncture.[25] Coming from Mannix, this

---

[22] The Profumo Affair, which broke during the European spring of 1963, was a notorious political scandal involving, among others, John Profumo, Conservative defence minister, and two London call girls, Christine Keeler and Mandy Rice-Davies; as well as Yevgeny Ivanov, a Russian spy; and Stephen Ward, an artist, osteopath and high class pimp. Calwell was visiting London in the European summer of 1963 when the scandal was peaking in the media and the law courts.

[23] 'Dr Mannix Hits at Lab Leaders', *Sun Herald*, 7 July 1963.

[24] 'Calwell, Arthur Augustus (1896–1973)', G. Freudenberg, *Australian Dictionary of Biography*. Calwell remained a regular caller at Mannix's residence Raheen until Mannix's death.

[25] Mannix had earlier also issued a controversial press release on the eve of the 1958 Evatt vs Menzies election, advising Catholics to support the DLP (at the expense of the ALP). See M. Gilchrist, *Wit and Wisdom: Daniel Mannix*, North Melbourne, Freedom Publishing, 1982, pp.243–244. Calwell, ALP deputy leader, was

CHAPTER ONE

latest public assault, an attack that included the gratuitously offensive reference to the Profumo business, had been felt as a very low blow for Calwell.

As for Calwell's then position among Catholic congregations, it can best be summed up in an anecdote of West Australian MP for Fremantle, Kim Beazley Snr.

Beazley remarked that when Calwell asked Irish-born Labor MP Danny Minogue to sound out his sisters (many of whom were nuns) about the ALP leader's election chances, Minogue's reply was that while his sisters were praying for Calwell they were not voting for him. The response became a standing joke in the parliamentary ALP.[26]

At the federal ALP conference in Perth in July-August, outgoing ALP national secretary Joe Chamberlain spoke forcefully against state aid in a high profile attack on the 'certain persons' who had tried to change ALP policy by 'backdoor methods'. This was a reference to the New South Wales state branch's suggestion that their ALP government provide science laboratories and 'other science facilities' for Roman Catholic schools.[27] The New South Wales proposal failed. A week after Chamberlain had publicly denounced members of his own party, a Gallup poll showed that, for the first time since the 1961 election, the Menzies government was ahead of the ALP, with 5 per cent of voters having, during the past year, drifted from the

---

'deeply saddened'. In the 1961 election campaign, Mannix had publicly described Santamaria as 'the saviour of Australia' in an ABC interview. See Gilchrist, *Wit and Wisdom*, p.257.

[26] Kim E. Beazley, *Father of the House: The Memoirs of Kim E. Beazley*, North Fremantle, Fremantle Press, 2009, p.108.

[27] 'Labour's State Aid Policy', *Sydney Morning Herald*, 2 August 1963. NB, at this time there seemed to be no settled editorial policy on how to spell Labor.

ALP to the Coalition. Crucially, this Gallup poll analysis showed that DLP preferences would, at that stage, have given the Menzies government an easy win over its opponents.[28]

Making matters even worse for Calwell and his party, at an October 1963 conference of the ALP's national executive, in Adelaide, another fight about state aid broke out between Joe Chamberlain and the clearly resilient New South Wales delegates. They were there to advocate for premier Heffron's state-aid proposal for secondary school student allowances. Chamberlain denounced the proposal as a 'drastic sectional decision which would mean a change to basic ALP policy', of which Chamberlain had been a ferocious champion since his election as ALP state secretary in 1949.[29] The New South Wales proposal was defeated.

The publicity surrounding the Adelaide meeting was disastrous for the ALP and for a by now punch-drunk Calwell who, according to the conservative-leaning *Sydney Morning Herald*, was 'publicly humiliated'. The *Herald*'s analysis also included the view that Menzies had just witnessed another damaging ALP fiasco which contained yet again the two explosive elements in the story that infuriated Catholic and non-Catholic conservative voters alike. These were: leftist (read Communist) union interference in ALP decision-making processes and the ALP national executive's negative attitude towards the state-aid issue. The *Sydney Morning Herald*'s parliamentary correspondent had tested opinion on both sides of politics and was in no doubt where matters stood:

---

[28] 'Vote drift to Federal Govt.', *Sydney Morning Herald*, 21 July 1963.

[29] B. Oliver, 'Chamberlain, Francis Edward (Joe) (1900–1984)', *Australian Dictionary of Biography*, http://adb.anu.edu.au/biography/chamberlain-francis-edward-joe-12304.

CHAPTER ONE

> The Federal A.L.P. executive meeting ended today with many delegates convinced that the decisions against the N.S.W. pupil allowance scheme will be the deciding factor in the Prime Minister, Sir Robert Menzies, seeking an early election. Many Liberals hold the same view, but it is not likely that Sir Robert will make the decision until next week. Some Labour men believe that the rejection of the N.S.W. Government's pupil allowance scheme will enable Sir Robert to cry again that Labour Governments are continually subjected to directions from outside bodies.[30]

The ALP was demonstrating yet again its talent for playing into the Coalition's hands with its internecine battles between appointed (mainly union) delegates and parliamentary representatives and by prolonging ongoing inner turmoil over the state-aid question.

These were the external political factors that helped Menzies make up his mind up about school funding. There have been several putative contenders for role of the conservative public figure who finally brought about Menzies' change of mind over state aid. According to historian Rob Chalmers, Queensland Liberal Senator Neil O'Sullivan may have been the instigator. And there were reports that it was Tasmanian DLP Senator and dedicated anti-communist George Cole.[31] Even Bob Santamaria claimed to have played a part in shifting Menzies' position. In 1997, towards the end of his life, Santamaria gave an extended interview for the *Australian Biography* project and spoke of his 1962–63 negotiations with Liberal politician Harold Holt. Characteristically, the shadowy but self-aggrandising Santamaria placed himself at the centre of events:

---

[30] 'A.L.P. Decision May Bring On Election', *Sydney Morning Herald*, 4 October 1963.

[31] R. Chalmers, *Inside the Canberra Press Gallery: Life in the Wedding Cake of Old Parliament House*, Canberra, ANU Press, 2011, p.66.

> [O]n the eve of the 1963 election – and that took place, I think it was on the 22 November, give or take a day – he [Harold Holt] got in touch with me and asked me to see him.[32] And he said that he'd discussed the [state-aid] matter again with Menzies, and Menzies intended to make some gesture – that's all that he said – and that I could tell Archbishop that something would be done to acknowledge the principle of state aid in the Liberals [*sic*] policy speech.[33]

Even so, such urgings from marginal political figures seem unlikely to have moved Menzies, who was very much his own man, frequently not even taking his Cabinet into his confidence.[34] Indeed, it is much more likely that the prime minister, who was at that time still ahead in the November 1963 Gallup poll, was not particularly attracted by any immediate political advantage to be gained or by unpredictable reports of DLP voting intentions.[35] If there is one clear candidate for the role of the Menzies associate who persuaded the prime minister to take on state aid, it is John Leslie Carrick, at that time the General

---

[32] Santamaria's memory is at fault here. According to historian Michael Griffin, Santamaria had already told Mannix on 1 November 1963 that the deal was sealed. The 'gesture' was publicly announced by Menzies on 12 November.

[33] *Australian Biography Online*. Screen Australia, http://www.australianbiography.gov.au/subjects/santamaria/interview1.html.

[34] Malcolm Fraser, then an ambitious backbencher, commented much later that in his view, a Liberal Party vote on state aid prior to the election would have been lost on sectarian grounds. Menzies almost certainly played his state-aid cards close to his chest until the last minute because he was anxious not to stir up sectarian divisions within the Cabinet. Carrick disagreed, arguing that post-war recruitment of younger ex-servicemen into the party had reduced entrenched sectarian attitudes. See I. R. Wilkinson, B. J. Caldwell, R.J.W. Selleck, J. Harris and P. Dettman, *A History of State Aid to Non-Government Schools in Australia*, Brighton, Educational Transformations Pty Ltd., 2006, p.45.

[35] There had been a slight swing towards the ALP just after the election had been called in October, but the swing moved the other way as Election Day grew closer. At the time, media reports mentioned that (what are now called 'shy') DLP voters played their pre-election cards close to their chests, which could have affected the Gallup results.

CHAPTER ONE

Secretary of the New South Wales Liberal Party and later senator and education minister.[36] Carrick, an unobtrusive but important party tactician and strategist, had the ear of the prime minister: in Carrick's view, while the state-aid issue was tricky and socially divisive, it could be worked to his party's advantage.[37]

In the early 1960s, Carrick had quietly gathered a like-minded crew of state Liberals around him, a group that included country Liberal member Wal Fife (later federal education minister), Eric Willis (later premier of New South Wales) and a young John Winston Howard (later prime minister), who were prepared to work within the party to advocate for state aid on the principle that state-aided Liberal 'variety' in education was a better model than Labor 'uniformity' and would set the scene for the Liberal Party's espousal of 'choice' as a parental right.[38] This was to become the Liberal party's version of school-based social justice. Carrick's argument was that in the short and the long term, a Menzies-led Commonwealth Government would need to address the issue if the Liberals were to claim for themselves (without the DLP's help) the role of a broad-based party, even if such a move might be temporarily unpopular within the Liberal Party, and might carry some electoral risk. The solution that Carrick offered was to provide a limited program of state aid for all schools, commenting some years later: 'What we decided was the real breakthrough. Now certainly

---

[36] Carrick also persuaded a reluctant Robert Askin, premier of New South Wales (1965–75), to bring in per capita funding for non-government schools in 1969.

[37] See G. Starr, *Carrick: Principles, Politics and Policy*, Ballan, Victoria, Connor Court Publishing. Starr deals with the context on pp.168-173.

[38] Fife was at that time state MP for Wagga Wagga, Willis was MP for Earlwood and Howard was president of the NSW Young Liberals.

it wasn't done to win votes, I can tell you that. And in any case, one didn't get far winning votes in Canberra'.[39]

Menzies sized up the overall political situation and decided to take advantage of the ALP's abject electoral situation, factoring in his interest in science education together with Carrick's views about broadening the vote. On 15 October, just over a week after the ALP's Adelaide brouhaha and, characteristically, without consulting his colleagues, Menzies called a 30 November election for the House of Representatives (his second snap poll).

Fate then struck once more, and yet again in Menzies' favour. On Melbourne Cup Day, Tuesday 5 November, the day before the election campaign was to begin in earnest, 99-year-old Daniel Mannix collapsed. Calwell, who had recently made peace with the archbishop, rushed to see him. On the next day Calwell paid another visit to Mannix's residence, Raheen, where he wept at the dying prelate's bedside. Mannix passed away at 12.35 pm, prior to Calwell preparing to give his televised speech that evening at the Royale Ballroom in Melbourne's Exhibition building. Meanwhile, the prime minister's televised speech was scheduled for the following Tuesday, the extra time giving Menzies a tactical advantage.

For Menzies, as opposed to Calwell and the ALP, the omens could scarcely have been better. After having damaged the ALP's electoral position in mid-year, Mannix's death had come at a very convenient time for a Liberal prime minister contemplating a spring election – the much reviled (by Protestant opinion) national leader of the Catholic state-aid cause was gone, leaving middle-of-the-road Protestants more able to soften their views about

---

[39]   Starr, p.172. The Canberra votes reference was to the significance of state-level politics in the federal Liberal party.

CHAPTER ONE

Commonwealth funding for Catholic and other denominational schools, including their own. With the irksome Mannix out of the way, Menzies now had more room to manoeuvre within his party on the state-aid initiative.

The 1963 general election was to be Australia's first televised campaign and, to his party's immense benefit, Menzies was a telegenic star, an authoritative and mellifluous performer who spoke direct to camera in a relaxed manner, employing a level gaze and a confiding voice. In contrast, the earnest and stolid Calwell was more comfortable as a deliverer of speeches in the party room or at the hustings, where he could emphasise his key points with a firm right forefinger. Unlike Menzies, Calwell was also stilted and uncomfortable when giving carefully written speeches and was particularly awkward in front of television cameras. As an indication of the effect of these kinds of occasions on Calwell and Menzies, respectively, the opposition leader generally ate little on the day and sweated profusely during a performance, so much so that his shirt and singlet had to be changed after the event. Menzies, who preferred a good meal and a glass of wine before giving a customarily urbane performance, was not a nervous television performer.

Calwell's general election speech (only his second as leader) was couched in general terms and based on his publication *Labor's Role in Modern Society* and his criticism of an allegedly worn-out and aloof Menzies government. When it came to education, the ALP leader steered clear of state aid in his policy offerings. He announced an insipid education package which included secondary school, technical school and teacher training scholarships and a meagre grant to the states of £10 million to assist with what was seen as a widespread crisis in school education. Calwell also promised a national inquiry into the condition of schools and of teacher education and a proposal to form a new Commonwealth Ministry of Education and Science.[40]

In his 12 November general election speech (his sixth) Menzies listed twenty-three manifesto items, starting with foreign policy and defence. Education came twelfth, tucked in between Trade and Child Endowment. Buried in Education's 847-word section lay the following promise:

> ... there is a special need for improved science teaching in the secondary schools, if we are to keep in step with the march of science. As some recognition of this need, we will make available £5M. per annum for the provision of building and equipment facilities for science teaching in secondary schools. The amount will be distributed on a school population basis, and will be available to *all secondary schools, Government or independent, without discrimination* [my italics].[41]

The most interesting part of the whole education section, overshadowed by the state-aid issue, was a promise of 10,000 Commonwealth upper secondary school scholarships (Forms 4 and 5 only) worth £4 million. The ALP was anyway in favour of individual bursaries and scholarships and the states and territories already awarded a host of minor subsistence grants to scholars, so there was no controversy there. What was notable about the Commonwealth scholarships was that they were available for the final two years of secondary schooling and were not means-tested. This meant that they would be applicable only to about 20 per cent of government and Catholic school students (given their post-compulsory retention rates) while non-Catholic

---

[40] Australian Federal Election Speeches, Museum of Australian Democracy, https://electionspeeches.moadoph.gov.au/speeches/1963-arthur-calwell.

[41] Australian Federal Elections Speeches, Museum of Australian Democracy, https://electionspeeches.moadoph.gov.au/speeches/1963-robert-menzies.

students attending Protestant denominational schools, with an 80–90 per cent retention rate, would benefit disproportionately. Menzies knew this. According to public servant Ken Jones, then serving in the Cabinet secretariat: 'The secondary scholarships idea was probably Menzies's own and certainly was based on the sorts of scholarships that he'd competed for, of course in a much tougher contest, when he was a scholarship boy himself. But these were to reward the elite not to encourage the less able.'[42] This Jones remark bears out Santamaria's comment that Menzies had played down the significance of the state-aid legislation for Catholics, telling Holt that his intention was merely a 'gesture'.[43]

While Menzies-style direct state aid may have been an educational gesture it was far from that in political terms. Promising very limited direct state aid to all schools in the form of largely controversy-free science laboratories and secondary school scholarships would satisfy Catholic opinion grateful for both a prime ministerial gift and imprimatur, neutralise most Protestant objectors to state aid, please the states and territories and keep the ALP divided by shoring up the anti-Labor Catholic vote.[44] Moreover, an unequal amount of money would go to the senior students of the Liberal-Country Party's kind of non-government schools. This would be certainly of some importance to an imperialist prime minister who valued the patriotic culture of the kinds of school he and most of his Cabinet had attended.

---

[42] K. Jones, Interview with Ken Henderson, 1985, TRC/1858/2/58.

[43] *Australian Biography Online*. Screen Australia, http://www.australianbiography.gov.au/subjects/santamaria/interview1.html.

[44] The hard-line [Protestant] Council of Churches in New South Wales was not at all happy. See, 'Churches Reply to Election Policies: Attack on Pledges to Private schools', *Sydney Morning Herald*, 22 November 1963. A handful of independent schools also objected on the grounds that government grants would mean government interference in their internal affairs.

Menzies was still not completely confident of gaining his improved majority. In late November he commented to young public servant Ken Jones, when they briefly crossed paths at Canberra airport, that the Coalition were 'not doing as well as they should', despite what Jones referred to in his memoir as ideas 'pinched from the Labor Party in New South Wales'.[45] However, as if to confirm Menzies' intuitive genius in calling a snap election based largely on fear of Communist expansion in Asia, a Gallup poll published on 18 November 1963 (on polling taken after Calwell's televised policy speech but before the Menzies policy speech) showed that while the Coalition vote had gained 1 per cent since October, the ALP's has dropped 2 per cent, with one of those percentage points having gone to the DLP.

Then came several larger matters. First, President Diem of South Vietnam was assassinated on 1 November and the South Vietnamese government was overthrown, adding to existing fears of instability in South East Asia. Indeed, one of the Menzies election posters was headed, 'Look North', a more restrained version of the racist late nineteenth- and early twentieth-century 'Yellow Peril' cartoons. On 22 November, just four days after that November Gallup poll was published, US President J. F. Kennedy was assassinated in Dallas, a traumatic event which, it is generally acknowledged, helped the Liberal-Country Party vote, on the basis that Menzies represented stability and continuity at a time of international uncertainty. In Australia, Kennedy had been perceived as strongly anti-Communist at a time when there were three Asian communist states to Australia's

---

[45] K. Jones, Interview with Ken Henderson, 7 August 1985, National Library of Australia, NLA ID 1648415/TRC/1858/2/57. Jones was in Menzies' Cabinet Secretariat and went on to become founding head of the post-election Commonwealth Activities in Education and Research department under the Prime Minister. He stayed in that post during its various iterations as a full department from 1963–83.

north, the People's Republic of China, North Korea and North Vietnam, and the nation was faced with an unstable South Vietnam.

State aid was all but buried as an election issue by these headline events. In the election, Menzies' coalition gained a 22-seat majority. The first preference vote for the ALP dropped by 2.43 per cent (compared with 1961 figures) and the Liberal-Country Party had benefited from a very handy 407,416 first preference votes for the DLP.[46]

An indignant Calwell, who had, among his other campaign humiliations, been obliged to sit through an anti-ALP sermon in St Francis Xavier Cathedral, Geraldton, held very firm opinions on where responsibility for his party's defeat lay. DLP election advertisements were, he said, 'shocking, filthy and scandalous', and church schools had been used to 'indoctrinate children against Labour ... Some women may have been affected by President Kennedy's assassination. Certainly the Prime Minister used President Kennedy's death rather shamefully to win votes'. On state aid for private schools Calwell said: 'I think State aid was used in conjunction with the threat of Communism – although there is no real threat of Communism in this country ... [and the DLP] took money from the Liberals'.[47]

With the election won and Calwell's political career in serious decline, the Menzies government brought in the promised education legislation in May 1964. Commonwealth state-aid funding was to commence on the 1st July the following year.

---

[46] DLP first preferences rose to 417,411 in the 1966 general election, fell to 367,977 in 1969 and fell again to 346,415 in 1972. By 1974 the DLP first preference vote had dropped to 104,974.

[47] 'Bitterness By Calwell in Review of Labour's Defeat', *Sydney Morning Herald*, 3 December 1963.

The 1963 announcement of the Commonwealth's science laboratory contributions was an expression of a long-held Menzies ambition for a national enhancement of science education, an attempt to broaden the appeal of the Liberal Party, and a last-minute, low-cost public relations exercise to give an extra DLP fillip to the Liberal-Country Party vote just before the general election. Menzies was fairly certain he could win the election with or without buttering up the DLP. His political experience, the Gallup polls and John Carrick told him so. When Menzies directed Holt to tell Santamaria that the prime minister was intending to make 'a gesture' towards Commonwealth funding for Catholic schools, he was not exaggerating.[48]

As for the social justice value of the Menzies initiative, there remain doubts about the real benefit of direct Commonwealth state aid for the second-class Catholic citizens of Australia. This was because the 1963 science and scholarship schemes proposal would provide Commonwealth funding to mainly Protestant secondary schools. This accorded with Menzies' elitist view that these socially, financially and intellectually selective schools should be given some supplementary aid. In 1970, Menzies was to make his preference for non-government schools clear:

> In my declining years, witnessing a world in which moral values are treated with such complete contempt in some intellectual, or more accurately, pseudo-intellectual circles, and in which the powerful influence of the Press seems to be, all too frequently, hostile to all received standards of social behavior, I retain my belief in the ancient virtues, and value the services which the church schools and colleges render unto them.[49]

---

[48] Bearing in mind Menzies' last minute nerves. See above p.39.

[49] Menzies, *The Measure of the Years*, 1970, p.95.

CHAPTER ONE

After more than a century of bitter debates about state aid for any denominational schools, the way was now open for state aid for all schools.[50] How that process was handled would be the subject of further rancorous political disagreement for more than half a century. As for the controversial new school lavatories at Our Lady of Mercy Preparatory School, they were eventually paid for, not by the state but by Catholic private subscription.[51]

---

[50] The dispute goes back to Governor Richard Bourke's failed attempt to introduce the government-funded, non-denominational Irish National School system in 1836.

[51] 'The genesis of state aid', *Canberra Times*, 14 July 2012.

Chapter Two

SNOB VALUE

The Menzies Gesture and Educating for Inequality

After his 1963 election victory, when speaking as guest of honour amidst the friendly, even rapturous environment of Sydney's annual Cardinal's Dinner, Menzies restated his motivation for his government's state-aid decision in clear and unambiguous terms. This was 30 July 1964 – the same month that saw his state-aid legislation introduced into Parliament. Prior to the prime minister's speech, Sydney's auxiliary bishop Thomas Muldoon had contributed to the euphoric nature of the evening by introducing the prime minister and declaring Menzies to be 'perhaps the greatest Australian of all time'. Menzies responded:

> Why did we do it? Well, we had various things in mind. In the first place, Australia in this scientific technological age, needs more people trained in science, better trained in science. The Australian universities need to have better equipped students coming up to them in science. We need to have, so far as we can, in the secondary school stages, such an encouragement of talent by teaching and equipment and every other way as to produce more people who will teach in these universities, maintain the standards of the past and increase them, improve them, as they ought to be improved for the future. And, quite frankly, whether it is through stupidity or otherwise, I just don't understand how any such distinction can be made. For us to discriminate in

making a grant in aid for a purpose of high national significance, for us to discriminate between Government schools and non-Government schools, would open up a world of discrimination in other fields to my mind equally unjustifiable.[1]

On that night, Menzies was the Catholics' hero of the hour, an unaccustomed position for the self-styled 'simple Presbyterian' prime minister. Whether or not his heroic status among Catholics in 1964 was justified is one of the issues to be examined in this chapter, which will look in detail at the workings of the Menzies school funding scheme.

In June 1964, an Education Division was set up within the Prime Minister's Department to oversee school and university funding (the latter handled by a Sydney-based Office of Education). As already noted, public servant Ken Jones was elevated from the Cabinet Secretariat to head the new Canberra division, a position that made him one of the most influential figures in the development of Commonwealth support for school education over the next nine years. His new boss was to be Liberal Senator John Gorton, Minister for Works (1963–67) and Education (1963–68).

Jones, who had been promoted without any consultation with Gorton and over the heads of two more senior public servants, was to work closely with his minister on the new funding system, but he did not make a promising start in his new appointment. Gorton could be an irascible character and the Jones appointment, which had come out of the blue to disrupt Gorton's preliminary planning sessions for the new school funding scheme, was not what the minister needed. According to Jones:

---

[1] 'Menzies gives Church Assurance', *Sydney Morning Herald*, 31 July 1964. Menzies was suitably modest about Muldoon's excitable encomium.

CHAPTER TWO

> Gorton had a disrespect generally for the public service because he thought many public servants who applied the book of rules were not interested in getting off their backside and doing things and things had to be done ... Gorton wasn't at all that pleased. Why did there have to be a change? Why can't I continue to work with the people I am [working with]? ... he treated me with pretty short shift [*sic*] ... I had a torrid time, or I thought a torrid time, for about three weeks.[2]

However, bridges were mended as Jones worked hard on the details of administering the science funding program which became a model for Commonwealth capital grants schemes during the subsequent McMahon and Whitlam governments. Gorton quickly became reconciled to the Jones appointment, and after that initial frisson they became close collaborators over education policy, staying in professional touch about education matters after Gorton succeeded Holt as prime minister in 1967.

The nature and significance of the Menzies government's funding largesse for secondary schools was less generous than had been anticipated by popular opinion and by education systems, especially when it came to Catholic schools. Within two years, Catholic education in New South Wales and in Australia generally was in crisis yet again (see below). A closer look at the secondary school science grants scheme reveals part of the reason for the continuing predicament of the Catholic education system. Despite prime ministerial rhetoric, the Menzies scheme had little beneficial effect on the funding of Catholic schools.

Reassuring the states and the smaller (mainly Catholic) non-government schools that the selection process would indeed be equitable, the 1964–65 grant allocation process was outlined by Menzies

---

[2] Jones, TRC 1858/2/60.

in the House of Representatives and by de facto education minister John Gorton in the Senate on 6 March 1964.[3] The £3.75 million available for government schools would be channelled through the states on a pro rata population basis. Individual applications (based on questionnaires) for the remaining £1.25 million, for non-government schools, plus the £2.5 million maximum promised for the 10,000 Commonwealth secondary school scholarships, and the 2,500 technical school scholarships, were to be decided by Gorton's new Commonwealth office. Menzies pointed out that in the first year of the science scheme's broad but thin operation, non-government school applications for science funding would be decided on the basis of need and not all applicant schools might be successful in that first year of funding, 1964–65.[4]

The best way to evaluate the overall significance of the science grants and estimate how far the £5 million per annum for laboratories might have gone, and where it actually went, is to note what Menzies himself said about the grant when allaying sectarian Protestant fears. Menzies commented that it was only a small part of the total of the additional £572 million spending promised in the 1963 election campaign. Further, if we look at the Australian Bureau of Statistics (ABS) calculations of the total of all students at school at age eleven or above in 1964 (just over one million), we have a £5 million annual capital grant being made available to a gross figure of just over one million students, at a mere £5 per annum per student. This was not a grand level of support for school science facilities.

---

[3] Gorton was officially Minister-in-charge of Commonwealth Activities in Education and Research under the Prime Minister, 18 December 1963–14 December 1966.

[4] 'Menzies Gives Details of Plan to Aid Science Education', *Sydney Morning Herald*, 6 March 1964. Not made public at the time was the influence of the Headmasters' Conference Industrial Grants scheme on the Commonwealth's approach.

CHAPTER TWO

As for distribution by school, it is almost impossible to ascertain precisely the number of eligible secondary schools that existed in Australia in 1964, the year when the state-aid legislation was passed. First, primary to secondary transition years varied from state to state and within each state. Second, in rural and remote areas, children of secondary school age often received their education in shared primary/secondary premises. Third, there were different kinds of secondary schools. In New South Wales for example, most government secondary schools were comprehensive establishments (moderate retention), some were selective (high retention), while others were specialist (high retention). In other jurisdictions too there were specialist technical, commercial or domestic science high schools. Fourth, in the 1965 *ABS Yearbook* the calculations for types of schools (primary or secondary) for the states and territories did not include Tasmania, South Australia or Western Australia. One thing we do know is that many secondary schools were small in the 1960s. The bigger 1000-student high schools only began to appear in any numbers during the 1970s. And there is another distribution factor: the gender gap. Most students who went on to study science in senior forms were boys.

Looking at the figures in a slightly different way, and allowing for school size disparities at the state and local level, a very crude reckoning can give us a national total of about 2500 secondary schools. In 1962 it had been calculated that the average 420-student school needed at least three science laboratories. If every Australian secondary school successfully applied for a Commonwealth grant for its three laboratories, each school would have received just £2000 of the capital funding per annum available to build, equip and supply science laboratories, many from the floor up and without including the recurrent cost of laboratory assistants.[5]

By 1962, the cost of fitting out a large secondary school along these lines was estimated at £144,000, which indicates that the cost of building and fitting out a medium-sized high school with three up-to-date laboratories would have been in the order of £72,000, far above the then maximum of £6000 over three years allocated to successful applicant schools by the Menzies plan.[6] This meant that the science grants were helpful but were not quite helpful enough for the disadvantaged Catholic systemic schools, nor the often-struggling government schools which could also count on state government assistance. The real beneficiaries were the mainly Protestant, established, non-government schools that already had science laboratories and could use the additional money for extensions, minor works and equipment top-ups, leaving a larger than customary proportion of a school's private income to be diverted from capital works into recurrent funding – a loophole that was later to become a feature of a more astute, established non-government school's financial modus operandi.

As for long-term funding for Catholic schools, the 1963 breakthrough moment had provided little in the way of financial support for what were system-wide structural problems. The Catholic Church persisted with its inefficient diocesan and parish-led attempts to administer the distribution of meagre Commonwealth and other

---

[5] $55,923 in 2016 terms.

[6] The figures on laboratory costs are based on the 1962 calculations of Sir Graham Savage, assessor for the British Industrial Fund for the Advancement of Scientific Education in Schools as quoted in 'The Sorry State of Science in Schools', *Sydney Morning Herald*, 23 January 1962. School student figures are based on *ABS Yearbooks* 1964 and 1965.

funds. The structural failings of this uncoordinated process were highlighted by a major financial crisis in the Catholic education system in 1966–68, principally caused by the rising number of salary-based lay teachers (as opposed to the poverty-bound clerical teachers who effectively taught for bed and board), declining parish-level revenue, building costs in growing outer suburban areas overseen by amateurish and inefficient lay committees, parental fee defaulting, and the consequent drift away from Catholic schools due to increased school fees that had been put in place to remedy the system's money problem. Despite frantic efforts to raise loans and increase parish levies as well as school fees, by 1967 the Catholic schools of New South Wales seemed to be back where they had been in 1962.

The eventual solution to these problems in New South Wales was not the Menzies scheme but the 1969 award by Sir Robert Askin's Liberal state government of per capita funding for all non-government schools, along with the return of educational finance management back into the clerical orbit. From 1974 onwards, the formation of professionally-organised Catholic education offices at a national and state level, founded to deal more efficiently and more equitably with increasing levels of Commonwealth funding, also helped the Catholic system.[7]

When it came to the secondary scholarship system, little of the annual scholarship money went to government school students.

---

[7] See for example, *Sydney Morning Herald*: 'Rise in Roman Catholic Fees', 26 January 1966; '$1m fund for Church school aid', 26 September 1966;' Bishop announces higher school fees', 18 November 1966; 'School Fees $1m owed', 8 December 1966; 'The Widening Gap', 7 April 1967; 'Church school fees to rise to $6-$10 a term', 4 January 1968; 'School Expenses to Priests', 11 January 1968; '100,000 Catholics go to state schools', 19 January 1968; 'Church planning to retrench teachers', 6 July 1968. Askin's per capita funding policy awarded schools $27 for primary students and $36 for secondary students.

Some did go to Catholic schools but a disproportionate amount still went to students entering the final years of established non-government schools, which, in the late 1960s, were beginning to charge increasingly high fees, widening the gap between scholarship income and school fees, which generally did not include obligatory 'extras'. By 1970, Victoria's Geelong Grammar was charging $2073 per annum for boarders. Most other boys' schools in Victoria and New South Wales were charging $1500–$1700 for boarders and $600-$800 for day students (girls' schools charged slightly less), at a time when the average Australian working wage was $3172.[8]

If we take $700 as the notional mean for day school fees in a boys' school, just over one fifth of an average single-income household's earnings would need to be spent on fees from Form I to Form III (after which competitive Commonwealth scholarships were available for Forms IV and V), severely reducing disposable income over that initial three year period, which was really a hurdle requirement.[9] There was a $300 per annum maximum tax rebate on school fees, but this was a bonus which disproportionately benefited wealthier middle-class parents. A sceptical observer might comment that the scholarship system disadvantaged the less well-off.

There was another problem with non-government school affordability. With the gateway to Commonwealth capital grants and scholarships now open, the road had been cleared for Canberra to provide and oversee capital and recurrent grants to both government

---

[8] 'School fees in Victoria costliest', *Sydney Morning Herald*, 8 October 1970, and 'Weekly Wages, Average Compensation and Minimum Wage for Australia from 1861-Present', *Measuring Worth*, https://www.measuringworth.com.

[9] The wealthier non-government schools did offer competitive bursaries (not large) from Form I onwards, but students from the growing number of fee-paying preparatory schools attached to these secondary schools were generally better placed to pick up these bursaries than students from the public education system.

and non-government schools, within a national and supposedly non-discriminatory grant system that was based on an annual, systematic budgetary arrangement. From 1964 onwards, however, the annual grant figures were not adjusted to mark an increase in secondary school students. By 1968, an estimated $39.6 million had been allocated for science education capital works in the states, a figure that maintained the annual funding level of the original 1963 promise but did not increase, despite a 21 per cent increase in secondary school student numbers in the six states.[10] Not only that, but with an annual inflation rate in 1965–69 hovering between 3.96 and 2.92 per cent, the real value of Commonwealth funding declined during the mid-to-late 1960s. Both these factors reinforce the view that Menzies was only really interested in kick-starting a national science education policy that was to be sustained by the states and the non-government systems.

In summary, the Menzies gesture, based on a combination of political and educational circumstances, allowed the Commonwealth to initiate a policy of state aid in 1963, laying to rest at long last the socially divisive spectre of sectarianism but clearing the way for a successor controversy, a class-based approach to school funding. This change of direction would eventually give the ALP one less dispute to argue about, with Menzies having unintentionally allowed Labor to focus on class inequality and social justice themes, more familiar Labor refrains when it came to education. Furthermore, in all but ending sectarian educational squabbles, Menzies had

---

[10] Calculated from 'Government and non-government schools: pupils, by grade, etc. and sex, states and territories', *ABS yearbooks* 1966 p.596 and 1969 p.492. The ACT and the Northern Territory were funded by a separate system of loans for capital works. The lack of annual increases 1964–68 may have been a sign that the 1963 grants had originally been intended as short-term contributions rather than part of a continuing and expanding program.

inadvertently freed up the ALP to develop a rapprochement with the Catholic Church and its electorally powerful bloc of parishioners, slowly turning away from a fading DLP, whose anti-Communist and pro-state aid raisons d'être were beginning to lose traction with the Catholic community in the late 1960s and early 1970s.[11]

This sectoral divide between the mainly striving government schools and the wealthier non-government schools provided a newly-defeated and still internally divided ALP with a unifying social justice battle cry. Indeed, in March 1964, at an ALP dinner in Smithtown, Tasmania, Calwell's charismatic deputy leader Gough Whitlam spoke up for an inquiry into all levels of education, criticising what he called the compartmentalisation of education and arguing that the role of all schools, including the non-government schools, should be about interpreting the society in which they lived, transforming it and reshaping it. Whitlam went on to say that schools were not just about getting a job and climbing the social ladder, arguing that they were not there just to create 'snob value'.[12]

Calwell, too, joined in the anti-elitist refrain in September 1964 with a parliamentary speech criticising the science grants legislation because, providing capital grants, it did not go far enough. He went further, attacking the scholarship scheme because it would lead to what he regarded as a 'savage competition' for scholarships that would, he alleged somewhat tenuously, produce 'a race of neurotics'. Calwell went further, painting a dismal picture of miserable 'average' (working-class) parents whose equally miserable children would

---

[11] The ALP was still self-harming on the issue until July 1969 when Gough Whitlam put an end to most of the in-fighting (see below).

[12] 'Snob Value' Not Role of Education', *Sydney Morning Herald*, 23 March 1964. A national inquiry into school education was a common ALP demand in the 1960s and early 1970s.

CHAPTER TWO

enter the scholarship examinations in competition with children of the same ability supported by parents in the higher income brackets and who would, 'because of social, cultural, environmental and economic factors[,] do better at school than the children of the same basic intelligence but who come from less fortunate homes'.[13]

Craig McGregor, journalist, critic and leftist social commentator, observed and commented on this class-based phenomenon in August 1965, when he wrote the first of two op-ed articles for the *Sydney Morning Herald* entitled 'Education for Inequality'. In the first of these, 'Scales weighted against the poorer children', McGregor pointed out that a 1962 Australian Council for Education Research (ACER) study of 114,000 school leavers showed that while 35.9 per cent of middle-class male school leavers entered university, only 1.5 per cent of working-class school leavers took the same educational path. The gist of the findings was summed up in McGregor's second article and his comments are worth quoting at length:

> More scholarships would obviously make a lot of difference; in fact there is room for a radical expansion of scholarships at school and university level. But Dr Radford [Director of the ACER] warns that these should not be granted through competitive examination which would once again favour children from high-status backgrounds. He suggests that they should be in the form of 'aid to living' allowances to the families of children who have the ability but come from poor backgrounds.
>
> The granting of scholarships regardless of socio-economic class produced some bizarre results. Melbourne University found that [university] Commonwealth scholarships 'tend to be held by students from wealthier families'. Since the scholarships were introduced a larger proportion of medical students in

---

[13] Reported in 'In Federal Parliament', *Sydney Morning Herald*, 18 September 1964.

NSW has been drawn from an upper-echelon background than ever before.[14]

These issues, however, were to be the focus of a later campaign, after a weary and despondent Calwell made his exit from politics in 1967.

Menzies also retired, in 1966, and was busy enjoying writing and visiting friends as well as fulfilling his 1965 ceremonial appointment as successor to Sir Winston Churchill in the role of Lord Constable of Dover Castle and Warden of the Cinque Ports. In an honourable gesture, Menzies supported Calwell's 1967 appointment as Privy Councillor, the last ALP politician to join that council. Later, Menzies sponsored Calwell's 1970 nomination for an honorary doctorate of laws at the University of Melbourne where the former prime minister was Chancellor.

Calwell died in 1973 and Menzies followed five years later, the latter after having suffered an incapacitating stroke in 1971. Both men are buried in family plots in the Melbourne General Cemetery in Carlton North, Melbourne. By 1978, the year of the former prime minister's death, the Commonwealth Government had created a separate Department of Education, was spending $787.7 million on school education, with an additional $30 million on administrative costs, and $3.1 million on school transport costs: a long way from the 1963 £5 million 'gesture'.[15]

After Menzies retired, education minister John Gorton, an alumnus of Sydney Church of England Grammar School and of Geelong Grammar School, a supporter of the established non-government

---

14   'Age of Inequality (II)', *Sydney Morning Herald*, 19 August 1965. The emphasis on male students was typical of its time.

15   *ABS Yearbook*, 1980 p.291.

CHAPTER TWO

school system and of Commonwealth intervention in education, began a campaign to expand and extend Commonwealth state aid for non-government schools.

Chapter Three

THE GORTON STYLE AND BETTER-ESTABLISHED SCHOOLS

In a smooth act of transition, the popular and energetic Harold Holt succeeded Menzies on 26 January 1966 as leader of the Liberal Party and as Australia's prime minister. Holt's 1966 elevation was no surprise. In 1939 he had been promoted by Menzies to become Australia's youngest junior minister, an appointment followed by a very brief period of wartime military training.[1] In the 1940s, 50s and 60s Holt went on to successive ministerial appointments, including as Treasurer (1958–65). Seen as an accessible and appealing politician of the new era, Holt was characterised presciently by a contemporary current affairs publication as 'gay, debonair [and] vaguely reckless'.[2]

Holt decided to keep Gorton on as a Cabinet-based education 'minister assisting', later formalising Gorton's role as an inaugural Minister for Education and Science after the Coalition's general election victory in late 1966. Gorton was to serve as education minister from 1963 to 1968. He was to set up the Commonwealth's education

---

[1] Menzies pulled Holt out of the military after a serious RAAF plane crash near Canberra killed ten on board including three Cabinet members and the Chief of the General Staff.

[2] Cit. Tom Frame, *The Life and Death of Harold Holt*, Crows Nest, Allen & Unwin, p.145.

bureaucracy; efficiently foster Australia's scientific, technical and higher education reforms; successfully oversee the expansion of state aid programs for government and non-government schools; and put in place the foundations of the Liberal Party's ideological approach to school education.

Holt and Gorton were similar in background and character. Born in 1908 and 1911, respectively, they were alumni of famous independent schools (Wesley and Sydney Church of England Grammar) and had been successful athletes at school and university. Both had served in World War II, although, unlike Holt, Gorton had experienced active service as a gung-ho fighter pilot in the RAAF's 1941–45 campaign against the Japanese. Leaving aside his combat sorties, Gorton had survived what had been for him an eventful war. He had been badly disfigured in January 1942 in Sumatra when crash-landing his Hurricane, was one of those rescued by HMAS *Ballarat* from a torpedoed ammunition ship, MV *Derrymore*, in February 1942, crash-landed his Kittyhawk in the Northern Territory early in 1943, and then made a forced landing in a second Kittyhawk in Milne Bay in March 1943.

As politicians, Holt and Gorton were known for their charm, their hard-working dispositions (14–15 hour days), for their informality and for their spontaneity. Although they were both in supportive and stable marriages, they were also known for their fondness for female companionship.[3]

They did differ in several important respects, however. Holt was a mediator and an ideological pragmatist while Gorton was forceful

---

[3] Holt had a famously close relationship with friend Marjorie Gillespie, and Gorton had as his Principal Private Secretary and close confidante Ainsley Gotto, a relationship that provoked gossip.

CHAPTER THREE

in discussion, held strong political opinions (he was a constitutional federalist or centralist), was impulsive, had clear views about the role and value of education in modern Australia and, as related previously, the role of the public service. In Gorton's case this impulsiveness, combined with a famously fiery temper and contempt for convention, became known as the 'Gorton style'.[4]

According to Ken Jones, who, as we have noted, had been appointed head of the Menzies Cabinet Secretariat before moving on to Education, Gorton had been one of the few ministers who would stand up to Menzies. But he had nevertheless been constrained from expanding Commonwealth aid in his education portfolio by the prime minister's late-career policy caution.[5] Under Holt, however, Gorton was much more able to strike out on his own as an educational reformer and as a defender of the independence of the non-government sector, particularly of the wealthier schools. Indeed, while it was Menzies who had opened a back door to state aid in 1963, it was John Gorton and his successor as education minister, Malcolm Fraser (1968–69 and 1971–72), who were to be the real change agents. They increased the scope of the support to provide a more substantive level of Commonwealth provision for the non-government school sector through grants and scholarships, and a cross-sectoral secondary school library scheme which began funding schools in 1969–70 with an initial grant of $3 million.[6] At the same time, as funding levels for non-government schools grew, Australia's more affluent Protestant schools were increasingly being

---

[4] Gorton had originally been a member of the Country Party but moved over to the Victorian Liberals in 1949.

[5] K. Jones, Interview with Ken Henderson, 1985, TRC/1858/2/56.

[6] Falling to $2.8 million in 1973–74.

seen by Liberal politicians as strongholds of Coalition politics, with their middle-class parents and alumni providing the Coalition with electoral support and parliamentary recruits.

With all of these initiatives, however, Gorton remained a careful custodian of Commonwealth money, especially when it came to higher education. He adopted only some of the major expansionist recommendations of the 1964–65 Martin Report (for more universities and new higher education colleges) in the face of outright opposition to change from Holt's Minister of Labour and National Service, William 'Billy' McMahon, and against the advice of the Treasury.[7] For Gorton, a particularly pleasing achievement in his attempts to develop Australia's higher education network was the foundation of Canberra College of Advanced Education, the first institution in what was to become a national network of advanced colleges and institutes – although Gorton did not envisage them as sub-university, degree-awarding organisations in a revised Australian higher education system.

Although happy to initiate what he hoped would be an Australian system of polytechnic-style institutions, Gorton was no supporter of Commonwealth funding for teacher training. He had two objections. First, a large proportion of Catholic trainee teachers would be employed by Catholic schools, which meant that if their training colleges were to be supported by the Commonwealth, the Catholic education system would receive an indirect higher education subsidy from Canberra. This was a sectarian issue which he had no desire to

---

[7] *Tertiary Education in Australia: Report of the Committee on the Future of Tertiary Education in Australia to the Australian Universities Commission*, Canberra, Government Press. The Committee's chair was Leslie H. Martin, physicist and higher education adviser.

CHAPTER THREE

revive. Second, Gorton's federalist views stopped short at training teachers. He believed that colleges of education were the business of the states and, when it came to the Catholic education system, the business of the Catholic Church.

As foundational minister of education and science, Gorton was no fan either of what he considered to be a post-war fad of emphasising science and technology at the expense of the humanities. Gorton was a follower of Matthew Arnold's nineteenth-century view of the perfectibility of the human spirit through the experience of a liberal education – in both schools and universities – that emphasised the study of history, literature and religion. At the same time, however, he recognised the value of the scientific and technical elements within a broad liberal education, seeing the enlargement of scientific and technological advances as part of a modern Australian industrial revolution which would be underpinned by merit-based Commonwealth Government support.[8]

Gorton became a public advocate for individual and institutional betterment in competitive educational environments. Indeed, as an inaugural and pioneering education minister he laid the groundwork of late twentieth-century Coalition educational thinking when he spoke out for Commonwealth Government support for 'various avenues' ('choice' in other words) in educational provision. These were to be free from needs-based institutional means-testing, which he argued discouraged initiative and would be too complicated.

In a revival of Victorian-era values of hard work and the rewarding of virtue Gorton dismissed the idea that because some parents were relatively wealthy, their children should be excluded from state

---

[8] See I. Hancock, *John Gorton: He did it his way*, Sydney, Hodder, 2002, pp.106-108.

assistance. For Gorton, it was absolutely a matter of social justice that parents who paid taxes, who could afford to pay high fees because of the rewards of their industrious behaviour and whose children performed well in competitive examinations, should benefit from access to Commonwealth support in a non-government education system. Gorton had thus turned the commonly accepted definition of social justice on its head, publicly providing the Liberal Party with its foundational philosophy when it came to school funding.[9]

When it came to managing the funding process, under the guidance of Ken Jones, the Gorton ministry's appraisal of all non-government school applications were assessed against fixed criteria rather than on individual merit. The new system focused, among other things, on school size, numbers studying science, existing school facilities, and a vaguely framed requirement of showing evidence of intent to improve. In other words, small schools with low science enrolments and poor facilities, but with an evident resolve to further the cause of science education, would be given a higher priority for grants over large schools that already had an established science culture and good facilities. To assist Gorton in administering the non-government school scheme, each state was to have Catholic and non-Catholic advisory committees, while Sydney Church of England Grammar School's headmaster L.C. Robson would offer advice to all non-government schools as chair of a national advisory committee, reporting to Gorton.[10]

---

[9] Gorton outlined his ideas on social justice in a major speech at the Second Melbourne Catholic Education Conference, 26 August 1966, cit. Ian Hancock, *John Gorton*, p.110.

[10] Robson, however, died of cancer in December 1964.

CHAPTER THREE

At that time, in the 1960s and 70s, many 'better established' Headmasters' Conference (HMC) and equivalent girls' schools were particularly beset by building renewal and maintenance concerns.[11] Their elite status may have come in part with venerability, but that venerability also came with structural obsolescence and decay as well as with increased running costs. To the principals of these schools, increased Commonwealth funding was a necessity rather than a bonus.

While HMC schools had registered Gorton's commitment to equitable distribution, they had also noted with some apprehension Gough Whitlam's March 1964 comments about 'snob value'. In mid-1964, anxious that their elite status might potentially draw some public anger over being awarded Commonwealth funding, as well as ideological fire from future ALP governments, the HMC set up a Public Relations Committee and accepted the offer of free consultative assistance from the National Fund Raising Council of Australia.[12] The Public Relations Committee's job was to present a unified front when dealing with politics and the media, and to present the 'best possible image of the independent schools'.[13]

---

[11] 'Better established' was originally a neutral Ken Jones term used in official communications about wealthier non-government schools. See K. Jones, 1985, TRC 1858/2/69.

[12] Avoiding the then despised term 'publicity'.

[13] J. Wilson Hogg, *Our Proper Concerns: A History of the Headmasters' Conference of the Independent Schools of Australia*, Parramatta, Macarthur Press, 1986, p.168. After ten years of negotiations across 1975–85, the HMC, formally 'The Headmasters' Conference of Independent Schools of Australia', joined with the Association of Heads of Independent Girls' Schools of Australia in 1985 to form a powerful lobby group, The Association of Heads of Independent Schools of Australia or AHISA. In 2000, AHISA began a collaboration with the Independent Schools Council of Australia or ISCA, the latter group representing schools rather than head teachers.

Aware of the growing cost of secondary schooling, especially in science education, one of the Public Relations Committee's first actions was to conduct a sample survey (31 of the then 71 HMC schools) of self-funded science spending from 1950 to 1964. The survey showed that the sampled schools had spent £8.5 million on science facilities during that period, with another £2 million allocated for 1965–66, an average of £338,000 per school over the sixteen-year period.[14] The idea behind publicising the survey was to impress upon public and political opinion the self-funded nature of HMC schools and their taking the lead in Australia's science education initiatives long before the Menzies scheme had been opened up for applications in 1964.

It was not just the HMC that was trying to make a good impression. During that settling-in period while Gorton and Jones liaised with representatives from individual 'better-established' Protestant schools and the HMC/HISGS schools, they also frequently met Archbishop James Carroll of the Catholic education system. Later, during the early 1970s, the education department officials also had meetings with the Catholic Education Commission and with their overseers, the Bishops' Central Committee.[15] During Gorton's ministry, ad hoc encounters between government ministers, officials and non-government school stakeholders were to be replaced by more orderly and more systematic forms of consultation.

Recognising the importance of making direct personal contact with all of the HMC schools and continuing to reassure them about the government's position, Gorton spoke at their thirteenth

---

[14] $9 million in today's terms.

[15] K. Jones, 1985, TRC 1858/2/69.

CHAPTER THREE

triennial conference on 30 August 1965, where he spent an entire morning taking questions and discussing the implications of the Menzies changes for HMC schools. The minister's thoughts were that the Commonwealth scheme needed to be extended into teacher professional development, libraries and language laboratories, but he advised his listeners that there were still 'latent and deep resentments' among the wider public about this kind of Commonwealth funding for independent schools, especially for socially exclusive schools. Gorton counselled the previously aloof HMC that it was time for its members to engage with the broader community in an attempt to dispel claims of 'elitism, privilege and snobbery'.[16]

Accordingly, the HMC realised that future growth, prosperity and reputation depended not only on fund-raising efforts among traditional sponsors, but also on effective publicity and getting their educational and financial messages across to the general public. Thanks to the carefully framed advice of John Gorton and the work of its Public Relations Committee, the HMC was about to move from the genteel Anglophile world of neo-gothic cloisters into the hurly burly of pressure group politics.

In a not particularly tactful keynote speech, the newly appointed HMC chairman, Colin Healey, attempted to reach out to likeminded members of society by vigorously defending the HMC way of life.[17] In a passionate address, he effectively aligned the HMC with Liberal Party politics by including references to the importance of spiritual and moral values, the idea of parental choice, hostile materialistic

---

[16] Cit. J. W. Hogg, *Our Proper Concerns*, p.167.
[17] Headmaster of Melbourne's Scotch College and former headmaster of Sydney Church of England Grammar School.

ideologies (Socialism and Marxism), the importance of social cohesion and the crucial nature of individual charitable compassion:

> Let us not forget that our schools actually are very great ones ... Our picture has been blurred in the past by ignorance of our composition and personality by emotional misjudgements and by unsound political philosophy. The greater responsibility lies upon us because of our independence to show that we are trying to guide our schools according to the Divine Illumination. We do not wish to make our schools dividers of the nation's society. But we wish to maintain the principle that diversity is not necessarily the enemy of social cohesion and that an assertion of faith, because it is an old faith, is not contemptible conservatism ... To call our schools now the preserve of the rich is absurd. We all of us know the many cases of parents of very straitened means whose sons we educate. I think of instances I know of widows whose incomes are well under £1000 a year with sons at independent schools. Such people are helped by their schools, and we must continue and increase our measures to help them.[18]

However, providing widows with assistance did not make up for the deficiencies in the government's senior secondary scholarship system, which was still geared towards middle-class students at HMC (and HMC-aligned) schools who were staying on beyond the minimum school-leaving age.

The Commonwealth scholarship subsidy was largely an irrelevance for most non-government school students who, from the mid-1960s onwards, had been eligible for state relief for textbooks and other school-related activities. After 1967, the states, following Victoria's example, even awarded small per capita bursaries. Furthermore, the more able of these students could be subsidised by various state

---

[18] The HMC had taken on the role of mentor and protector of aspirational non-HMC private schools.

CHAPTER THREE

governments and by Catholic bursary schemes.[19] While it is true that Commonwealth scholarships were helpful for senior students in the Catholic school system, transition numbers into the non-compulsory years of systemic Catholic schooling were about the same as the equivalent figures in government schools, and far below retention rates in HMC and similar schools. All in all, in the late 1960s the Commonwealth scholarship scheme still provided a disproportionate benefit to students attending the wealthier non-government schools.[20]

Meanwhile, in 1966, the ALP had continued on its path of political self-harm. In June 1966, a ferociously worded minority report of the ALP's national education advisory committee was presented by deputy leader Gough Whitlam and four supporters.[21] They forcefully advocated a national education inquiry and an impartial schools commission along the lines of the Australian Universities Commission, which were also recommended less stridently by the majority report. The proposals were opposed by the ALP's national executive.

Seven months later, however, Whitlam had been elected to lead the ALP, and by late 1968 the establishment of a Schools Commission had become official ALP policy. The Coalition government had no such embarrassing public quarrels and in 1969, in a significant and radical

---

[19] By the late 1960s governments in all states had introduced minor per capita grants for non-government primary schools, a development that was to put increasing pressure on the Commonwealth to follow their example.

[20] While dealing with broader state-aid issues, Gorton was also beset by an intense campaign from 1966 onwards by the Library Association of Australia (LAA) to improve school library provision by funding primary as well as secondary school libraries. The situation was resolved in the LAA's favour by the Whitlam government.

[21] The four supporters were Tasmanian Minister of education W.H. Neilson, West Australian State MP J. T. Tonkin, Tasmanian Lance Barnard, and L.J Reynolds of News South Wales.

move, Gorton followed the example of Victoria's Liberal premier Sir Henry Bolte by increasing his level of support for non-government schools. Gorton moved on from just capital grants and scholarships to introducing general recurrent grants for all non-government schools, a scheme which came into operation from 1970 onwards. This was a major development since recurrent costs included salaries, normally a large proportion of a school's operating expenses. The growing level of expense involved in that new system can be seen from the figures. In 1969–70, the Commonwealth cost for recurrent expenditure disbursed to non-government schools was a (by now decimalised) $12.1 million. By 1973–74, general recurrent grants had risen to $54 million, a 348 per cent increase over five years. In contrast, all capital grants to non-government schools (science and libraries) in 1973–74 totalled $6.7 million.[22] Gorton's 1969 decision provided a new level of relief for non-government schools and marked a major turning point in Australia's school funding saga.

Back in the world of politics, towards the end of 1967 the Holt government was heading into trouble. The Coalition government was running out of steam after nearly twenty years in power and a 5 per cent swing to the ALP had been registered by a Gallup poll in September 1967. The prime minister had also lost some of his allure and his political touch in badly mismanaging a bothersome and lingering domestic scandal over the use of the RAAF's VIP fleet. The November 1967 Gallup poll then recorded the Coalition's worst showing since 1961, a Senate election was won by the ALP

---

[22] The aim was to help Catholic schools, still struggling with their recurrent costs. The amounts were $35 per primary school student and $50 per secondary school student. From 1973 onwards, recurrent grants were fixed at 20 per cent of the cost of educating a child in a government school. See I. A. Wilkinson et al., *A History of State Aid*, Table 2.1, p.40.

CHAPTER THREE

in November 1967, and Labor also gained two seats in by-elections at Corio (Victoria) and Dawson (Queensland).[23] Additionally, the war in Vietnam was about to take an unpopular turn among Australian voters.

A New South Wales state election was due in 1968 and a general election scheduled for 1969. John Carrick, still an energetic and highly capable General Secretary of the New South Wales Liberal Party, wrote to Gorton in December 1967 suggesting that an extra $20 per capita be added to the existing Commonwealth secondary scholarship grants (set at a $400 maximum) to help with these upcoming election campaigns. While Carrick, Holt, Gorton and other Liberal Party leaders were well aware of the past benefits of the 1963–66 drift of disillusioned Catholic voters to the DLP, they were now anxious about a possible drift back by Catholics to a resurgent, Whitlam-led ALP. Gorton accepted the politically-motivated proposition: Commonwealth scholarships were to be increased in 1968.[24]

Perhaps because of the unusual circumstance surrounding his sudden elevation to the prime ministership and his equally sudden departure from the same office, Gorton's educational achievements are little remembered in conventional histories of Australia.[25] On 15 December 1967, while on a working holiday in the Mornington Peninsula, Holt decided to take a swim in rough surf off Cheviot

---

[23] 'Poll indicates a swing of 5 p.c. to Labor', 13 September 1967 and 'Govt. popularity lowest since 1961 says poll', *Sydney Morning Herald*, 17 November 1967.

[24] Even so, the 1969 DLP vote fell and a renascent ALP, while losing the election, managed to claw back eighteen seats from the Coalition. School scholarships were increased in August 1968 in Gorton's first budget as prime minister.

[25] Gorton stepped down in controversial circumstances in March 1971 after publicly losing Fraser's support and a consequent tied vote of no confidence in the Liberal party room. Gorton never forgave Malcolm Fraser for his allegedly subversive actions.

Beach and was never seen again. Holt was officially declared dead on 19 December; a memorial service took place on 22 December and was followed by some Christmas-season internal Liberal Party politicking. On 9 January 1968, Gorton, who had been a very capable Senate leader for his party, was elected leader of the Liberals and sworn in as prime minister, while remaining in the senate. That anomaly was fixed in February when he was elected member for Higgins in a by-election.

Gorton's period as prime minister was overshadowed by the publicity surrounding the Holt drowning, the unusual and remarked-upon rapport the prime minister had had with his young parliamentary secretary Ainsley Gotto and the fact that he occupied a political space between the sentimentalised Menzies era and the contentious Whitlam and Fraser eras. Nevertheless, as education minister, Gorton was remembered by his administrative head of department Peter Lawler as 'impressive', by his assistant secretary Ken Jones as 'magnificent', and by historian and biographer Ian Hancock as 'an outstanding success'.[26]

Gorton's term as education minister led to a watershed series of events in the development of school education policy-making and of higher education development in Australia. As far as state aid was concerned, the Coalition, at both Commonwealth and state levels, had committed itself to continuing to provide generous financial support for its natural allies, Australia's leading non-government schools. At the same time, equivalent Commonwealth support was, of constitutional necessity, guaranteed for all Catholic schools, thus forming an unlikely but powerful alliance between old rivals: the

---

[26] Hancock, *John Gorton*, pp.105 and 121.

CHAPTER THREE

Catholic schools and the mainly Protestant non-government schools systems, which were quick to realise the benefits of a united front. Moreover, but Gorton's decision to provide recurrent funding for non-government schools opened the way for state funding equivalence with government schools.

Seeing this, the ALP was quick to realise that a new approach to school education policy would be beneficial: one which argued that elitist non-government schools drained the pool of Commonwealth Government funding, which should by rights go to government schools. As for the ALP's relations with the Catholic schools, the time had come for reconciliation with the hope that such rapprochement might drive an electorally advantageous wedge between conservative Protestants and ALP-forgiving Catholics.

Meanwhile, in February 1968, John Gorton, newly-installed as prime minister, offered the Cabinet position of Minister of Education and Science to Liberal MP Malcolm Fraser. The Cabinet appointment was a reward for Fraser's support during a bitterly contested post-Holt internal campaign for the prime ministership, and Fraser took up his new job on 28 February 1968. The former army minister had been, and remained, a strong advocate for an Australian forward defence policy, a supporter of the 1964 revival of conscription and a defender of Australian involvement in the war in Vietnam. Education was not his political passion of the moment, but a Cabinet post was a Cabinet post.

Chapter Four

MALCOLM FRASER

Let's Pitch It a Little Higher and See How We Get On

During Holt's prime ministership, Fraser had been an assiduous army minister and an ardent enthusiast for Australia's civil assistance program in Phuoc Tuy province, South Vietnam. He was now leaving the army portfolio during a tense time with the ferocious January-February 1968 Tet Offensive still underway, and when US public opinion and (secretly) US strategic opinion was turning against the war in Vietnam. Accordingly, the new education minister came to his job with half his mind still caught up in the complexities of South-East Asian politics and Australia's role in Vietnam, issues that were publicly and privately to preoccupy him over the next twenty-two months before Gorton appointed him Minister of Defence in October 1969.[1] At the same time, Fraser's new position offered him a chance to oversee a containable set of policies that were far removed in distance, in character, and in order of difficulty from the Vietnam entanglement.

---

[1] Following his close to four-year stint in the Gorton administration, the two men fell out badly in March 1971 and Fraser went to the backbenches until his return to Cabinet as Prime Minister McMahon's Education Minister in August 1971. See below p.75.

As with Gorton, Fraser's school and university days provided him with inspiration for his very clear anti-collectivist views about education.[2] Unlike Gorton, however, Fraser had no faith in the perfectibility of human behaviour, which, in his view, was the flawed argument of political romantics who favoured ideological determinism and state intervention. Overall, Fraser's ideological position was that individual rights and freedoms trumped state intervention. Despite his cautious approach to theory, he was at that stage interested in Keynes and, in keeping with his stubborn individuality, an admirer of controversial Oxford historian AJP Taylor, as well as a fan of wide-ranging philosopher and historian Arnold Toynbee. In summary, Fraser was a stern anti-communist who was in favour of individual endeavour within a clear, humanistic moral framework.

As a person and as a politician, Fraser was a reserved and commanding figure (6'5" tall in the old scale) combining a gruff, emotionless and unyielding demeanour with a relentless work ethic. Fraser operated from within a fixed set of principles; he had a capacity for ruthless action which came out particularly strongly during a challenge, when he would remorselessly enter into a confrontation if it affected his position or his values. On the other hand, he welcomed the advice of those in politics and in the public service who disagreed with him, as long as their differences of opinion were carefully argued. In line with his principles, he was an early and individualistic conservative activist for social diversity, human rights, the right to protest peacefully, Indigenous land rights, environmental conservation and multiculturalism.[3] At the same time, because of his

---

[2] Melbourne Grammar School and Magdalen College, Oxford (his father's old college).

[3] Fraser was a leading advocate of 'multiculturalism', a term he used in 1969, four years before it was first used by Whitlam's controversial minister for immigration Al Grassby.

CHAPTER FOUR

landowning background, his university education, his conventional views on social issues such as abortion and his haughty manner, he came across to colleagues and outside observers as a dyed-in-the-wool Liberal traditionalist.

As education minister, Fraser worked slowly and cautiously to develop his own views about funding schools and at first he kept a relatively low profile. Fraser did receive delegations from the HMC and the Catholic schools system in 1968, each group wanting what they considered to be the next stage in increased Commonwealth funding: per capita recurrent support.[4] Fraser jibbed at that idea on sectarian grounds and his only major policy initiative during that first year in office was to announce a national ministerial conference on education issues in September 1968, which was to discuss the operating principles of the new Colleges of Advanced Education.[5]

With education policy proposals still mired in debates about social division, Fraser responded by taking a strong and unambiguous stand on school funding. In October 1968 he addressed the issue during his speech at a college dinner at the University of Adelaide. He told the attendees that non-government schools had a right to state aid and, following Gorton's line, he maintained that there was neither justice nor equity in attempting to deprive all non-government schools of Commonwealth funding.[6] Not only that, but in what was to become

---

[4] During a tight 1967 state election campaign and at the urging of Santamaria over DLP preferences, limited per capita support was offered to non-government schools by Victoria's Liberal premier Sir Henry Bolte. The rest of the major jurisdictions followed suit 1968–69, putting pressure on the Commonwealth to follow Victoria's lead.

[5] This was the first of a series of annual meetings of all education ministers. A national network of CAEs, as they became known, grew rapidly. By 1973 there were 101 colleges of various sorts, including teacher training colleges.

[6] 'Govt. support for independent schools a 'right'', *Sydney Morning Herald*, 26 October 1968.

– 63 –

a repeated Fraser and Coalition theme, he warned his audience that any drift of enrolments from non-government schools towards government schools that might be caused by an ALP-imposed reduction in state aid would lead to an increased economic burden on taxpayers.[7]

In December 1968, Fraser followed up his October remarks by provocatively – and characteristically – rejecting a New South Wales request for a funding loan for government schools, while simultaneously announcing a $3.6 million outright 'gift' to the non-government schools of the Australian Capital Territory. The ACT was still a Commonwealth jurisdictional enclave where, according to an acerbic *Sydney Morning Herald* editorial, 'the general standard of schools in Canberra would be the envy of State or independent authorities'.[8] Sir Robert 'Bob' Askin, the then outspoken premier of New South Wales, who had been persuaded by John Carrick and John Howard to move into providing direct state aid in late 1966, was furious that his state's schools had not also benefited from Fraser's generosity. The following year saw a revival of political tensions over state aid with Fraser asserting his position at a number of public forums.

On the other side of politics, as we have already seen, in June 1966 Whitlam had moved towards a schools commission and, when it came to establishing such a commission, Whitlam was not alone. Even the normally conservative *Sydney Morning Herald* thought a schools commission was a good idea because it would reduce political opportunism across all school and college education policy areas. The

---

[7] Cit. Philip Ayres (1987), *Malcolm Fraser; A Biography*, Richmond, William Heinemann Australia, p.135.

[8] 'Christmas gift', *Sydney Morning Herald*, 13 December 1968.

CHAPTER FOUR

ALP federal executive, Whitlam's 'twelve witless men' of ill repute, was still dominated by anti-state-aiders who loathed Whitlam and regarded him as a subversive progressive. They refused to accept the minority report's recommendations.[9] Seven months later, however, Whitlam had been elected to lead the ALP and in late 1968 the establishment of a Schools Commission became official ALP policy.

The result of such a move was that, in an election year, the Coalition was on the point of losing education as a political wedge. Fraser immediately attempted to push back against Whitlam by demanding the ALP leader give 'strong support' in parliament to the non-government sector. Whitlam countered by demanding that Fraser give a ministerial statement in parliament which could lead to an open debate. Nothing came of that idea and each protagonist backed off on these parliamentary challenges while pressing on with public confrontations.[10] State aid, however, was still anathema to the ALP hierarchy.

On 26 February 1969 Fraser attended the opening of a Catholic college at the Australian National University. At this event he informed his listeners that the Commonwealth Government would 'expand and cater for that section of the population which had always been educated in independent schools', a clear reference to both Catholic and non-Catholic non-government schools. In his address, Fraser took up the justice and equity theme again, arguing further that he could 'see no reason why three-quarters of the

---

[9] The 'witless' remark was made by Whitlam in February 1966 on television, and had almost led to his expulsion.

[10] 'Caucus backs Whitlam in $25m State aid', *Sydney Morning Herald*, 27 March 1968. Whitlam had announced his decision on 23 February and the ALP Caucus had backed it on 19 March. The backing of the ALP's National Executive was yet to come. *Sydney Morning Herald*, 7 May, 1969.

population should be educated in Government schools while the remaining quarter were educated in independent schools without Government aid.'[11]

Using carefully phrased prose that was meant to be both guarded and persuasive, Whitlam's position on state aid remained unequivocal. He supported Commonwealth support for all educational institutions, government and non-government. To Whitlam this was an equal opportunity issue and a matter of social justice. He explained his position in a letter to the readership of the (at that time) anti-ALP *Sydney Morning Herald* on 7 May 1969:

> It is part of a precise and consistent plan to ensure that Australia's national Government should do for all schools, Government and non-Government, at least as much as it does for universities and at least as much as the national Governments of comparable countries do for their schools.[12]

In the same letters column, Fraser, denying that he had said, as the *Herald* had previously reported, that 'only private schools can rescue today's youth', outlined his position on the non-government sector, based on two key assertions. First, 'there is value in diversity ... [which] improves the general quality of education'. Second, in a democracy, the efforts of those involved in supplying 'their own educational needs carries with it a right to reasonable support from the Government both state and Federal'.[13]

The embarrassing 'today's youth' quote actually belonged to Attorney General Nigel Bowen (soon to be Fraser's short-lived and

---

[11] 'Hint on state aid', *Sydney Morning Herald*, 27 February 1969.

[12] Letters Column, *Sydney Morning Herald*, 7 May 1969.

[13] 'Mr Bowen's Kite', *Sydney Morning Herald*, 7 May, 1969. *The Herald* apologised for putting words in Fraser's mouth.

CHAPTER FOUR

unexceptional successor in the education ministry), who had been speaking at a 5 May 1969 Sydney meeting of Catholic parents attended by, among others, an almost certainly disconcerted Gough Whitlam and an equally startled Fraser. Bowen then floated the possibility that the Commonwealth might even take over all secondary schools, going well off message with a rant about modern youth:

> I believe it could be a real danger for Australia if all our youth grew up without access to spiritual values, without training in our accepted conventions of behaviour – searching for beliefs and conventions and open to every way-out'ism.[14]

The pre-election state-aid debate heated up in late autumn of 1969 with the next major confrontation at Sydney Town Hall on 31 May, where a mass meeting was convened by the New South Wales Teachers' Federation; they were still opposed to state aid in any form, while at the same time demanding improvements in salaries and working conditions. This was followed by a 1 June mass meeting (one of eight Sydney gatherings in May and June) of Catholic parents, teachers and clergy to be addressed by leading Coalition and ALP figures.

In a heated atmosphere where the issue of Catholics as second-class citizens was raised once again, both Fraser and Whitlam spoke in a circumlocutory manner, with Fraser promising 'significant support' during government discussions preceding the August budget, and Whitlam reiterating his promise, if elected, of a $25 million grant to non-government schools. The Catholics were unimpressed. They

---

[14] 'Bowen Sees New Aid to Non-state Schools', *Sydney Morning Herald*, 5 May 1969. Incidentally, the *Herald* also carried the story of the Los Angeles launch of the destroyer *USS Harold E. Holt*. The launch bottle bounced seven times before it smashed.

wanted sustained state aid based on Commonwealth per capita recurrent funding, not vague promises of Coalition support, nor an Opposition promise of a large, one-off payment. The states had moved to per capita recurrent funding and the Catholics upped the stakes. Commonwealth grant handouts were no longer enough.

Meanwhile, important by-election campaigns in Bendigo and Gwydir (western New South Wales) were under way and state aid was at the heart of the Bendigo campaign. Gorton spoke at Kyneton, promising increased aid for all schools on the narrow grounds that all schools should have 'the same facilities', with a rambling justification for state aid for non-government schools based on his aversion to 'frozen syllabuses' in a prevailing and 'monolithic' government system. He added in the school closures scare factor of a Goulburn-style, collapsing non-government system, proclaiming that if the non-government schools expired because of lack of funding it would be a national economic problem and children would have to be 'forced to attend state schools'.[15]

The 7 June 1969 by-election results were a mixed outcome for all concerned. The ALP retained Bendigo but with a reduced majority. The Liberals also had a slightly reduced vote. In Gwydir, the Country Party retained their seat despite a 7 per cent swing to the ALP.

Sydney Morning Herald political journalist Ian Fitchett saw the Bendigo result as a plus for the ALP in a state where the ALP was at a low ebb, but he also saw the Gwydir result as a blow for the Country Party. As for the state-aid issue, it was generally held that, beyond Victorian hardcore ALP opponents of state aid and a few stubborn ALP holdouts elsewhere, the sectarian element in

---

15 'P.M. openly backs aid for schools', *Sydney Morning Herald*, 4 June 1969.

CHAPTER FOUR

the political debate was dead. Whitlam reinforced the point at a Catholic parents' meeting at Wollongong on 8 June, explaining that because of the population explosion, it was as inevitable that the Commonwealth would have to help schools as it had been for Canberra to assist the universities.[16]

Whitlam took the caucus's full state-aid decision to the Victorian ALP conference in Collingwood on 14 June where, while he was warmly applauded after a typically resonant speech, the diehard Victorian state branch voted against recurrent state aid as well as against Whitlam's foreign and defence policies.[17] The state-aid argument within the ALP had taken a familiar turn.

With a general election due later that year, Whitlam's party remained split, with its Victorian branch in conflict with the ALP national executive over state aid (and other matters). Most of Victoria's left-leaning members favoured phasing out state aid altogether and regarded some of the other branches, particularly the New South Wales branch, as sell-outs. Whitlam, having been publicly rebuffed at Collingwood, believed that the ALP was all but unelectable if it pursued such a divisive agenda. He decided that it was time to intervene.

On 17 July 1969, the ALP held a preliminary meeting of state and federal party leaders in Sydney. The meeting unanimously endorsed Whitlam's policy of recurrent state aid for government and non-government schools. Whitlam also got his way at the biennial national conference in Melbourne on 2 August, despite rumblings from Western Australia's still active Joe Chamberlain and the anti-

---

[16] 'After the by-elections', *Sydney Morning Herald*, 10 June 1969.

[17] 'State Aid a 'Must' – Whitlam', *Sydney Morning Herald*, 15 June 1969, and 'Victoria ensures Gorton's return', *Sydney Morning Herald*, 17 June 1969.

Catholic Victorian Left. His victory only came after a promise to form an Australian schools commission to 'examine and determine the needs of students in Government and non-Government primary, secondary and technical schools'. On the next day, the national conference modified his proposed $50 million 'emergency grant' to government and non-government schools from an outright fifty-fifty split to a per capita arrangement, while at the same time endorsing the principle of Commonwealth support for all schools.[18] Meanwhile, Whitlam and the ALP were busy reforming the party structure and abolishing the turbulent Victorian branch, moves still regarded by some veteran members of the ALP Left as acts of treachery.

In what was characterised by the *Sydney Morning Herald* as a 'bidding war', Opposition leader Whitlam then promised the non-government schools a disproportionate 50 per cent of a huge, ALP caucus-approved $50 million grant to all schools in 1970–71 should the ALP be elected.

On 28 June, Malcolm Fraser, having anticipated the ALP's next move and looked for a new demarcation line, persisted with his warning that non-government schools were not being given 'common justice'. In repositioning the Coalition on the issue, Fraser used the school closures scare tactic in a second attempt to wedge Whitlam and his party:

> The problem of providing places in Government schools will be aggravated if a number of independent schools are forced to close, which I believe, would be the situation, if additional aid were not forthcoming … [The disproportionate nature of the promised $50 million grant] is a clear recognition by Mr

---

[18] 'Labor defines State aid policy', *Sydney Morning Herald*, 2 August 1969.

CHAPTER FOUR

Whitlam of the fact that the independent schools have special problems not shared by State schools.[19]

Fraser's line on state aid was becoming clearer. Initially, he had opposed per capita recurrent funding because of its potential to be criticised as sectarian. By late 1969 he had changed his mind. During mid-1969, Fraser had commissioned a departmental survey of non-government schools, to be directed by Ken Jones, the results of which went to Cabinet late in 1969. The survey, which told Jones and Fraser what they already knew, showed that Catholic schools were still in what Jones called 'dire straits' and, still struggling with pay issues, had not gained any real advantage out of a block capital grants system.[20]

Recurrent and capital state aid were by now a bipartisan policy. What differences remained were now about how the aid was to be distributed. In that regard, the Left-instigated plan for a schools commission, on the face of it a sensible enough idea, was a danger signal as far as Fraser was concerned. If Whitlam gained power, it would be the Left of the ALP that would have a hand in determining the proposed commission's terms of reference, which were unlikely to be favourable to the non-government schools sector.

Fraser would have to look at Coalition policy again if he wanted to neutralise the latest Whitlam triumph, and pre-empt any attacks on non-government schools by a subsequent ALP government. The

---

[19] 'Schools – State Aid or Closure ... Warning by Minister', *Sydney Morning Herald*, 29 June 1969. Only the Coalition side of politics had mentioned school closures.

[20] K. Jones, 1985, TRC 1858/70. Jones said that the survey was teed up to support a recurrent funding policy. The Australian Education Commission had commissioned a national survey of education needs in August 1969 which had also pointed out the inequities in the current funding arrangements. Gorton passed the survey's report on to a working party led by progressive Liberal Don Chipp which fed its findings into a National Goals Sub-Committee. I R Wilkinson et al., 2006 p.41.

education minister acted quickly. In the House of Representatives on 13 August 1969, he promised per capita, non means-tested Commonwealth recurrent funding as a policy to be included in the Coalition's platform for the forthcoming spring general election. During the planning stages of the recurrent funding scheme, Fraser was discussing the possible extent of recurrent funding with Ken Jones, and in an uncharacteristically spontaneous move, Fraser suggested that Jones should 'pitch it a little higher and see how we get on'. If the Coalition won the next election, at both state and Commonwealth levels, the richest schools would be given the same per capita allowance as the poorest. Fraser's barrier to later ALP governmental interference had been put in place.[21]

Fraser had reached that position because his solution to recurring state aid crises had to be a Coalition per capita grants scheme to assist with recurrent costs. As far as Fraser was concerned, the issue was neither a class nor a sectarian issue but a matter of pragmatism and principle. His reasoning was simple. Catholic schools needed yet more help because block capital grants alone and state-level subsidies had not worked. If the Catholic school system collapsed for lack of money, Commonwealth and state jurisdictions would suffer. On the other hand, if the Catholic schools were to receive direct per capita recurrent state aid to provide a stable and viable educational level of provision for their students, the mainly Protestant (and mainly

---

21 One of the political problems associated with state-aid funding was dismantling already-established arrangements that favoured any particular voting bloc. An administrative issue was the lead-in time required to make legislative amendments. To give schools time to adjust over four-year funding periods, the process normally started with a May budget announcement, went on to the November/December final legislative processes and was then introduced during the following year or even the year after. In this case, Fraser's pre-emptive plans might not be introduced until the 1971 school year at the earliest.

financially secure) non-government school sector would have a socially-just right to be given help as well, whether their schools needed it or not. Needs-based education policies were not suited to non-government schools because the disparities between the financial circumstances of Catholic and established Protestant schools would lead to an inequitable allocation of resources where Catholic schools would gain more than their Protestant allies. Government schools were out of the equation, already well cared for by the states and by the Commonwealth, with the latter providing up to 50 per cent of government school costs.

In making this decision, Fraser laid down the basis for later Liberal Party policy on state aid in which he outlined, yet again, the Liberal social justice argument. In his view, the fact that Commonwealth funding supplemented already generous income from private sources was simply a sign of a non-government school community's worthy industriousness. Moreover, as he stated:

> We believe it is the democratic right of persons to be allowed to establish independent schools such as we have in Australia. We do not believe in government monopoly ... We categorically reject the argument that because a significant number of citizens choose to seek a form of education for their children which they preferred to the state system and are prepared to make financial sacrifices, those citizens cannot expect any help from the state even though they are easing its financial and physical burden ... To deny a school assistance on the grounds that it was already producing good academic results would be to penalise excellence.[22]

---

[22] Cit. Malcolm Fraser and Margaret Simons (2015), *Malcolm Fraser: The Political Memoirs*, Carlton, Melbourne University Publishing, p.175.

The Coalition won the 25 October 1969 general election with a reduced majority. But Whitlam was an inspiring leader, the previously divisive state-aid issue seemed to have been resolved at last, and the ALP was now within reach of victory after two decades in opposition. The newly founded Council for the Defence of Government Schools (DOGS) fielded nineteen general-election candidates across four states, a move that came to nothing in parliamentary terms but which gave the organisation a good deal of publicity.[23] The state-aid issue was not quite dead and buried yet.

With the House of Representatives election won, Gorton moved Fraser to the position of defence minister in his new cabinet. This was a post that Fraser held for almost two years until he fell out badly with his former mentor in 1971, when Gorton was in charge of a government in steep decline.[24] The Gorton style, which had deteriorated into erratic impulsiveness, was no longer working. In addition, Fraser was at loggerheads with the prime minister over the Vietnam imbroglio, was furious about Gorton's back-channelling with Defence, and was anxious about a wilting Gorton's ability to deal with an ascendant Opposition led by parliamentary virtuoso Whitlam.

In March 1971, Fraser acted. After delivering a vitriolic resignation speech in the House of Representatives, criticising Gorton for his

---

23   See for example a full-page feature article by Margaret Jones, 'DOGS are putting the bite in the election', *Sydney Morning Herald*, 15 October 1969. The article included a telling cartoon of schoolboys Whitlam and Gorton standing next to a recumbent hound which had DOGS painted on its back and was gripping a bone-shaped document marked 'state aid' in its mouth. The caption reads 'I thought between us two we had buried that bone once and for all!'

24   Fraser was succeeded in his first term as education minister by lawyer Nigel Bowen (1969–71) and by pastoralist David Fairbairn (1971–72). Neither distinguished themselves in the position.

CHAPTER FOUR

interventionism and disloyalty, Fraser returned to the backbenches. He was reinstated in August 1971 as education minister by incoming prime minister McMahon, after Gorton had used his casting vote to remove himself from office. Although he had been the second most senior member of the Gorton Cabinet and had performed well as Treasurer (1966–69), McMahon was distrusted and disliked on both sides of politics mainly because of his fondness for career-enhancing leaks to the media. 'Tiberius with a telephone' was arguably Whitlam's least insulting description of his opponent.[25]

Fraser's second period as education minister (August 1971 – November 1972) came following that post-Gorton party leadership reshuffle, and was noteworthy for the education minister's support for an expansion of Commonwealth funding in tertiary education and determined insistence on the expansion of aid to non-government schools. Fraser's second term was also noteworthy for his unusual tactic, based on his leadership intent, of deliberately paying little political attention to his talented education opposite number, Kim Beazley Snr, focusing instead on the charismatic Whitlam. At the same time, the HMC began a campaign to develop an even closer relationship with the Coalition government.

In November 1971, Basil 'Jika' Travers, chairman of the HMC, reported to his Standing Committee that, together with the Chairwoman of the Association of Heads of Independent Girls' Schools (AHIGS), he had recently had a formal meeting with Fraser and had also attended a meeting of the Senate Select Committee

---

[25] Cit. Julian Leeser (2012), 'McMahon, Sir William (Billy) (1908–1988)', *Australian Dictionary of Biography*, http://adb.anu.edu.au/biography/mcmahon-sir-william-billy-15043. This was an unkind reference to the Roman emperor Tiberius (14–37 AD) who in later life became a reclusive tyrant.

on Education. Travers was principal of Sydney Church of England Grammar School (1959–84), a well-known former sportsman, a keen networker and forceful advocate of the non-government schools' cause. According to J Wilson Hogg, the HMC's historian, the November meetings had gone well and 'valuable contacts had been made'.[26]

Six months later, in May 1972, Travers was in Canberra again, this time accompanied by JM Dixon, Chairman of the National Council of Independent Schools. Travers and Dixon arrived in Canberra with a specific agenda: to find out what Fraser had meant in a recent statement on increased capital funding for government and non-government schools. Again, the meeting went well. According to Hogg, 'The Minister for Education made it clear that he would welcome comment and advice which might assist in framing the appropriate legislation'.[27]

During Fraser's second ministry, recurrent grants for non-government schools were increased, and a new level of capital grants for government and non-government schools was set to be introduced in 1973. The plan was for 40 per cent of the educational costs of a student at a non-government school to be jointly funded by the jurisdictions and by the Commonwealth. Not all states were happy about that proposal. The less wealthy states of Tasmania, South Australia and Western Australia (all ALP at that time) were critical, on equity grounds.

Fraser's motivation for stepping up the tempo in 1971–72 was his concern about ongoing funding problems within the Catholic

---

[26] J.W. Hogg, p.207.

[27] J.W. Hogg, p.207.

CHAPTER FOUR

systemic schools at a time when the next House of Representatives election was due in late 1972. In May 1972, polling predictions were already looking dire for the Coalition, and Fraser wanted to get his per capita system and the new 40 per cent scheme up and running prior to the forthcoming election. As noted, this would make it harder for any incoming ALP government to reverse the 1963–72 Gorton/Fraser achievements of providing increased capital funding and introducing recurrent subsidies for Catholic schools, many of which were still struggling to stay solvent. Dearer to Coalition hearts was Commonwealth support for the more comfortably well-off Protestant schools, and that would also remain in place if and when Fraser could get his latest changes established, which he did.

The figures tell the story. When Gorton first became education minister in January 1966, the Commonwealth was committed to providing up to $5 million in capital grants to all schools for science laboratories and up to $10 million per annum in upper secondary school scholarships. Six years later, according to the 1972 *ABS Yearbook*, the Commonwealth had budgeted for up to $43.3 million for school laboratories. Under the 1968 libraries act, $27 million in capital grants had been made to the states over the three years, commencing 1 January 1969, to finance buildings and associated capital facilities for libraries in government and non-government secondary schools. As for recurrent grants, under the non-government schools legislation, payments were made to the states, for transmission to non-government schools. These payments were for contributions to school running costs at rates of $35 per primary pupil and $50 per secondary pupil per annum as from the beginning of 1970.[28]

---

[28] The States Grants (Science Laboratories) Act 1971 (extended for the four years ending 30 June 1975), the States Grants (Secondary School Libraries) Act 1968

Of the science grants, as we have seen, a disproportionate amount of that funding would have gone to non-Catholic, non-government schools and the same was the case with the library funding. The non means-tested per capita approach to funding for non-government schools was a direct and unabashed contribution to recurring expenses in line with Fraser's moral reasoning that tax-paying parents who chose to send their children to wealthy non-government schools were making a democratic individual choice, and each student needed pro rata financial support. This was written into a Commonwealth Department of Education publication, *Achievements of the Commonwealth Government in Education*, at Fraser's instigation, as 'The Government firmly supports the fundamental right of the individual to choose his [*sic*] system of education, and that is why the Government's programs are designed to promote equality of opportunity in all schools'.[29] Interestingly, when it came to post-compulsory tertiary education, Fraser later reversed his logic while in opposition. In the face of Whitlam's proposed policy of free university and college studies he remarked in an April 1974 radio broadcast, 'Labor's policy of free tertiary education would result in the giant inequality of a wharf labourer paying taxes to subsidise a lawyer's education.'[30]

Prior to the approaching 1972 general election Fraser, with typical determination, conducted an election campaign of his own using his newly-developed reasoning regarding the state-aid issue as a tactical

---

and the States Grants (Independent Schools) Act 1969. *ABS Yearbook* 1972, Public Finance p.550.

[29] Cit. I.A. Wilkinson et al, 2006, p.43.

[30] Cit. P. Ayres, 1987, p.200. Among other issues, the comment presumes that children of working class families would never become lawyers.

CHAPTER FOUR

device to tempt Whitlam and the ALP into a fight and bring out old divisions in the Labor opposition.[31] Fraser pointed out that his progressive measures had included increased funding for both government *and* non-government schools, as well as a move by the Commonwealth Government into funding state-based teacher training colleges and pre-school training colleges. Additionally, Fraser gained Cabinet approval of the Australian Universities Commission's and the Australian Commission on Advanced Education's requests for combined triennial funding 1973–75 of $1.4 billion, a 45 per cent increase on the previous triennium. Within that figure, the growth of Colleges of Advanced Education funding 1973–75 would eventually reach a staggering 117 per cent increase over the 1969–72 triennium.[32] Furthermore, Fraser approved increased spending on secondary scholarships, support for Indigenous and migrant students, set up the Commonwealth Teaching Service to provide staff for ACT and NT schools, and allocated $274,688 for research into education.[33]

The closer the election date came, the more Fraser ramped up his rhetoric, continually playing the 'centralist' card, accusing Whitlam of attempting to create a government school 'monopoly' and of trying to create 'government by commission'; these were phrases that, to a Catholic audience, might smack of Soviet-style collectivism.[34] Taking his cause into public meetings, Fraser even taunted his opponents when,

---

[31] The election was to be held on 2 December, announced on 10 October by the increasingly hapless McMahon who had omitted to inform his Country party colleagues of the election date.

[32] P. Ayres, 1987, pp.198–200.

[33] '$274,688 granted to support research into education', *Sydney Morning Herald*, 20 November 1972.

[34] 'Centralism in Labor's Plans', *Sydney Morning Herald*, 16 November 1972.

for example, at a Campbelltown election meeting on 24 November, he attacked a phalanx of ALP supporters, noticeable by their 'It's Time' buttons, for not taking him on. After twenty-five minutes of an uninterrupted Fraser tirade against allegedly mendacious teacher unionism, one audience member dared to interrupt the politician. 'I wish I had more like you' was Fraser's quick reply, and, turning to the rest of the audience he complained, 'It's a struggle to get a reaction out of you'.[35]

Not all of Fraser's colleagues were convinced of the appropriateness of his aggressively disdainful strategy, especially regarding the funding of wealthy private schools. Their own positions, as members of a disliked, scandal-affected and error-prone government led by the ineffective and unpopular McMahon, was becoming more precarious by the month and Fraser's belligerence was not helping. It is clear from contemporaneous political commentary that Coalition MPs, many of whom were not fond of Fraser the man, thought that pushing for more money for well-to-do schools was a dangerously provocative tactic that played into the ALP's hands.[36] Fraser did acknowledge that there might be a problem with such an unremitting approach and, sticking with the idea of private initiative, he urged non-government schools to award more bursaries and, reaching hard for justification, argued that more funding for the non-government schools would mean lower fees. The HMC schools were supportive of the idea of more bursaries but, in practice, they failed to respond.[37] And history

---

[35] 'Teachers making false claims', *Sydney Morning Herald*, 25 November 1972.

[36] See for example Max Walsh's feature column, 'Minister punts heavily on his party's handout', *Sun-Herald*, 28 July 1972.

[37] 'Private school bursary plan commended', *Sydney Morning Herald*, 1 July 1972.

CHAPTER FOUR

demonstrated that in the period 1962–72, non-government school fees tended to go up rather than down, whatever the circumstances.[38]

As part of his assertive election strategy, Fraser continued to take on Whitlam directly, all but ignoring Opposition education spokesman Kim Beazley Snr. Fraser argued that the ALP used selective statistics as part of their intention to cut state aid to non-government schools and that Whitlam was planning to set up a Schools Commission to implement those cuts. Moreover, the ALP was, he alleged, intending to set up a state monopoly.[39] He also pointed out that he had reviewed the scholarship system to remove some of its inequities. Before the election date was announced, Fraser even challenged the Opposition leader to a 5 October debate in Whitlam's own constituency of Werriwa.

As it transpired, the proposed locking of antlers in Werriwa was overtaken by two events: the election announcement on 11 October and the *Sydney Morning Herald's* awkwardly-timed (for the ALP) publication of damaging excerpts from Arthur Calwell's memoirs, which contained revelations regarding his fraught relations with Whitlam.[40] Calwell's vengeful 5 October endorsement of union

---

[38] A search of the *Sydney Morning Herald* archives from 1 January 1962 to 30 December 1972 reveals no entry under 'school fees fall' or 'school fees down'. A similar search for 'school fees rise' or 'school fees up' shows seven mentions about annual rises.

[39] 'Fraser Defends Education System', *Sydney Morning Herald*, 6 April 1972; MP attacks Plan to Reduce Aid to Schools, *Sydney Morning Herald*, 9 July 1972; 'State Aid Labor Under Fire Again, *Sydney Morning Herald*, 20 November 1972; 'Centralism' In Labor's Education Plans', *Sydney Morning Herald*, 16 November; 'Fraser calls on Whitlam to debate education', *Sydney Morning Herald*, 21 September 1972.

[40] 'The Calwell Story: Gough Whitlam and I', *Sydney Morning Herald*, 2 October 1972. Calwell had been hit hard in the November 1966 election campaign by Whitlam's 21 November announcement that, contrary to ALP policy, regular Australian troops might stay in Vietnam. In Calwell's opinion, Whitlam lost the ALP the election.

leader Bob Hawke as 'the ablest man in the ALP' did not help the ALP's cause either.[41]

But Fraser's single-handed election campaign and Calwell's sabotage came to nothing. It was Whitlam who, having promised innovation and renewal with a vaguely framed offer to replace per capita funding and make it the fastest growing area of Budget expenditure, seized the education policy initiative prior to Election Day. McMahon's election offer consisted of a list of worthy but uncontroversial assurances followed by a rejection of needs-based funding. Neither set of promises seemed to be a significant factor in the election result except that Whitlam promised change and an improvement in quality of life, and McMahon promised a familiar route, which, since Menzies had retired, had seen a succession of prime ministerial misadventures, blunders and gaffes.[42] On 2 December 1972, McMahon's government failed at the polls and the brief but incandescent Whitlam era began.

In the event, the Coalition government was ousted because McMahon had neither the manner nor the capability of a prime minister, because the Coalition was divided over finance issues, because the DLP was no longer a valuable ally and because the Liberal Party was visibly suffering from low morale. After twenty-three years of conservatism, the electorate was suffering from Coalition fatigue. In the election itself, a 2.64 per cent swing to the ALP combined with the second preferences of the progressive Australia Party and a continuing (slight) reduction in the DLP vote gave the ALP a nine-

---

41 'Hawke is ablest in ALP – Calwell', *Sydney Morning Herald*, 6 October 1972.

42 The term 'quality of life' became an increasingly common motif in popular debate from 1968–72. The phrase referred to a perception that there was a growing contrast between Australia's national prosperity and uncertainties about individual and sectoral wellbeing.

CHAPTER FOUR

seat majority, although Whitlam would still have to contend with a hostile senate.

Once the ALP victory had been declared, Whitlam wasted no time waiting for the final results to be called, quickly convening the ALP caucus to elect ministers. He and his ever-reliable deputy, Lance Barnard, were sworn in on 5 December 1975 as ministers in a two-man government, with Whitlam temporarily in charge of thirteen portfolios and Barnard momentarily responsible for fourteen.[43] Almost immediately, Whitlam gave the non-government schools temporary reassurance by announcing that the McMahon government's school funding arrangements for 1973 and 1974 would remain in place.

Probably the best summary of how these latter events unfolded – and how Australians reacted to these events – can be found in this 1973 commentary in *The Australian* by then-journalist Robert Drewe, a commentary cited several times by Whitlam in his speeches and writings. Drewe's observations have the same kind of feel about them as Wordsworth's exultant response to the commencement of the French Revolution, particularly the poet's remarks on the passing of 'forbidding ways / Of custom, law, and statute', and his comment that the revolutionaries had, 'The Chance to Put Their Schemes into Practice'. Here is Drewe's more modern assessment:

> You're aware of a certain rare feeling of national self-respect these days. It's not as if we're suddenly a big-shot country ... but the fact is that Labor restored some dignity to the conduct of our national affairs at a time when we had all come more or less to expect nothing but ill from political action.

---

[43] Technically it was a three-man government. The Governor-General Sir Paul Hasluck was an ex-officio government member during the interim period.

Without precedent in the history of British-style governments, it set out to make up for lost time by immediately implementing its campaign promises. Australians blinked as within weeks we recognized China, ended conscription, abolished race as a criterion of our immigration policy, began reform of the health service, supported equal pay for women, abolished British honours, increased arts subsidies, put contraceptives on the medical benefits list, took the tax off Australian wine, moved to stop the slaughter of kangaroos and crocodiles and searched for a new national anthem. Along the way, the Government attempted to make our relationship with America ... a bit less one-sided. The End of The Ice Age, is how Russell [sic] Ward describes the new era in a current Meanjin article.[44]

When the duumvirate had been replaced on 19 December by a fully-manned and sworn-in Cabinet, the new education minister Kim Beazley Snr began his work on switching from a per capita state funding model to a needs-based approach. And this is where economist Professor Peter Karmel, chair of a newly-established Interim Committee for the Australian Schools Commission, came in. The first task of the Committee was to establish a position somewhere between the abolitionist location of the remaining anti state-aiders, such as DOGS, who were resolutely against any form of non-government school eligibility for Commonwealth support, and the conservative view of undifferentiated eligibility, as enunciated by Malcolm Fraser's support for per capita funding, where parent and school prosperity were immaterial elements in deciding who should

---

[44] Taken from a transcription of a Whitlam speech at Old Parliament House 3 December 2002 and reported in *The Age*, http://www.theage.com.au/articles/2002/12/02/1038712880799.html. Interestingly, in this speech Whitlam omitted the original Drewe reference to the formation of the Schools Commission. Perhaps he forgot or perhaps he left it out because the actual Schools Commission was set up in December 1973.

CHAPTER FOUR

be awarded Commonwealth support. The Karmel solution was differentiated eligibility within a needs-based funding framework.

However, whatever Karmel was to propose, it had been Fraser's 1969 decision to adopt per capita funding for non-government schools that became another major turning point in the story of the development of state aid policy in modern Australia. Fraser's work, building on Gorton's policy improvisations, laid the practical and philosophical foundations of the Coalition's later highly politicised educational initiatives – manoeuvrings that were originally based on a matter of principle, but which were soon to become matters of partisan class-based opportunism.

Chapter Five

THE WHITLAM GOVERNMENT

The Chance to Put Their Schemes into Practice

At a press conference on 12 December 1972, Gough Whitlam announced the formation of an Interim Committee for the Australian Schools Commission to be chaired by Peter Karmel. A cultured educational reformer with immaculate academic, administrative and public service pedigrees, Karmel had begun his rise to policy pre-eminence working as a statistician in the Commonwealth Bureau of Census and Statistics, before and during Australia's post-war reconstruction phase.[1] More recently, he had been foundation vice-chancellor of Flinders University (1966), chair of a 1969–70 Committee of Enquiry into Education in South Australia, and was, in 1972, chair of the Australian Universities Commission, which was to provide the model for Whitlam's planned Schools Commission. The Commission's organisation, rationale and *mode d'emploi* were to be established by the Interim Committee.

---

[1] Where he had not been afraid to offer his opinion in the face of countervailing social and economic views. See S. Macintyre, *Australia's Boldest Experiment: War and Reconstruction in the 1940s*, Sydney, New South Publishing, 2015, p.234.

The Interim Committee, quickly known as the Karmel Committee, included two independent school-sector representatives. They were Alice Whitley (former principal, Methodist Ladies' College, Sydney) and Father Francis Michael Martin (Catholic Education Office, Melbourne). Education lecturer Jean Blackburn, as deputy chair, represented the progressive end of the educational continuum. Blackburn, who was a former teacher, former communist and enduring feminist, had already worked with Karmel on the 1969–70 South Australian inquiry.[2] As it happened, the use of one of the South Australian inquiry's major research tools, a survey of all schools that covered their assets and the economic needs of their students, was to become a controversial issue for non-government schools.

The committee contained no representative from either Tasmania or Queensland.[3] Parents' associations and teacher unions were quick to criticise this and other omissions from the list; there were no parent or working teacher representatives.[4] After that initial outburst of grassroots exasperation, the Christmas and summer holidays intervened and, until the Committee published its findings in late May 1973, there was little further in the way of public criticism.

---

[2] Other committee members were Geoff Hancock (New South Wales Education Department); Edward T. Jackson, Technical Education Department Victoria; A.W. Jones, South Australian Education Department; Peter Tannock, Faculty of Education University of Western Australia and Catholic educator; M.E. Thomas, Education Department New South Wales and Wilfred White, teacher liaison officer Department of Education, South Australia. Interestingly, nobody picked up on Jean Blackburn's former Communist party membership, almost certainly because this was a pre-digital information age and because she had kept a low profile until she left the party in 1956.

[3] Tasmania's premier was 'Electric Eric' Reece, a confirmed anti-centralist who was just about to engage in a struggle with the Whitlam government over states' rights and the Lake Pedder environmental issue. Queensland was led by Premier Joh Bjelke-Petersen, a dyed-in-the-wool enemy of Whitlam and all that he stood for.

[4] 'Education groups hit commission', *Sydney Morning Herald*, 14 December 1972.

CHAPTER FIVE

Coalition opposition to the work of the Interim Committee was hamstrung by Whitlam's appointment of the politically-unaligned Karmel. Indeed, when still in office, in March 1972, Malcolm Fraser had asked Karmel to investigate the problem of graduate employment, unintentionally cementing Karmel's virtually untouchable status as chair of this new Committee.[5]

In the meantime, new education minister Beazley kept a low profile on school policy. His major concerns during January to May 1973 were teacher unemployment in New South Wales, Indigenous education issues, pre-school expansion, setting up a technical education commission, dealing with the idea of an open university and the announcement in March of his 1974-onwards free tertiary education policy, seen as yet more 'creeping centralism' by the *Sydney Morning Herald*.[6]

During the period preceding the publication of the Karmel Committee's findings, the independent school sector remained anxious about any carryover of the ALP's fierce 'wealthy schools' election rhetoric. Keen to sound out the intent of the new government, the HMC took the unprecedented step of inviting ALP leaders Whitlam and Barnard as guests of honour to the March 1973 Canberra dinner of the HMC's Standing Committee. Chair of that committee 'Jika' Travers spoke first. Whitlam then spoke briefly in general terms, followed by Barnard who spoke at length. According to HMC chronicler J Wilson Hogg, who was present:

> It was clear that what he [Barnard] said had been most carefully prepared: it was at once far-reaching and profound, and at times

---

[5] 'Leave pupils at school, says Fraser', *Sydney Morning Herald*, 7 March 1972. Fraser slipped the Karmel remark into a televised talk about state aid.

[6] 'Masked Centralism', *Sydney Morning Herald*, 31 March 1973.

brilliant. Nothing that the Prime Minister or Minister for Education had to say betrayed the faintest bias for or against any particular form of schooling. Indeed, all three addresses revealed vast areas of common ground.

Reassured, the HMC decided the occasion had been a great success.[7]

This feeling of harmony and good will was to dissipate, however, once the Karmel Committee report was published in late May 1973. Unsurprisingly, the report was to become the main preoccupation of the August 1973 HMC conference where it was to divide opinion, with disagreements hindering a common HMC response.[8]

The Catholic sector had been very busy long before Karmel. Following the 1964 awarding of Commonwealth grants, the Catholic Church had set up a federal Catholic Education Commission, first convened in 1969 with annual meetings until 1971, followed by the formation of a Standing Committee, which lasted until the 1974 formation of a National Catholic Education Commission (NCEC). In preparation for new political circumstances and in light of the formation of a proposed Schools Commission, the Church's hierarchy followed Western Australia's example in supplementing the work of local diocesan education offices by setting up state-level commissions in Melbourne (1973), Sydney (1974), Brisbane (1973), Hobart (1978) and Adelaide (1973). The work of these commissions was to oversee and coordinate Catholic school systems within their respective bailiwicks, deal with internal funding allocation policy and act as forceful supra-diocesan advocates for a Catholic education system that had previously been dispersed and disconnected.

---

[7] J.W. Hogg, 1986, p.207. As chair of the HMC Standing Committee, Hogg had himself previously invited the more politically congenial pairing of Menzies and Dame Pattie to the only other occasion of this kind.

[8] J.W. Hogg, 1986, pp.208–209.

CHAPTER FIVE

When the Karmel report was published on 30 May 1973 the initial response was mixed. The 178-page report, a clearly laid-out document that combined statistics with analysis and with consequent policy suggestions, argued that students within the major education systems suffered from a variety of injustices, mainly to do with staffing, resourcing and the provision of educational opportunity. The committee proposed that, while curriculum and management should be diverse, there must be a basic level of educational provision for all children. The report contended that per capita funding did not address the current injustices since, to put it simply, the wealthier schools were adding their per capita funding to other forms of income (including fees, bequests, fund-raising and loans). Meanwhile, the less well-off non-government schools were struggling to maintain a decent level of educational provision, even with state or system funding plus Commonwealth per capita funding.

The report further asserted that Commonwealth funding should be based on identified needs, not just on raw student numbers. To make this happen, and having surveyed independent schools, the report proposed a seven-point school-needs classification which would assist in determining who got what. The soon-to-be-established Schools Commission's funding programs were to cover general needs, special needs and educational improvements. The needs categories were recurrent funding, capital funding, libraries for primary and secondary schools, funding for special schools, funding for disadvantaged schools, money for teacher professional development, and a funding allocation for special projects and innovations. Controversially, all schools would be classified within an A to H set of priority categories (a South Australian initiative), with wealthy independent schools in the A group having their per capita funding cut altogether.

There were other recommendations, including the plan to democratise school management by forming parent councils (opposed by the teacher unions), and a proposal to hold recipients of Commonwealth-tied grants more accountable for their expenditure. To alleviate the shock of the per capita cut-offs, the Karmel Committee recommended that funding for Category A schools would be phased out in stages to avoid sudden financial crises. The remaining schools would gain Commonwealth funding on a sliding scale based on net income. The government expected government schools would receive $461 million in Commonwealth aid while all independent schools, which had lost their per capita annual grants ($104 per secondary student and $62 per primary student) would still receive $179 million in other grants.

The report anticipated that 140 independent schools would gradually lose Commonwealth funding, a calculation that was overtaken by events when the Whitlam cabinet abruptly announced on 13 June that the per capita funding cut-off point for all Category A schools would be at the end of 1973.

The education community's responses to the report were varied. The Karmel Committee's recommendation that schools should set up governing bodies or councils that involved parents proved to be a step too far for some teaching organisations. Politically, the Coalition had little room to manoeuvre since the Karmel Report was not a partisan set of arguments but a calmly-expressed analysis laid out in systematic, black and white detail by a committee chaired by a reputable academic whom Fraser had once considered for another

CHAPTER FIVE

key investigative post. And wealthy Category A schools did not have many defenders among the wider electorate.

The Catholic reaction to Karmel was generally positive.[9] Indeed, the Catholic representative on the Karmel Committee, Father Francis Martin, Director of Catholic Education in the Melbourne Archdiocese, revealed that he had supported the Category A cuts.[10] The Bishops preferred per capita funding but, of the three major education systems, the Catholic schools overall did stand to be the main beneficiaries of the new system since most Catholic schools were in the lower needs-based categories. The official Catholic position was that as long as the new system was not centralist, over-bureaucratised, did not impinge on the autonomy of the Catholic education system and treated all children in all independent schools equally, the bishops were satisfied that there would be a spirit of 'harmonious co-operation between federal and state governments, parents and their organisations and the various bodies which conduct schools in the independent sector'.[11]

As we have seen, five of the Catholic systems had already moved or were quickly moving into state-level, Commission-friendly mode (Tasmania rather slowly) to provide a national network of Catholic bureaucracies. In the new system, their job would be to distribute the additional funding, coordinate school activities and staffing, liaise

---

[9] Late in the day, a Bishops' conference in August did, somewhat unrealistically, suggest that the Catholic schools that benefited from the A-H grading should hand back money to support those schools that received none. That idea came to nothing. 'Catholic schools may renounce aid', *Sydney Morning Herald*, 1 September 1973. Santamaria's response was to denounce Karmel.

[10] 'Catholic member backs "A" cut', *Sydney Morning Herald*, 10 August 1973.

[11] See, 'Bishops Spell Out Policy on Aid to Schools', *Catholic Weekly*, 7 June 1973. The complaint about bureaucracy seems to have been a pointed remark about Church-State relations when it came to authorising and building new schools.

with diocesan offices, deal with state governments and advocate for the Catholic education system. The Church's post-Karmel optimism was later partially dissipated once each archdiocese worked out the cost of these new Commissions, expenses that would have to come out of the Church's share of Commonwealth largesse.

As might be expected, the response of the other non-government schools was unenthusiastic, especially when it came to staffing implications. Most of the larger (c. 600-student) non-Catholic schools had received about $60,000 each per annum in Commonwealth recurrent funding through per capita grants alone, money that was largely spent on staffing. The bigger independent schools (c. 900-student) stood to lose as much as $97,000 per annum in recurrent funding at a time when an average graduate secondary teacher's annual salary lay between $4000 and $6000.[12] Leaving aside scholarships and capital grants, if we take $5000 to be an average salary, this means that, in New South Wales at least, Karmel's Category A schools would have to make swingeing teaching staff cuts. Indeed, some medium-to-large schools might lose as many as twelve full-time teachers in staff rooms that would normally accommodate about 30–40 teaching staff.[13]

The HMC's reaction was largely negative. At their November 1973 annual meeting it was argued by the chair, 'Jika' Travers, that the Karmel Committee had tried to do too much too quickly, lacked 'breadth of educational understanding and knowledge', did not fully appreciate the workings of independent schools, and was 'superficial

---

[12] The lowish salaries of New South Wales independent schools had recently come more into line with union-gained state school salaries. The salary range takes into account jurisdictional variations.

[13] Based on a 1:20 whole school staff student ratio which would have been a normal figure for the time.

and limited in concept'. This line of attack became a recurring HMC theme, along with the view that school communities that worked hard to raise voluntary contributions were being penalised for their success.[14]

Colin Healey, the thoroughly conservative headmaster of Scotch College, Melbourne, was at his 'choleric best' in his criticism.[15] Healey pronounced that 'the mountain has brought forth a mouse ... We should not waste too much time on, nor over-emphasise, our disgust at the ridiculous differentiation of schools in categories of per capita grants ... the Report appears to be a pagan product of materialistic needs [read, socialist] which pay lip service to independence but really aims at the destruction of independence by making it too expensive'.[16] In contrast, Jesuit headmaster Father John Hawkins of Xavier College, Kew, suggested that the HMC members should look for the positives in the report, a cautiously optimistic comment reflecting the fact that the Catholic Church seemed to have benefited most from the Karmel changes, even if his own college had not. As it happened, Healey's financial problems were to be alleviated by increasing school fees and by promises from Victoria's education minister and deputy premier Lindsay Thompson of increased state-level grants. In other words, he promised a low-profile aid package that would almost certainly have been available to the rest of Victoria's Category A schools.[17] This kind of handout would also have occurred

---

[14] In a report to the HMC, cited in Hogg, 1987, p.209.

[15] J.W. Hogg's description p.209. In 1977 Scotch College was one of the largest schools in Australia, with 1173 senior students and 422 students in junior classes. Healey's school stood to lose about $130,000 per annum which would, according to the Reserve Bank of Australia inflation calculator, be a massive $1.17 million per annum in 2016 terms.

[16] Cit. J.W. Hogg, 1986, pp.209–210.

[17] See *The Scotch Collegian* (1973) pp.6–7 for details.

in other states and could explain the more or less resigned, rather than outraged, attitude of HMC schools to the Karmel changes. A $100 per annum per capita fee rise plus a state-level subsidy might even leave Category A schools better off than they were before the proposed Karmel cuts.[18]

On the final day of the November HMC conference, Commonwealth education minister Kim Beazley Snr entered the lion's den to speak and to take questions. He did mollify some attendees by announcing that schools could appeal against their Category A designation but he remained firm on the principle of needs-based funding. The general tenor of the non-Catholic independent schools' response, apart from Healey's fulminations, seemed to be a resigned acceptance of the Whitlam government's policy and a decision to adjust to new circumstances by raising fees. It was almost as if the headmasters felt they had been let off lightly. The schools did argue that such a move would force out that proportion of their students from families with a limited capacity to pay fees, leading to the independent schools becoming 'the preserve of the rich'. That was their argument, at least.[19] The reality was that Category A schools, even with their very long waiting lists, their supplementary assistance from the states and their increased fees, did little to expand their in-school bursary programs.[20]

The political response was much more hostile. At first, state governments (three Coalition and three ALP) seemed perfectly happy with the Karmel Committee's findings and recommendations,

---

[18] See for example, 'Lost school aid may raise fees', *Sydney Morning Herald*, 14 June 1973.

[19] 'Fees may rise $100', *Sydney Morning Herald*, 15 June 1973.

[20] As it happened, Scotch College's numbers went up to 1721 in the college in 1977. The figures in the junior school followed the upward trend to 463.

CHAPTER FIVE

which included an increase in funding for mainstream government schools, for technical education, for special education, disadvantaged schools and teacher professional development. New South Wales Education Minister Eric Willis, while not rhapsodic in his response, was cautiously welcoming, especially about the funding increase. On the day after the report was released, he commented that 'my initial reaction is to commend the report with certain reservations. The proposals for NSW parallel closely my own department's assessment of the situation', adding that the money to cover new initiatives needed to be available.[21] In Victoria, education minister Lindsay Thompson's reaction was more begrudging, using education to pick up on a long-standing jurisdictional issue over state autonomy when it came to the management of Commonwealth grants. Victoria was not happy about the idea that Canberra should audit a state's disbursement of Commonwealth money.

While the initial reaction of the education community to the funding changes was generally positive at the time when Kim Beazley Snr met his State counterparts on 14 June, matters soon took a sour turn. An irate Lindsay Thompson went head-to-head with Beazley over the accountability issue, so much so that Thompson, normally a sanguine political operator, had to be calmed down by Eric Willis. In the grander scheme of things though, the states remained positive about the proposed educational reforms even when the premiers convened on June 28 for their annual meeting with the prime minister, on this occasion under the public gaze, a Whitlam innovation.

---

[21] 'Schools report realistic - Willis', *Sydney Morning Herald*, 31 May 1973.

The main items for discussion were related to Whitlam's use of Section 96 of the Constitution to move into social improvement areas (including education) normally managed by 'tied grants' to the states.[22] Other items for discussion included Whitlam's ending of appeals to the Privy Council, taxation issues, special financial assistance to the states, unemployment relief, sewerage projects in Victoria, assistance to local governments, migrant labour for railways and so on. Whitlam, a centralist who was exasperated by the states' unsystematic approach to the disbursement of Canberra's money, held firm on not increasing the Commonwealth's ad hoc hand-outs. Education was indeed an agenda item but it provoked little debate. The meeting ended in rancorous grandstanding with accusations that Whitlam had breached faith with the premiers and was intent on 'starving out' the states.[23]

Following that conference, Whitlam attempted to intimidate the discontented premiers. Undeterred by falling opinion polls, the prime minister announced in August that he would be having no more collective talks with state premiers. From now on, Canberra's inter-jurisdictional business would take place through correspondence and private meetings.[24] A year later, it was business as usual. The premiers' conferences took place in June 1974 and 1975.

The Opposition's spokesman on education, Nigel Bowen, took a not unexpected stance, attacking the cuts to Category A independent schools as a broken promise. Beazley was targeted as the Opposition's

---

[22] Commonwealth aid to States if and when 'it sees fit'.

[23] The premiers at that meeting were Sir Robert Askin (NSW), Rupert Hamer (Victoria), Joh Bjelke-Petersen (Queensland), Don Dunstan (South Australia), John Tonkin (Western Australia) and Eric Reece (Tasmania).

[24] 'Whitlam to abandon Premiers' conference', *Sydney Morning Herald*, 20 August 1973.

CHAPTER FIVE

main offender, for it was he, according to Bowen, who had said prior to the election that no independent school would be the worse off as a result of any Whitlam government changes. Furthermore, cutting per capita grants off so abruptly in 1973 was a 'savage discrimination against a particular group of schools'. Using the HMC argument that students would be forced out of independent schools, Bowen further suggested, in something of a stretch, that the savings gained would be outweighed by the additional cost to the state schools of taking in new students.[25]

Beazley's response to criticism of the Karmel Report was to take a different tack from his previous position of advocacy for state aid for all schools. Addressing the July 1973 ALP conference, Beazley attacked Nigel Bowen's point of view. Beazley declared that it was time to end education's dominance by 'the articulate middle classes' who, he asserted, gained a disproportionate amount of educational aid while the poor were disadvantaged by their social position of 'political impotence'. 'What are the values of our society?', Beazley queried. 'What are the priorities of Australia when one tiny select group of schools received more public attention and concern than the other 98.5 per cent?'[26]

Quoting a carefully selected passage taken from the Karmel Report as an illustrative example highlighting the financial problems still troubling the Catholic education system, Beazley outlined a case where a Catholic school had been forced to salvage desks from a junkyard, desks that had been dumped by better-resourced government and non-government schools. Beazley then stepped up

---

[25] 'Opposition attacks school grant cuts', *Sydney Morning Herald*, 15 June 1973.
[26] 'Education Directed By Middle Classes', *Sydney Morning Herald*, 11 July 1973.

the rhetoric: 'These are the conditions which are retarding intellectual growth, stunting achievement, destroying satisfaction – in effect making schools a prison and education a sentence'.[27] And that was why, in Beazley's view, an independent Schools Commission was needed to oversee the development of a more equitable process of school funding.

As if to support Beazley's case, when the New South Wales school categories were announced on 6 August 1973, of the State's eight aspirational De La Salle (Catholic) secondary schools, none achieved a Karmel grading higher than H. The ALP position was that this kind of problem would best be remedied by a needs-based funding model managed by a stand-alone Schools Commission, taking the school funding issue beyond the reach of partisan political and sectoral manoeuvring.

Such a Schools Commission had been a long time coming. In 1963–64, progressive Victorian ALP members Race Mathews and David Bennett, both Fabian reformists who were close to Whitlam, drafted *Looking to the Future*, an education policy statement in which the authors, keen to get it past the Victorian Junta, skirted around the state-aid issue and focused on educational need in the Catholic system. In order to bring about ALP-friendly change, Mathews and Bennett advocated a national education inquiry and the provision of needs-based state aid to independent schools as long as government schools were brought up to the same resource levels as their more successful independent counterparts. The best way to make this happen, they argued, was, among other steps, to found an independent national school commission similar to the

---

[27] 'Education Directed By Middle Classes', *Sydney Morning Herald*, 11 July 1973. Beazley's example came from p.46 of the Karmel Report.

CHAPTER FIVE

existing New Zealand Commission on Education, answerable to the Commonwealth minister of education. This proposal worked its way around internal party opposition and, as we have seen, was accepted by the ALP in August 1969.[28]

Accordingly, in July 1973, with the wind of the generally positive response to the Karmel Report in his sails, Beazley started work on setting up the Schools Commission. He rang Ken McKinnon, at that time Director of Education in Papua New Guinea, with whom he had a direct connection through the Moral Rearmament Movement, and invited him to become chair of the new federal body. A month later McKinnon arrived in Canberra and his appointment was announced on 24 September.

In McKinnon's view, the Commission should not be just a funding agency, disbursing Commonwealth money in a fair and equitable manner. The Schools Commission should also consult widely, investigate educational issues, and disseminate new ideas to bring about positive change in Australia's schools.

McKinnon and Beazley then began work on recruiting suitable senior staff. There were to be twelve commissioners, four of whom would be full-time. Beazley wanted West Australian Catholic academic Peter Tannock, David Bennett (Monash Education, full-time), Peter Moyes (Christ Church Grammar School, Perth) and Desmond Wood (special education). McKinnon invited Jean Blackburn (full-time) and Greg Hancock (NSW Education Department, full-time) to

---

[28] Mathews, a Fabian and Cooperative socialist, later became federal MP for Casey (1972–75) and state member for Oakleigh (1979–92). Bennett, also a Fabian, was at that time Chief Researcher for the Australian Council for Education Research. He was a notable and passionate progressive educator who began his teaching career in Moe, Victoria. Bennett was also a grandson of John Monash, a fact which, out of modesty and self-reliance, he did his best to conceal. Sadly, he died early of cancer in 1983.

join the Commission. The other recruits, who came as representatives of stakeholder groups, were Joan Kirner (Australian Council of State School Organisations and representing parents), Ray Costello (Australian Teachers' Federation, teacher unions), Alby Jones (South Australia, Director-General of Education) and Tony McNamara (Catholic education system). The work of the Commission was to be authorised and funded by the parallel passage of two bills. The first of these was the Schools Commission bill, and the second was a States Grants bill.

While McKinnon watched the parliamentary process unfold in an optimistic and energetic frame of mind, a brooding Malcolm Fraser was also watching in a far less constructive mood. Fraser's political ambitions had temporarily been blocked by his appointment as Snedden's primary industry spokesman, normally a Country Party post and a political cul-de-sac for the ambitious Liberal. Throughout 1973, Fraser had bided his time, steadily building a media and political reputation as a formidable champion of liberal conservative values (anti-abortion; hard line foreign policy; free trade; anti-permissiveness; anti-centralist). However, his media and political reputation also included observations about his perceived aloofness, his impersonal demeanour (seen as arrogance) and his supposedly uncaring Western District squatter mentality. Fraser hired a public relations consultant, Jon Royce, who moved his media image more into warm, family man territory. As for politics, Royce advised Fraser to move from defence of conservative values into attack mode, but to pick his targets carefully. One such target was the Whitlam government's education policy. His principal line of attack was a familiar one, the superiority of per capita funding over any alternative and the insidious nature of leftist collective ideology hidden in the two education bills coming before parliament.

The Schools Commission bill and its accompanying States Grants bill moved through parliament in November 1973. Of the two measures, the Schools Commission legislation, not a money bill, was the more vulnerable.[29] Reaching the Senate on 13 November, the bill was subjected to a period of political manoeuvring where it was twice blocked in the upper house and referred back to the House of Representatives for amendment. The main objection of the Opposition was Karmel's A–H categories, which had, in their view, been based on poor decision-making and would lead to injustices which would affect the non-Catholic independent schools more than others. One particularly egregious case was cited by John Carrick (now a Senator) in which the Australian International School in Ryde, an experimental institution, had been designated Category A despite the fact that its classrooms were former chicken sheds, the school's recreation centre was a former double-decker bus and the headmaster's office was a caravan.[30] On appeal the school had been downgraded – to Category B.

Another key issue for the Opposition was the role of the minister of education in making appointments to the Commission (should be reduced to avoid ALP bias) and the size of the Commission's executive committee (should be expanded to allow a wider representation for independent schools). The composition of the current Commission

---

[29] The States Grants bill could be delayed but, by convention, not blocked.

[30] 'Experimental school an 'A', *Sydney Morning Herald*, 14 November 1973. John Carrick, a survivor of brutal Japanese imprisonment in World War II went on, among other things, to become education minister (1975–79) in Fraser's first two cabinets. See 'Ex-PM salutes father of state aid John Carrick'. *The Australian*, 11 September 2012.

also needed close scrutiny (too many progressive appointees). A third problem was the Opposition's desire to include a clause stating that parents had a right to choose which kind of school they might send their children.

With the Schools Commission bill moving back and forth between the upper and lower houses, Fraser, acting as the Opposition's education spokesman in the House of Representatives (with Senator Peter Rae as the ex-officio minister) intervened. On 5 December 1973, Fraser delivered parliamentary speeches and asked aggressive questions which focused on justice for private schools as a theme, and on the progressive makeup of the Commission. As far as Fraser was concerned, there had already been 'tragic errors' in managing the school category scheme and the Commission needed restructuring so that 'the interests of all schools can be properly safeguarded', a swipe at the efficiency of pre-Commission decisions about funding and its effect on the morale, reputation and workings of non-government schools. For Fraser, unless these demands were met, 'we will have a situation in which injustice is perpetuated within the Australian community'.[31] Fraser wanted to push hard against the proposed Karmel reforms, publicly threatening to use the Opposition's Senate numbers to block the forthcoming Schools Commission bill and arguing for an election over the issue. However, with the Karmel Report and the Schools Commission initiative being so popular, Senate DLP leader McManus counselled his Liberal colleagues that this would be 'as popular as killing Santa Claus at Christmas.'[32]

---

[31] *Hansard*, House of Representatives, 5 December 1973.

[32] Cit. Freudenberg, 1977, p.279. Fraser had supported the bipartisan Australian Universities Commission but believed that the Schools Commission was stacked

CHAPTER FIVE

Part of Fraser's argument was that the Australian Parents' Council (APC) should be represented within the Commission, to which Whitlam minister Lionel Bowen replied that the APC was a well-known front for the Liberal Party, responding during a heated debate about the Senate amendments, 'But whom does the Council represent? It represents the Liberal philosophy which is against the whole philosophy of this Government. Their philosophy is one of bolstering up privilege and guaranteeing that there will be inequality because of the stupid policy of across the board grants irrespective of need'.[33] On 6 December, the Senate amendments were rejected for a second time. All of this was happening while the Opposition had rejected or blocked the Family Law bill as well as the Petroleum and Minerals Authority bill, and was simultaneously obstructing the Government's health insurance (Medibank) legislation which the Senate put on hold on 12 December.

Meanwhile, even though the Senate and the House of Representatives were still battling over the second passage of the Schools Commission bill, an eager McKinnon began to recruit staff for the Commission by advertising for a Secretary at a starting salary of just over $19,085 and two Assistant Secretaries at $17,300 each.[34]

This pre-Christmas blocking behaviour of the Opposition, which included a Senate filibuster, led to talk of a possible forced double dissolution over the two education bills, although Bowen brushed off that suggestion by saying that the government could always

---

with ALP placemen. Santamaria and his National Civic Council were livid that the ALP had stolen their state-aid clothes, effectively ending their *raison d'etre* and the bargaining power of the DLP.

[33] *Hansard*, House of Representatives, 5 December 1973.

[34] *Sydney Morning Herald*, 17 November 1973. $19,000 was a professorial salary in 1973.

continue with the Interim Committee until the matter was decided. However, in characteristic crash-or-crash-through mode, Whitlam contradicted Bowen, telling a parliamentary caucus meeting that he had no intention of being a lame duck prime minister and he would call a double dissolution if it was necessary.[35]

The impasse was becoming exasperating to both sides of parliament, with the Government crying foul over the Opposition's tactics. A sizeable proportion of Opposition members from the Country Party were also anxious that the Fraser-led campaign against the Schools Commission legislation was being seen by the electorate as unnecessarily divisive and elitist, and that it might even deprive rural schools of funding increases.[36] At a press conference on 11 December, Whitlam announced, in response to a question, that if the Opposition in the Senate passed the Schools Commission bill, his government would consider phasing out the Category A funding reduction program instead of cutting off the grants on 31 December.

Following on from Whitlam's concession, the bill's prospects then improved still further when, behind Fraser and Snedden's backs, Country Party leader Doug Anthony began negotiations with Bowen, who was still in temporary charge of education while Beazley recovered in hospital after collapsing from overwork. With the Fraser-led impasse generating bad press for the Coalition, Bowen and Anthony agreed to join forces – the latter normally an anti-ALP hardliner – and bypass the Liberals, on the understanding that the Whitlam government would bring in an education bill that phased out per capita funding instead of implementing the sudden

---

35 'Education Wrangle: Poll or Retreat? and 'No Point', *Sydney Morning Herald*, 12 December 1973.

36 'Opposition split over education aid bill', *Sydney Morning Herald*, 12 December 1973.

CHAPTER FIVE

cut-off, and the government would drop its objection to the 'choice' amendment. Accordingly, Country Party support in both houses allowed the Whitlam government to get its education legislation through an antagonistic Senate. Snedden was furious at what he considered a betrayal by his deputy prime minister.

The consequence was that agreement was reached between the government and the Country Party that Category A schools were to retain a scaled-down version of per capita funding for two years. On 13 December the two bills were carried in both houses thanks to nineteen Country Party MPs crossing the floor, to ironic ALP cheers, and to DLP support for the Country Party in the Senate. Snedden, still outraged by events, vented his anger on Whitlam, who had been intent on tabling and commenting on a summary of his government's achievements in 1973. The Opposition leader initiated a move to force Whitlam to read out the 62-page document verbatim, a task which took two hours to perform while Snedden sat opposite, signing his Christmas cards. The Schools Commission bill received the Governor-General's assent just before Christmas Day.

With the seasonal break in sight, the year had, on the face of it, ended reasonably well for the government with two major bills passed and the Opposition in disarray. This was a circumstance which did not go unnoticed by even the fervidly anti-ALP *Sun Herald*, whose senior political columnist Maximilian (Max) Walsh, a moderate, pronounced that education had been a 'bad issue' to use as a trigger for an election and that, 'Labor finished the year looking and sounding better in Government than perhaps at any time during the year.'[37]

---

[37] 'Improved political image for Labor as year ends', *Sun Herald*, 16 December 1973. According to Graham Freudenberg, by November 1973 Whitlam's government

As for Fraser, his campaign, which was mainly about building his leadership profile within the Liberal Party, had come unstuck because of his tendency to overreach. It had taken the actions of one of his few close parliamentary friends, in the form of Doug Anthony, to rescue the Coalition from its Fraser-created impasse. What was much more interesting about the Schools Commission parliamentary campaign, though, was that there seemed to be a popular, media and political consensus that such a circuit-breaking authority was a move in the right direction. That was until the Commission went to work.

---

had made 1675 decisions, presented 254 bills to parliament, of which 223 had been passed, and commissioned (and tabled) 39 reports of 94 governmental task forces, inquiries and commissions (Freudenberg, 1977, p.290).

Chapter Six

THE SCHOOLS COMMISSION

Too Radical,

Too Expensive, and

Likely to Raise Expectations Too High

The government's 1973 pre-Christmas battle over education funding, a short-lived victory for Whitlam and Beazley, was a response to a much larger and increasingly bitter struggle by the Coalition to bring down the prime minister. Encouraged by a string of 1973 opinion polls showing rising criticism of the government, the Coalition had been working on a broad anti-ALP strategy based on the alleged illegitimacy of the Whitlam government.[1] In 1974, the Coalition added the accusation of incompetence to that of illegitimacy. This was a struggle that was to intensify in 1974, when global, domestic

---

[1] The polls had gone up and down over the year with Sydney's tabloid *Sun Herald* specialising in banner headlines along the lines of ALP COULD HAVE LOST APRIL ELECTION (6 May 1973) but by late October the Gallup poll suggested that Whitlam's government, serially blocked in the Senate, was steadily losing support at a time when an April 1974 double dissolution was being touted as a legislative circuit breaker. Coalition politicians, still smarting at being out of office after twenty-three years, were convinced that the Whitlam government was a cuckoo in the parliamentary nest. See Hocking, 2014, pp.97–99.

and internal governmental forces were to combine against the Whitlam government.

Away from the parliamentary shouting and in an atmosphere of 'innocent hopes', the official work of the Schools Commission began immediately after the passage of the legislation.[2] On 19 December 1973, the newspapers carried re-advertisements for Schools Commission positions, including one for a Secretary.[3] On 22 December, the Commonwealth announced that it had already started work on two School Commission projects: the $2.6 million education innovations centres program and the $6 million innovations in school initiative. By now the Schools Commission was recruiting executive officers for its four branches: (1) Policy Development Planning and Research, (2) Public Policy Planning and Research, (3) Professional Policy Development, and (4) Programs.

Interestingly, according to Ken McKinnon, the Commission's setting up had been hindered at the public service level by Frederick Wheeler, Secretary of Treasury (1971–79), and by Alan Cooley, Chair of the Public Service Board (1971–77), who were both politically opposed to the government's education policy.[4] On the face of it, obstructionism of some sort might have been expected. Wheeler, one of the Canberra public service's formidable 'Seven Dwarfs', described by an obituarist as 'a master of guerrilla warfare in the bureaucracy', was a powerful influence within the public service and in government, as was his Deputy Secretary (Economic), the

---

[2] McKinnon's expression, see McKinnon, 2010, p.4.

[3] A professorial level stipend in 1973. See University of Sydney advertisements, *Sydney Morning Herald*, 23 June 1973.

[4] McKinnon, 2010, p.3.

conservatively-inclined and tough-minded John Stone.[5] Cooley too was a capable and daunting public servant.[6]

It is possible that McKinnon, a provincial arriviste in public service terms, may have mistaken establishment arrogance for outright sabotage, but it is more likely that his assessment of Treasury's and PSB's attitudes towards the setting up of the Schools Commission was an accurate one. While McKinnon was an innovator with an open disposition, Wheeler, a champion of 'Treasury Line' economic orthodoxy, was neither of these things.[7] Wheeler was almost certainly aghast at the government's plan to splash an additional $467 million on schools in 1974–75, on top of an already planned $193 million. This proposed increase came at a time when the Treasury was already anticipating a domestic inflation crisis, and when the signs were clear the world would soon be facing the dire inflationary consequences of the late-1973 Middle East oil embargo.[8]

---

[5] For more on Wheeler see John Farquharson, 'Wheeler, Sir Frederick Henry (1914–1994)', *Obituaries Australia*, National Centre of Biography, Australian National University, http://oa.anu.edu.au/obituary/wheeler-sir-frederick-henry-1567/text1630, accessed 26 September 2016.

[6] See J.R. Nethercote, 'Unearthing the Seven Dwarfs and the Age of the Mandarins', *Obituaries Australia*, National Centre of Biography, Australian National University, http://adb.anu.edu.au/essay/5/text26981, originally published 5 October 2012, accessed 28 September 2016, and S. Furphy, ed., *'The Seven Dwarfs and the Age of the Mandarins: Australian Government Administration in the Post-War Reconstruction Era'*. Canberra, ANU Press, 2015. Wheeler and Cooley were alumni of Melbourne's Scotch College and Stone had attended Perth Modern, a selective state school.

[7] The 'Treasury Line' was mainly anti-spending and anti-inflation. Whitlam went around Wheeler and the Treasury, looking for alternative views.

[8] Wheeler, who had been shut out of Whitlam's very early discussions with major department heads, was contemptuous of Whitlam's poor grasp of the importance of economic policy. By 1974, Whitlam was convinced that Wheeler and his circle were trying to destabilise his government. The Treasury Secretary did eventually play a key part in bringing down the Whitlam government because of its freewheeling approach to the 1974–75 Khemlani Loans Affair. See Whitlam, 1985, pp.205–206; Macintyre 2015, p.116 and Hocking, 2014, pp.129-130. Malcolm Fraser too was to become a critic of Wheeler, in his case because of poor advice. One of the interesting

There was another setback for the Schools Commission. As far as McKinnon was concerned, the passage of the Schools Commission legislation had been an excellent start but he had noticed an organisational problem with the Act. The compromise draft of the bill included no reference to the status of Commonwealth aid as either a provider of needs-based funding for all schools or for just a selected number of comparatively disadvantaged schools. He also noticed that the draft did not clarify the nature of the relationship of the Schools Commission's work with the overarching framework of the Commonwealth Grants Commission (established in 1933), which had responsibility for advising the government on vertical and horizontal funding imbalances and distributing non-specified general purpose funding payments and specific purpose funding known as 'tied grants'. With the latter, both the Schools Commission and the Grants Commission operated on a perceived needs basis, but their parallel (yet-different) funding arrangements had the potential to skew the Grant Commission's overall data, which was meant to act as a basis for its funding allocations. According to McKinnon, the problem was swept under the carpet and never resolved.[9]

Nevertheless, in the New Year, McKinnon and his team began the process of setting up a national network of voluntary State Planning and Finance Committees to deal with disbursement of recurrent and capital Commonwealth funding. Each committee was chaired by a member of the great and good, for example, former High Court Judge Sir Ronald Wilson in charge of the West Australian committee

---

features of this period in Australia's educational history is just how quickly the sums allocated for state aid for all schools rose from £5 million, or $10 million, in 1964, to a total of $661 million by 1974.

[9] McKinnon, 2010, p.4.

CHAPTER SIX

and former Monash University Vice-Chancellor Louis Matheson chairing its Victorian equivalent. The disadvantaged schools program was handled by state-based committees while the innovations program initiative was run by David Bennett, who was assisted by local consultants to help applicants improve their submissions to the state committees, who then passed them to the Schools Commission of National Committee of Chairmen for final authorisation.

The Commission was responsible for seven funding and innovation programs during 1974–75:

- Recurrent grants related to the needs of schools.
- Funds for general buildings.
- Funds designated for the improvement of schools serving socio-economically disadvantaged areas. Supplementary building grants were provided for the running costs of compensatory education programs in these schools.
- Funds for the improvement of special education for handicapped children. Grants were provided for the building and replacement of special education facilities, and to augment the funds for the running costs of both government and non-government special schools and classes, and for special education teacher training and related teacher replacement.
- Funds for experimental programs of an innovative nature at the school level.
- The Teacher Development Program, including the funding of education centres for teachers, a school travel and exchange scheme, and the training of Aborigines for educational leadership.

- A school libraries program (1974–75 only) which provided funds for the development of library resource centres in schools and for basic courses in school librarianship for teachers (absorbed by other programs in 1976).[10]

McKinnon's 2010 recollection of that period is perhaps the best source for the atmosphere within and the operational practice of the Schools Commission:

> Now that I look back on that phase, it was a unique period of nation-wide voluntary involvement in delivering educational improvement. Some of the best and most energetic of educational thinkers (e.g., including outstanding people still around like Barry McGraw [sic], Michael Pusey, or Don Edgar,) willingly volunteered to become involved in the state committees, whether for deciding building priorities or assessing innovations applications.[11]

> We consulted incessantly with national and state organisations. For instance while we met with State representatives in the State, including the Director-General, annually the Commission also consulted the D-Gs as a group for two days each year in Canberra, a rare time for D-Gs to spend exclusively discussing educational ideas and needs. We met and discussed ideas with every group that had credibility and some that didn't. Overall, it was an approach that despite obvious success, in Canberra circles was sometimes criticised as being too radical, too expensive, and likely to raise expectations too high.

---

[10] Taken from the ABS 1975–76 *Yearbook*, p.654.

[11] McGaw went on to become a key figure in Australian and OECD educational reform. Pusey, a sociologist, gained fame in the 1990s following his criticisms of economic rationalism's capture of the Commonwealth politicians and the public service. In 1980, Edgar became foundation director of the Australian Institute of Family Studies.

CHAPTER SIX

Its up-side was enormous. Regular consultations made it normal for parents, teachers, State education officials, and other stakeholders, to civilly discuss the merits of different educational approaches. Initial Commission ideas were road-tested and often redrafted. Initially some State Departments had difficulty in open consideration of the merits of ideas, and to the reality that the ideas of parents, union leaders, or whoever, if backed up by empirical evidence, might be the most valid policy paths.[12]

During 1974, the year of an 18 May double-dissolution election, the Schools Commission continued to carry out its burgeoning responsibilities in an efficient, consultative, low-key fashion, scarcely raising a ripple among politicians who had so fervently opposed its Whitlamesque creation. There had, however, been a small pre-election education crisis in May when Victorian premier Rupert 'Dick' Hamer, in a mischievous act, authorised a High Court writ against state aid grants.

The writ had been sought by a Victorian DOGS group of state-aid holdouts that included ALP firebrand Bill Hartley (later known as 'Baghdad Bill' because of his unreserved support for Baathist tyrant Saddam Hussein), prominent trade unionist John Halfpenny and Schools Commissioner Joan Kirner. Whitlam was publicly furious with Hamer and must have been disappointed with his personal appointee Kirner, who had been recommended to him by his wife Margaret, though nothing was said about her in public at least.[13] As for McKinnon, he later invited Joan Kirner and spouse Ron to join

---

[12] McKinnon, 2010, 'The Schools Commission: A Review', University of Melbourne Seminar, September. The author owes a debt of thanks to Professor McKinnon for the first-hand backgrounding provided by this paper.

[13] 'Hamer defends aid challenge', *Sydney Morning Herald*, 15 May 1974. In Victoria, the Attorney General Vernon Wilcox had to authorise the seeking of a High Court writ. With Kirner, it is possible she had become involved in the DOGS case prior to her appointment as a commissioner.

him in the front row of the Sydney Opera House for an evening with Joan Sutherland as Electra in *Idomeneo*.[14] In any event, the DOGS case dragged on until 1981 when it was dismissed six to one. The dissenting opinion was that of former ALP Attorney General Lionel Murphy, a dedicated opponent of state aid.

Back in Canberra, and with an election due, the Coalition Opposition published its election manifesto in late April, announcing that it would not reduce Karmel-based funding and it would retain the Schools Commission. On the other hand, the Coalition, sticking to its electorally-damaging educational worldview, promised to give independent schools an additional 20 per cent of the cost of educating a government school student, in the form of per capita grants. Whitlam's key election speech focused on Opposition obstructionism and on his government's achievements. Education funding, now seemingly settled as an ALP issue, merited a mere eight words in Whitlam's 1587-word pre-election address.

After an election that was complicated by four referendum questions, Whitlam's government was returned with a reduced majority, facing a still hostile senate. An ineffectual Snedden, refusing to accept reality, commented that, 'We were not beaten. We didn't win enough seats to form a government, but I do not believe what has occurred was in any sense a defeat'.[15]

As for education funding, by this time it was reasonably clear that there were differences of opinion on the Australian political continuum. At one extreme was the DOGS position, namely that no government funding of any kind should be allocated to non-

---

[14] Joan Kirner in a repeat of a 2001 interview with Margaret Throsby, ABC Midday, 3 June 2015.

[15] Cit. Museum of Australian Democracy, https://electionspeeches.moadoph.gov.au.

CHAPTER SIX

government schools. In the centre came the more equitable, needs-based, top-up supporters who argued that both government and non-government schools should receive Commonwealth funding up to a base level but no further. Over to the right, an additional element in the political mix comprised the conservative supporters of non-government schools who insisted that because they paid federal taxes, the schools to which they sent their children were entitled to Commonwealth support whatever the financial condition of the schools. Also in that mix was a specific Catholic position that the Church had a duty to provide schooling in population growth areas, an open-ended commitment that led to dismay among the hardliners, the centrists and Kim Beazley Snr.

The Schools Commission, now endorsed by both major parties, got on with its job. To illustrate the kind of work, both large and small, that the Commission carried out, on 2 May 1974 Minister Beazley announced that, among other matters, the Commonwealth would be allocating a second (needs-based) capital grants distribution of $3.8 million from its 1974–75 $148.5 provision for government schools and $30 million for independent schools. Within that May 1974 allocation for 'urgently needed classrooms and other facilities', Queensland would receive $1.1 million, South Australia $888,500, News South Wales $857,561, Western Australia $394,000 and Tasmania $122,000. (Victoria had received $1.9 million in the previous round). The next day, the Schools Commission announced that it would fund fifty pilot libraries in non-government primary schools. At the same time, the Schools Commission oversaw the distribution of funds for a wide range of innovation activities. For example, $1408 was given to mathematics teacher Barry Hughes of Albury North High School, who wanted to purchase a 'minicomputer' which would have 'print-out and read-in attachments'. The computer would, Hughes hoped, 'take mathematics away from the textbook'. Further up the funding scale, a Mr DP Murkin of Rainbow Public School, Randwick, was given $4390 to help set up an open classroom. All in all, by May 1974 the Schools Commission had allocated $775,000 out of its $6 million innovations program, a result that disappointed Schools Commission director McKinnon since only one in eight applications had been successful.[16] At the end of May, Beazley then announced that new measures would be funded to assist 'extreme pupils', an alarming classification which actually referred, in a crass 1970s way, to gifted and talented students at one 'extreme' of the scholarly spectrum, and less able students at the other.[17]

By early 1975, with Snedden having effectively abandoned the anti-Schools Commission argument, there seemed to be a bipartisan consensus that the Commission was actually doing a good job. Even the *Sydney Morning Herald*, in a 3 February 1975 editorial at the start of the new school year, was mildly approving of the Commission's early progress, especially when it came to funding for disadvantaged schools. The newspaper also approved of McKinnon's public acknowledgement that 'financial realism was important because money for education is or should be unlimited and that education should automatically take precedence over other pressing needs'.[18]

Whitlam now had to confront the opposition over far bigger crises than state aid. Despite substantial achievements that included the

---

16 '50 Pilot Libraries', *Sydney Morning Herald*, 3 May 1974.
17 'Scheme to help extreme pupils', *Sydney Morning Herald*, 30 May 1974.
18 'School Priorities', *Sydney Morning Herald*, 3 February 1975.

CHAPTER SIX

eventual passage of the health insurance bill, the Whitlam government had been looking increasingly shaky throughout 1974 and early 1975 as a consequence of a series of crises. These included rising inflation and increasing unemployment, continuing fall-out from the 1973 global oil crisis and, towards the end of 1974, revelations regarding the toxic Loans Affair. Not only that, but external pressures on and internal tensions within the Cabinet had led, according to Beazley, to 'government by tantrum'.[19]

One consolation for Whitlam was the ineptness of the Snedden-led opposition, which had continued to stumble its way through 1974, raising Fraser's leadership hopes yet again. After five more months of Snedden still being routinely humiliated in parliament by an imperious Whitlam, enough had become enough for Fraser and a small coterie of supporters who mounted a November 1974 leadership challenge, which Fraser narrowly lost. In March 1975, Fraser and his supporters tried again, overthrowing Snedden in a bitter leadership coup that left the ruthlessly ambitious Fraser now face to face with Whitlam, a prime minister in haughty decline.

Not that the politics of the day interfered with the work of the Schools Commission. During 1975, the capital and recurrent grants were distributed as usual and without controversy and new special programs were authorised. The latter included a national scheme for thirty-two pilot teacher centres that were to act as meeting places where teachers could share professional experiences and plans. A national school-to-school teacher exchange program was set up, 'to allow short-term visits of teachers and administrators to other schools

---

[19] Cit. Clem Lloyd, 2013 edition, 'Edward Gough Whitlam', *Australian Prime Ministers*, Sydney, New Holland, p.342.

or situations which may be in other states and/or in systems different from their own, or even in different schools in the same system'.[20]

Within the 128-project Innovations Program, the nuns of The Holy Family School in Doveton, Victoria, received $1800 to set up a small zoo; Sister Marcia Rosa of St. Brigid's School Midland Western Australia was given $18,000 to improve relations between migrants and the school; Ms [sic] J Stoward was allocated $1100 to extend the work in schools of the Tasmanian Childbirth Education Association; Mr TJ Harden of Balaklava High School, South Australia was given $1413 to develop a driver education and automotive engineering project; and Peter Steel, an art teacher at Liverpool Girls' High School New South Wales, was given $2230 to restore a discarded offset printing press to print a student-edited school magazine.[21]

Probably the most startling innovation project was that of Marist Brother Barry Lamb, who received a grant to set up a community school annex in Kogarah Marist Brothers High School. The annex serviced the needs of disaffected Year 10s, who were allowed to smoke in class as well as in their comfortably furnished (with castoffs) common room while listening to, among other things, Lou Reed on a cassette player. The boys were obliged to seek outside work for one day a week and, excluding lesson time, they could come and go much as they felt, as long as they studied for their School

---

[20] Schools Commission Advertisement, *Sydney Morning Herald*, 22 March 1975.

[21] What is interesting about these announcements, which were almost all based on government press releases, is the prominence given to grants awarded to Catholic schools. This would suggest that there was a public relations campaign under way, auspiced by either the Commission or by Beazley's department (probably the latter) to highlight Catholic grants as a way of emphasising the needs-based approach of the innovations program.

CHAPTER SIX

Certificate.[22] There was nothing in the way of furious reaction from outraged taxpayers in the *Sydney Morning Herald*'s letters column.

While announcements about Schools Commission projects were regularly appearing in the press, the nation's economic and financial situation had been deteriorating to the point where Whitlam had set up an Expenditure Review Committee in January 1975 to advise an inner Cabinet on economic and financial matters.[23] McKinnon had been on the point of asking for a $2 billion budget allocation for the 1976–78 triennium, more than doubling the existing 1974–75 budget arrangements, but in light of the need to make budget cuts, that figure looked unrealistic. Nonetheless, when the Commission's first annual report was published in early June 1975, McKinnon put in for $2.07 billion dollars in school funding over the three years 1976–78. His request came just before the August Budget deliberations were to commence under the guidance of new Treasurer Bill Hayden, and at a time when economists were warning that Australia was heading for a $2–3 trillion annual deficit and 400,000 unemployed.

As well as dealing with funding recommendations, the Commission's 400-page 1975 report emphasised equality and diversity as its two main educational priorities, arguing that all students should be brought to a 'plateau of competence', with McKinnon suggesting that

---

[22] 'Where pupils can smoke and take jobs', *Sydney Morning Herald*, 1 April 1975 (the article was not an April Fools' Day joke). Barry Lamb was still actively doing community work in the early twenty-first century. He wrote a submission in to the 2000 Commonwealth inquiry into the 'social, cultural and educational factors affecting the education of boys in Australian schools' and moved to Heidelberg West, Victoria to carry on his community work in 2013.

[23] Whitlam had already set up a prime minister's departmental think tank, the Priorities Review Staff.

this could be achieved through 'improved quality in schooling' and more teacher and parental autonomy at the school level.[24]

In between the May tabling of McKinnon's annual report and the scheduled August budget, the Whitlam government was hit by three heavy blows. The most injurious of these was a series of revelations in late May – now known as the Overseas Loans Affair – about an ill-advised attempt to shore up Australia's economy through the offices of a shady, London-based Pakistani broker, Tirath Khemlani. Whitlam's trustworthy but unwell deputy, Lance Barnard, resigned to take up a diplomatic post in Scandinavia. In the resulting by-election for the seat of Bass, the ALP lost, with a catastrophic 17 per cent swing against. At the same time, such were the ongoing criticisms of the government's financial incompetence that on 2 July, Whitlam had been obliged to sack Treasurer Jim Cairns on a different loans matter, convening a special, clearing-the-air session of the House of Representatives on 9 July. In these tumultuous circumstances, and besieged from within and without, Whitlam had decided not to accept any of the education commissions' recommendations (schools, universities, technical and advanced) and the Schools Commission's first annual report faded into the political background.

Not that the politics of school education became completely overshadowed by the government's successive crises. There had been a portentous, if brief, educational controversy about the School Commission's views on curriculum in the midst of Canberra's other crises. The dispute was initiated by two conservative academic Professors, James McAuley and Leonie Kramer.

---

24   '$2070m plan for schools', 'Funds: report urges more say for schools' and 'Three-Point Plan for Federal Aid', *Sydney Morning Herald*, 4 June 1975. Beazley had tabled the report in parliament the day before.

CHAPTER SIX

Prior to the formation of the Schools Commission, Australian debates about the politics of schooling had been based on sectarian and sectoral differences and funding inequities. As we have seen, by 1975 sectarian controversies had all but faded into insignificance, leaving only arguments about distribution of funding. But the formation of the Schools Commission had unwittingly opened up a new area of political disagreement by bringing curriculum philosophy and design within its remit. With curriculum in Australia now a national issue, as opposed to a state-by-state matter, McAuley and Kramer attempted to create a moral panic based on the approach of conservative UK academics Brian Cox and Anthony (AE) Dyson, authors and editors of the UK's controversial *Black Papers* series (first published in 1969). These pamphlets had bemoaned a national decline in educational standards in England and Wales, attacked what were considered as the 'excesses' of progressive education, opposed the idea of comprehensive education and argued for the retention of selective grammar schools, with choice of selection to be delayed until age thirteen, as was the case with 'public' (non-government) schools. Contributing authors included novelist and philosopher Iris Murdoch, author Kingsley Amis and Rhodes Boyson, the flamboyant and successful headmaster of a London comprehensive school and later a Conservative Party politician.

An Australian version of a *Black Paper*-style assault began in mid-August 1975 at a New South Wales Liberal Party convention, where James McAuley, poet and professor of English at the University of Tasmania, delivered a philippic that railed against an alleged decline in Australia's school education. McAuley, a Catholic, had been founding editor of ultra-conservative magazine *Quadrant* in 1956 and was a serial controversialist with a taste for hyperbole.

His speech, published in full in the *Sydney Morning Herald* in a five-column opinion editorial, was entitled 'Education in decline: Towards a new barbarism'.²⁵ The gist of McAuley's largely evidence-free criticism was that a 'catastrophic' rise in educational radicalism had altered the traditional purpose of Australian schooling, which had, according to McAuley, once been based on a rigorous and discipline-based education system (and good manners) but had now been transformed into a non-scholarly, individualistic and socialistic experience based on an adoption of inter-disciplinary studies and mixed-ability classes.²⁶

It was an allegedly progressive curriculum discussion paper authored by the normally conservative New South Wales Board of Studies that had spurred McAuley into delivering his diatribe. His conclusion, disingenuously tying New South Wales Board of Education discussions into the Schools Commission activities was: 'If the Australian Schools Commission has its way in backing federally what it hails are "the emerging trends in Australian education at the present time", a new barbarism lies ahead'.

McKinnon replied on 21 August in a five-column article in the *Sydney Morning Herald* entitled 'Opposing the doctrine of inherited privilege'.²⁷ Briefly, McKinnon's carefully-worded response, based

---

25 18 August 1975. McAuley, a co-founder of the conservative periodical *Quadrant*, was known for his involvement in the 1944 Ern Malley spoof poetry affair. His first major venture into 1970s politics was a September 1972 address to a New South Wales Liberal Party convention. The talk was entitled 'Against Leftist Perversion'.

26 The only evidence offered by McAuley was that the New South Wales Board of Studies had circulated a discussion paper that included the teaching of 'personal development'. There was a case against poorly thought out 1960s progressivism in 1970s schools in the United Kingdom and in Australia, but by appealing to evidence-free prejudice rather than reason, McAuley was clearly not the person to make it.

27 'Opposing the doctrine of inherited privilege', *Sydney Morning Herald*, 21 August 1975.

mainly on a natural and distributive social justice theme, was that those who oppose change in educational practice fail to understand the nature and the value of equality of opportunity, and are the defenders of a privileged high culture that has traditionally been offered to an elite within a discriminatory education system. For example, he argued, there were real gender-bias issues in schooling which disadvantaged girls' education. McKinnon also pointed out that all school students were indeed expected to be literate, numerate, logical in their thinking, and acquainted with works of literature. At the same time, McKinnon did lead with his chin when he asked in his rejoinder, 'Is a vivid emotionally-involved description of surfing any less valid than exercises on lumpy opaque poetry?'

Leonie Kramer, Sydney University's professor of English literature then jumped in with a three-column discussion of McKinnon's article and of the Schools Commission's 1975 report. In her contribution, Kramer linked the Schools Commission's attitude to radical student activism and to militant trade unionism. She further argued, without citing any evidence, that 'equality of opportunity' was a form of 'levelling down', and accused the Schools Commission (again without evidence) of falsification by asserting that 'the forms of knowledge valued in schools and associated with power in the society largely represent the accumulated culture of ascendant social groups'.[28] Much of the article was in the same vein.

While there seems to have been no published response to the Kramer contribution, there was a brief flurry of correspondence

---

[28] 'A recipe for lower school standards', *Sydney Morning Herald*, 25 August 1975. Kramer, who had a distinguished academic and administrative career, was an alumna of Presbyterian Ladies' College, Melbourne and, as far as the author knows, had never spent time in a government secondary school during the course of her long and controversial life.

about McAuley's article by a supportive quartet of headmaster 'Jika' Travers, a chemistry lecturer, a professor of Italian and a teacher of modern languages, together with a letter from a principal of a western suburbs high school furious with McAuley.

The McAuley/Kramer initiative did lead to Fairfax tabloid journalist Chris Anderson publishing a follow-up horror-story, 'The Age of the Super-Illiterates', on 7 September 1975. Anderson, a political commentator (and later CEO of Optus 1997–2004) explained in a full-page feature piece that, 'many academics', 'various estimates' and 'recent surveys' showed that national educational standards were in decline and 'old-fashioned standards of "reading, writing and arithmetic" [were] going by the board', and 'many ... basically blame the school system'.[29] Anderson did manage to get a comment from one academic, Professor LF Crisp of the Australian National University, who had asked 25 of his 75 second-year students to attend remedial classes.[30]

The standards issue largely dropped out of media consciousness until June 1982, when Lachlan Chipman from the University of Wollongong took up where McAuley, his fellow right-wing philosophy professor, had left off.[31] Interestingly, the McAuley/Kramer axis set both the tone (aggressive), the perspective (elitist) and the

---

[29] 'The Age of the Super-Illiterates', Sun-Herald, 7 September 1975. The article was sub-headed, 'It's costing $2000m a year for education – but whatever happened to the three Rs?'

[30] An odd claim since it seems unlikely that the ANU was offering 'remedial classes'. However, 'Fin' Crisp was a notable and well-regarded ANU eccentric. In his latter years he argued that 'middle-class sprigs of this post-Spock generation' were more interested in political power than in hard study. See Scott Bennett, 'Crisp, Leslie Finlay (Fin) (1917–1984)', *Australian Dictionary of Biography*, National Centre of Biography, Australian National University, http://adb.anu.edu.au/biography/crisp-leslie-finlay-fin-258/text22227, published first in hardcopy 2007, accessed online 14 October 2016.

[31] 'Teachers' campaign deceitful: Chipman', *Sydney Morning Herald*, 24 November 1982.

CHAPTER SIX

methodology (largely evidence-free) of what was later to become Australia's 'dumbing down' educational controversy, a politicised crisis that was to peak in the first decade of the twenty-first century.

At the outset of this persistent anti-public education campaign, Kramer, McAuley et al. did not recognise that, with increasing numbers of students staying on beyond the leaving age, schools and education departments across Australia had to broaden the senior curriculum to accommodate those students who were not going on to university. What then transpired in these curriculum culture wars was a slowly developing, two-pronged attack on government schools. The first of these prongs, largely led by *The Australian* and other Murdoch outlets, was aimed at 'standards': in other words, elitist levels of expectation and achievement. The second prong, led by John Howard in the 1990s, was aimed at 'values': in other words, attachment to conservative 'Judeo-Christian' tenets, a misconstrued version of Australia's cultural heritage.

Meanwhile, in Canberra, an October 1975 stopgap budget, designed to see out the year and get through the first half of 1976, proposed to fund the Schools Commission at $342 million for the first half-year of 1976. This was an interim figure that was only slightly less (pro-rata) than McKinnon's proposed triennial $2.07 billion, but with no indication of what might come afterwards, leaving school planning in limbo until the economic and political situations stabilised.

In mid-October, there was some slight indication of what the Opposition might do about education if and when in office (a double dissolution was still on the cards at that stage). Senator Margaret Guilfoyle, the Coalition education spokesperson, outlined her side's policy on schooling in an anodyne speech in which she promised she would resume triennial funding and review the education commission's four sets of recommendations. At the same time, she reiterated the individual choice argument and argued for an increase in state and private effort at the pre-school level. There was little else she could do about policy formulation, operating as she was out of a small office in Melbourne with a single staff member.[32]

All of this educational jockeying for position came to nothing, however, when the budget was yet again sent back by the Senate, with Whitlam still insisting on what he thought would be his escape route of a half-senate election, and with the government contemplating unconventional ways of getting past the Senate barrier. Fraser stood firm on his demand for a general election and on 11 November Governor-General John Kerr sacked the Whitlam government on the grounds that the government's inability to obtain supply constituted a constitutional crisis that could only be resolved by his appointment of Malcom Fraser as interim prime minister, with Fraser committing to holding a general election as soon as possible. The Coalition won a 13 December general election in a landslide, giving the Coalition an unprecedented majority of 30 seats in the House of Representatives. What direction education might take under the new government was unclear.

---

[32] Guilfoyle, who went on to become Australia's first female cabinet minister, in 1978, described her lonely term as Opposition education spokesperson as her 'hardest year'. Margaret Guilfoyle, 'The Senate: Proportionately Representative but Disproportionately Male', *Papers on Parliament* No. 17, September 1992, http://www.aph.gov.au/~/~/link.aspx?_id=428C52E3AF2E4969B7A8B16FA0D1F4FD&_z=z. When elected senator she was dubbed the 'Iron Butterfly' by some patriarchally-inclined journalists who were following the man-framing clichés of the times (Imelda Marcos was variously an 'Iron' or 'Steel Butterfly', Rosalyn Carter was a 'Steel Magnolia' and Margaret Thatcher was an 'Iron Lady'). Guilfoyle went on to complete a distinguished senatorial career with a reputation as an efficient team player and consummate political operator. Interestingly, Guilfoyle later became a friend of Joan Kirner, Australia's first female premier and a member of the ALP Left.

Chapter Seven

THE SCHOOLS COMMISSION AND THE LIBERAL WAY OF PROGRESS

With the 1975 election result settled, Malcolm Fraser began to recruit his Cabinet. After filling in for six weeks in Education, Margaret Guilfoyle was transferred to head up Social Security. It was at this stage that Senator John Carrick received a phone call from the prime minister. Carrick, who had moved from being General Secretary of the New South Wales Liberal Party to the Senate four years prior, was not expecting a senior position in the new government. Much to his surprise, Fraser offered him the politically contentious and administratively complex posts of Minister of Education and Minister Assisting the Prime Minister in Federal Affairs. These appointments marked a rapid leap by Carrick from the backbenches to twin Cabinet-level posts.[1]

Carrick, like Guilfoyle, was energetic, enthusiastic and a good team player, qualities that Fraser valued in his cabinet ministers,

---

[1] In writing about Senator John Carrick the author owes a debt of thanks to Liberal Party member and academic Dr Graeme Starr whose excellent 2012 biography *Carrick: Principles, Politics and Policy* (Ballan, Connor Court) has provided very useful background for this section.

understandably given the McMahon and Whitlam Cabinet debacles. Carrick was still highly regarded as one of the Menzies-era party strategists and brought with him personal gravitas, a network of political connections and a firm and principle-based view about what Liberalism really meant. He also, as we have seen, had a longstanding interest in education, having been a key player in developing the New South Wales Liberal Party's approach to schooling in the 1950s and 1960s and assisted Menzies with the Commonwealth's post-1963 transition to school funding.

When in parliament, Carrick had also worked with Fraser when the new prime minister had been Minister of Education and Science and Carrick had been a member of the Senate Standing Committee on Education and Science. In all, the senator had been at work on education matters for two decades prior to becoming minister, an unusually informed background for a position normally regarded as a worthy – but dull – second-tier Cabinet post. Assisting Carrick with his transition into office was Fraser, who, from a distance, now guided Carrick in his new role. Also assisting the new education minister was the highly capable Kenneth 'Ken' Jones, the department's secretary since 1973. It probably helped the development of their mutual trust that Carrick and Jones had both fought against the Japanese in World War II, Carrick in Timor and Jones in New Guinea. As a minister who had helped define Liberal Party policy, Carrick eschewed the use of political advisers, preferring the advice of Jones and his senior departmental staff.[2] Carrick was open to representations from individual interest groups but not from paid lobbyists (such as ACSSO and the unions).

---

2   Graeme Starr, 2012, pp.24–246.

CHAPTER SEVEN

Carrick's pre-political life in Sydney tells us more about this latest education minister. He came from an aspiring Anglican middle-class family that had been adversely affected by the 1930s Depression. The young Carrick attended the local state primary school and a (selective) technical secondary school and in 1941 he graduated from Sydney University after studying part-time while working as an accountant. Prior to World War II Carrick had joined the Sydney University Regiment, transferring to the militia after war broke out in 1939. He transferred again from the militia to the Second Australian Imperial Force (AIF) late in 1940, where he was commissioned as lieutenant before being posted to an anti-tank brigade. The novice officer was then put in charge of an anti-tank troop as they trained for desert warfare.

Carrick and his troop were not posted to the Western Desert but instead sent to join the ill-fated Sparrow Force, one of several mid- to-late 1941 Australian 'Bird' ('Sparrow' and 'Lark') detachments set up to defend Australia's northern colonial neighbours, Portuguese Timor, the Dutch East Indies and New Guinea, against an anticipated Japanese invasion.[3] Carrick and his comrades were taken prisoner and sent to harsh prisoner-of-war camps in Timor and Batavia, then to the notorious Changi prison camp in Singapore and on to the Burma-Thai Railway in May-September 1943. Returned to Changi by the Japanese in late 1943, Carrick and his fellow prisoners were liberated by the Allies in August 1945. Carrick's youthful Depression-era travails as well as his wartime experiences played an important part in shaping his character as a resilient, individualistic

---

[3] Sparrow Force also included a British detachment of anti-aircraft gunners. All members of the two 'Bird' forces were captured or died.

and thoughtful politician who was determined to have his career guided by clear strategies and effective tactics.

Carrick also learned from his war experiences that a democratic society needed effective individual leadership for good, organised resistance in the face of totalitarian brutality: it was this worldview that led to him becoming a Liberal Party supporter.[4] In 1949 he wrote and published what became the party's early handbook, *The Liberal Way of Progress*. These beliefs included the view that while socialism was an ideology that favoured the wisdom of the state over the opinions of the individual, liberalism asserted that the authority of the state needed to be tempered by the potential of the individual.[5] In Carrick's view, the Liberal Party was and should be a non-sectoral, non-sectarian and anti-collectivist organisation based on spiritual (as opposed to secular) values. While schooling is not mentioned in the pamphlet, Carrick believed that everybody in Australia deserved a good general education.[6]

In a post-Whitlam environment that comprised national financial and economic anxiety as well as a conservative political and public reaction against optimistic and expensive nation-building, one might have expected an almost immediate change of policy and practice from the new minister of education, especially considering Carrick's reputation as a firm if courteous Liberal Party strategist. As it

---

[4] Interestingly, Tom Uren, who had experienced wartime experiences similar to Carrick's and shared his views about totalitarianism joined the ALP, eventually becoming a Labor thinker and a two-time ALP minister.

[5] See, J.L. Carrick, *The Liberal Way of Progress*, Sydney, Liberal Party of Australia (N.S.W. Division), 1949, and J.L. Carrick, *The Liberal Way: An Outline of Liberal Philosophy*, Sydney, Liberal Party of Australia, (N.S.W. Division), 1957.

[6] A good deal of anti-collectivist Liberal Party hostility to ALP political culture was based on the ALP's 'Pledge', an agreement by members to follow the party line. The Liberal Party had no equivalent requirement.

CHAPTER SEVEN

happened, such was not the case. Indeed, at first, Ken McKinnon developed a good, behind-the-scenes professional relationship with Carrick, who eschewed the kinds of publicity appearances engaged in by his predecessors Gorton, Fraser and Beazley. McKinnon regarded Carrick as an able, influential and patient minister who was firm in his desire carry out the policies of his party.

The Liberal Party's agenda was based on a conservative narrative that featured the government school system as a value-free wasteland of secularism and somehow at the same time a source of ideological radicalism. This militancy had allegedly been stirred up by young teachers who, having benefited from a free university or college education, had cut their political teeth in anti-war protests and were now members of anti-Coalition trade unions. A more detailed version of this narrative included the electoral support of the Teachers' Federation for ALP education and other social policies, government school teachers who as active union leaders at national, state and branch level used their paid school holidays to carry out union activities and used school printing and duplicating resources for political ends.[7] It was far better, the conservative narrative went, to support mainly Protestant non-government schools which were founded on a free-enterprise competitive worldview, had a well-developed school culture based on individual and team achievement, were committed to conventional middle-class values and had been established on various forms of conformist, spiritually-based values systems. An underlying conservative argument concluded that the Commonwealth should just focus on non-government schools, which deserved government funding because parents paid taxes;

---

[7] See 'Teachers tighten their grip on Labor', *Sydney Morning Herald*, 14 January 1983.

these schools had congenial values and Canberra should get out of government school funding altogether, leaving it to the states. However, just as it was impracticable for total withdrawal of state aid from all non-government schools, so also was the idea of total Commonwealth withdrawal from government schools, which were now heavily dependent on Commonwealth money. Both sides in the funding argument were locked in to a stalemate that had no apparent solution except sequential and politically-motivated catch-up funding decisions that might lead to a temporary advantage, soon to be reversed by any new education minister.

When implementing Liberal policy, Carrick was an imperturbable backroom wheeler and dealer who preferred to see policy done rather than talked about. One of the issues that his departmental head Ken Jones presented to him was the bureaucratic issue caused by the autonomous role of the Schools Commission, by now the main designer of Commonwealth school education policy and principal agent of funding provision. In effect, the Schools Commission was sidelining the education department and when it came to overseeing Commonwealth schools policy, McKinnon and Jones formed a very uneasy team, with McKinnon as the initiator, Jones as the respondent and Carrick as the final arbiter.

McKinnon's role as a de facto junior minister placed his departmental head and his minister in a mortifying position. Accordingly, a gradual erosion of the Schools Commission's autonomy was to become a central feature of the Carrick administration's strategy. As for Jones' relationship with Carrick, the former was delighted with his new minister for several reasons, one of which was Carrick's level of influence within the government:

CHAPTER SEVEN

> He became one of the four or five most influential Ministers and that's a help to any portfolio, because – not that you get preferred treatment – you get knowledge, you get information, you know what's going on and you're in on discussions.[8]

For most of 1976, known in Canberra for a time as 'The Year of the Pause', Carrick more or less left McKinnon to get on with his job.[9] Carrick's hands-off, low profile approach to school education in 1976 was a consequence of two other political matters. First, the education budget allocation for the first half of that year had already been settled in late 1975 and there would be no changes until the August 1976 budget was announced. Second, as part of Fraser's 1976 'New Federalism policy' the government was attempting to redefine the Commonwealth's financial relationship with the states. This was an initiative that was for Carrick in his role as federalism minister both time-consuming and politically fraught, taking up most of his time in the first half of the year. When Carrick did have more time for his education portfolio, relations between McKinnon and the government were to take a different tack, as Carrick and his successor as minister Wal Fife adopted an increasingly interventionist approach to the Commission, in pursuit of the Liberal way of progress. For the time being, however, taking into account the fraught post-dismissal political climate and the popularity of the Schools Commission, Carrick's move to curtail the Commission's independence was gradual rather than sudden.

In 1977, an election year, Carrick continued with his policy of leaving matters to the Commission, only intervening late in the

---

[8] Jones, 1985, TRC1858/2/91.
[9] Jones, 1985, TRC 1858/2/89.

year, but in an unexpected direction. Carrick announced, through a government pre-election press release, that 'The Schools Commission will continue to have full freedom to investigate and report without restriction and to respond to specific requests from the Minister'.[10] McKinnon appreciated such a constructive attitude, a disposition which seemed to match that of Carrick's predecessor Beazley.[11]

Meanwhile, the Schools Commission moved on with its existing grant disbursement tasks as well as with setting up new initiatives. One such project was tackling gender inequality in schools. During 1975, the Commission had, as part of its Karmel Report equality agenda, begun to push for social and political recognition that gender inequality in schools was a serious social justice issue that needed fixing. Accordingly, the Commission set up a study group which researched and published a formative report, *Girls, School and Society*, published in November 1975.[12]

The members of the study group were McKinnon, Jean Blackburn, Cathy Block (NSW Teachers' Federation officer), Jean Martin (Australian National University sociologist), Elizabeth Reid (Whitlam's adviser on women's affairs), Susan Ryan (Labor member of the ACT Legislative Assembly and ALP senator), Bill Thiele (University of Queensland's student counselling service), David Widdup (researcher with the Royal Commission into Australian Government Administration) and Daniela Torsh (Commission executive officer and later a noted film maker). The list of consultees and researchers

---

[10] 'Education', *Sydney Morning Herald*, 22 November 1977.

[11] McKinnon, 2010, p.10. The word 'specific' is a clue to Carrick's real intentions.

[12] Committee on Social Change and the Education of Women. Study Group & McKinnon, K. R. & Australia Schools Commission, *Girls, School and Society: Report by a Study Group to the Schools Commission*, Schools Commission, Woden, A.C.T., 1975.

CHAPTER SEVEN

resembles a pantheon of second wave Australian feminism, with Eva Cox, Wendy McCarthy and Anne Summers included among them.

The terms of reference of the study were to look for signs of underachievement of women and girls in education and to investigate the idea of gender-based anti-discriminatory legislation, ('sex-based' in 1970s terms). Among the conclusions outlined in the study's 194-page report were findings that gender-based stereotypes were dominant in educational resources, featuring male figures more often than female figures, represented as docile, delicate and domesticated. Men were represented as authority figures who were active, strong, decisive and adventurous. The report further remarked on low self-esteem among female tertiary students and noted that half of eligible tertiary female students entered Arts courses, while the comparative figure for men was 21.7 per cent. Of female students entering colleges of advanced education, two thirds became teachers. Accordingly, the working party recommended in its report that legislation should be enacted to end gender discrimination in schools.

These findings were greeted with both alarm and acclaim by feminists who saw the study as a confirmation of what they already knew and as a breakthrough moment in Australian gender relations. Alison McKinnon, starting her career as a scholar of the history of education, commented thirty-one years later: 'I still remember the excitement of the *Girls, Schools and Society* report and the sense of outrage at the overt discrimination it revealed.'[13] Unfortunately, the early December 1975 timing of the release date of the report was terrible. It followed on from the Whitlam government's dismissal, it came during the bitter post-dismissal general election campaign, it

---

[13] McKinnon, 2006, p.6.

coincided with the 7 December Indonesian invasion of East Timor and it was then followed by the annual summer holiday political and media hiatus. In the *Sydney Morning Herald* there was only one mention of the Commission's labours. This consisted of a brief preview of its findings on 27 November. After that came silence.

At this time, a Royal Commission on Human Relationships Whitlam established was ploughing on with its very broad-based inquiry. The three progressively-inclined commissioners, Felix Arnott (Anglican Archbishop of Brisbane), Anne Deveson (social commentator) and Elizabeth Evatt (lawyer and chair) were eventually to make 500 gender, sexual, social, medical, legal and housing recommendations, most of which were ignored by the Fraser government, with the notable exception of the establishment of the Family Court in 1976. Elizabeth Evatt became the Family Court's first Chief Judge.

This detour into gender issues is important for two reasons. First, these two investigations were Whitlam-era inquiries so loaded with progressive agendas and personnel that conservative politicians simply ignored almost all of the two sets of recommendations. Certainly, apart from divorce law reforms and the Family Court, the reports seem to have come to nothing substantive at Commonwealth level in terms of structural change in education. On the other hand, the reports did create a new public environment for informed discussion of what had previously been institutionally or personally closed-off topics. In education, the main new area for debate was gender inequity. In human relations, it was sex education and eventually the decriminalisation of homosexuality. While governmental strategic funding would have been valuable when it came to dealing with gender and sex education issues, changes in curriculum were more

CHAPTER SEVEN

important than funding, and the two reports opened up a whole new area of consciousness-raising debate.

The supportive response of the first Fraser government (1975–76) to the Schools Commission's work seems to have been swallowed by a mythology that this government damaged government schools.[14] Carrick gave carte blanche to the Schools Commission to carry out any new inquiries and he accepted without quibble the Schools Commission's first triennial report 1976–78 (mainly a statement of indicative funding which had been published in June 1975). The report had indicated that just over $2 billion, a massive figure for the time, would be needed to carry out the Commission's three strategic priorities over the triennium. These were the need for educational equality, the importance of 'more open attitudes to educational organisations', and a requirement that schools should adapt more to meet the needs of their different communities.[15]

There were progressive social reform agenda elements in the Fraser governments 1975–80. The Fraser government had been firmly behind the divorce reforms and the creation of the Family Law Court and Fraser had, without demur, recommended the judicial appointment of Elizabeth Evatt to Governor-General John Kerr. Moreover, the Coalition legally recognised Indigenous land rights in 1976, established the Federal Court of Australia in 1977, created the

---

[14] See for example C. Campbell and H. Proctor, *A History of Australian Schooling*, Sydney, Allen & Unwin, pp.202, 224, 2014.

[15] *Schools Commission Report for the Triennium 1976-1978: A Summary* (1975) Canberra, Australian Government Publishing Service. The recurrent grants program was expected to cost $1.1 billion ($1.3 million government/$598,000 non-government), capital grants $695,000 ($578,600 government/$116,457 non-government), the disadvantaged schools program $58,000 ($49,291 government/$9209 non-government) and all special projects $36,000. Services and development made up the rest at $79,880 ($17,920 government/non-government $4030).

multicultural-focused Special Broadcasting Service in 1978, and set up the Australian Refugee Advisory Council in 1979. Fraser was also a firm opponent of South Africa's racist apartheid system.

But by mid-1977 Jones and Carrick began to take a more active stance regarding the Schools Commission's attitude and role. The political relationship between Carrick's department and the Schools Commission began to change. Budget priorities and the continuation of Fraser's austerity regime led to a change in the government's attitude to education, with Carrick now obliged to renege on his initial acceptance of the Schools Commission's 1976 triennial report funding figures. With Treasury and the Cabinet pressing him to cut spending, Carrick reluctantly reduced growth in all education sectors to an overall 0.065 per cent in real terms, with schools losing $40 million overall. In those rearrangements, a net transfer of $9 million from proposed government school programs to non-government schools aroused publicly-expressed exasperation from educators and from state politicians. Joan Kirner too, still a Commissioner and by now president of the Australian Council of State School Organisations (ACSSO), commented that this government-enforced funding rearrangement marked the end of the Schools Commission as an independent body. New South Wales' ALP education minister Eric Bedford commented that the funding cuts were 'disastrous' for government schools.[16]

1978 saw a further hardening of Carrick's attitude towards the Schools Commission, following on from a spat between him and the Australian Teachers' Federation. The disagreement, running from late

---

[16] 'Guidelines put strain on schools body', *Sydney Morning Herald*, 6 June 1977 and 'Angry reaction to Carrick', *Sydney Morning Herald*, 4 June 1977.

CHAPTER SEVEN

1977 into the new year, began with a Schools Commission vacancy. In January the former New South Wales Teachers' Federation (better known as 'The Federation') president Ray Costello would leave to work with John Dawkins after four years with the Commission. David Bennett had also resigned as Commissioner, in December 1977, and had not been replaced. These crucial resignations came at a time when McKinnon needed unanimous support for a costly 1978 triennial report he was about to submit to the government for approval. In the New Year, however, the Commissioner was now in charge of an organisation split four ways at the board level with only one member from the Government school sector, three members from the private schools sector, two from State education authorities and three academics.[17]

The Federation had originally insisted on a simple swap, with its new and notably radical president Van Davy replacing Costello. In a move reminiscent of a *Yes Minister* tactic, Carrick and Jones outmanoeuvred the Federation by requiring that the Australian education unions provide the minister with a shortlist of suitable nominees rather than a single recommendation, insisting that the education minister would make the final choice. In March 1978, the unions finally complied and Carrick selected Alan Marriage as the Commission's new union representative. Marriage was President of the Technical Teachers Union of Victoria, a small breakaway group without the radical track record or the political clout of the Federation.

---

[17] 'Teachers lose a voice on money guidelines', *Sydney Morning Herald*, 9 March 1978. This detailed article, written by education reporter Sarah Monks, seems to have been the outcome of a background briefing by a Commissioner, possibly McKinnon himself.

In effect, Carrick was doing to the Schools Commission precisely what had been done to his side of politics during the Commission's establishment, namely, stacking the organisation with pro-government Commissioners.[18] Carrick's push back against the Whitlam-era culture of the Schools Commission increased in intensity when, instead of consulting the non-government lobbyists as a single group, the minister now insisted on dealing with them in private and as separate entities. This move disturbed the Catholic hierarchy, however, who, aware that their system was consistently gaining a larger share of the budget than it should, did not want to be seen as favoured lobbyists engaged in secretive special pleading.

Carrick's quarrel with the Commission continued into March 1978 and came at a time when the Commission was still preparing the new triennial report which would argue for a reduction in government control over funding guidelines. This was a tactical move to reduce Carrick's ability to allocate funding distribution at sectoral level.

From within the Commission, McKinnon was also working towards a new three-tier funding category system. McKinnon was eventually to come to the conclusion though that this proposed new system actually favoured the non-government schools. Under this new system, those schools able to raise large amounts of private funding would receive a correspondingly lower amount of money from the Commonwealth. A consequence of the new model would be that non-government schools could cut back on irksome fund-raising and be placed in a lower tier, gaining them an equivalent

---

[18] Commissioners were appointed for maximum seven-year terms and could, under the Schools Commission Act, only be sacked for misbehaviour, physical or mental incompetence, taking another job or absence for extended periods of time without ministerial approval.

CHAPTER SEVEN

handover of Commonwealth funding to make up the shortfall. Not only that, but the proposed formula meant that Catholic schools, many of which were still in transition from mainly clerical to mainly lay teaching staff, could put in for additional needs-based recurrent funding over and above the kind of funding given by the States and by the Commonwealth to government schools which were already fully established.

There was still another issue. In an expanding non-government school system, building new schools placed a much heavier burden on a needs-based model than maintaining established schools.[19] The consequence was that a demand-driven funding model allowed new non-government schools to claim what appeared to be a disproportionately high level of capital funding from the Commonwealth compared with long established government schools, some of which were losing students to the non-government system.

The effect of these three factors became evident in the April 1978 Commission report to Carrick for the 1979–81 triennium. The report recommended a rise of more than $45 million in grants to the minority sector non-government schools in 1979 (total $231 million) compared with a rise of just over $25 million to the majority sector government schools (total $367 million). These amounts, representing a 5 per cent increase on the equivalent 1977 figures, were well above new treasurer John Howard's guideline of a 1 per cent maximum increase per annum. The report was rejected by a Fraser cabinet still attempting to work within the boundaries of Howard's fiscal restraint policy.

---

[19] There had been a noticeable drift from the government system to the non-government system during the late 1970s, and Catholic schools faced the added funding problem of building for an expanding student demographic in newly-established suburban areas.

Instead, Carrick's June budgetary allocation for the forthcoming year gave a $14 million increase in recurrent funding to the non-government sector with a second successive denial of any increase for the government sector. All capital grants would be cut by $9 million in total, with an $8 million cut for government schools and a $1 million cut for non-government schools. The six-tier funding system was retained. Protests from the government school sector abounded. Carrick's justification when faced with protests was that government schools had been more than adequately funded during the post-Karmel period and were now close to the resource targets suggested by Karmel. In conservative social justice terms, it was now the turn of the non-government sector to catch up.[20]

The Commission's position worsened as the year went on. In June, Fraser announced that his government's austerity program would continue and there would be no financial concessions to the states during the annual premiers' conference due to start on 22 June. This announcement caused disquiet at the state level. The Schools Commission's continuing management of a large proportion of each state's education budget became a sitting duck for premiers eager to take control of the distribution of Commonwealth education money.

Indeed, after the premiers' conference it was announced that the anti-centralist premier of Western Australia, Sir Charles Court, had proposed that the Schools Commission should be shut down entirely and Commonwealth funding should simply be handed over to the states. This proposed move to abolish the commission and allow the states to allocate Commonwealth funding was supported by the equally anti-centralist Queensland premier, Joh Bjelke-Petersen,

---

[20] 'Group plans protest over school funds', *Sydney Morning Herald*, 13 June 1978.

CHAPTER SEVEN

but was diverted by Fraser and Carrick into a review of the role of the Schools Commission by Commonwealth and state education ministers in August-September that year. If the review did take place later in that year, its proceedings were apparently not published.

What was published in late October was a bold, 100-page Schools Commission criticism of the Commonwealth government's education policy. The Commission's accusations included allegations that the Fraser government tended to favour non-government schools, arguing that funding arrangements were, in contemporary terminology, a zero-sum game that adversely affected government schools. The Commission's second argument was that there was little progress being made in bringing disadvantaged (mainly inner-city and rural) schools up to mainstream government-school standards. The third criticism was that if special Commission education programs were to continue, the money for these programs would have to come out of overall Commission funding – again, a zero-sum arrangement.

Carrick responded a month later, pointing out that while the government had no intention of withdrawing funding from government schools, December's Education Council meeting would discuss these and other matters. The other matters included (alarmingly for the state education ministers and for McKinnon) a proposed change to full state funding for government schools and a reform of the Schools Commission. As it happened, the only public announcement that came out of the council meeting was a proposal to examine a plan to provide professional development to those teachers who were peripherally involved in careers advice.[21] In essence, this 1978 jockeying for position between Carrick and the states had been

---

[21] 'Plan to make teachers more aware', *Sydney Morning Herald*, 19 February 1979.

more about internal domestic politics than about education policy. Much of the political rhetoric of 1978 had been mere huffing and puffing with a bit of political positioning thrown in, with the Schools Commission, by now struggling to maintain what was left of its autonomy, caught in the middle.

The year ended peacefully enough, but there had been some indication already of where Carrick and the Fraser government were now heading when it came to funding schools. From now on, the Schools Commission, instead of being the sole statutory authority responsible for disbursing the Commonwealth's education dollar, was to be more of an advisory body and a consultative group now loaded up with newly-appointed non-government sector Commissioners.

The new year 1979 began quietly, but in March, Carrick, now pursuing an economic rationalist train of thought, announced that the government was not just in favour of parental choice in the private school system but was also now supportive of 'choice' in the government school system as well. On the face of it, this precursor to later Liberal attempts to boost the non-government sector was an impractical suggestion, but nevertheless Carrick had taken up the idea by allocating $200,000 of the Schools Commission's own money to explore the idea and come up with advice.[22]

It was not just that the Schools Commission was being reduced to an advisory body. Commonwealth government cuts to its educational programs continued apace. In May 1979 the *Sydney Morning Herald*

---

22 'Should parents have more choice?', *Sydney Morning Herald*, 20 March 1979. Such an idea was impractical in rural areas, difficult in regional centres where patterns of population growth were a determinant and in city areas where there would be strong opposition from education departments wedded to the catchment areas system of school choice. Also, internal information about schools that might allow informed choice such as examination results remained confidential.

CHAPTER SEVEN

pointed out that the Commission's innovations programs and disadvantaged schools programs had both been cut back within a reduction of special project funding from $4.8 million in 1978 to $3.9 million in 1979, compared with the Schools Commission's 1975 recommendation of $30 million.[23]

Matters did not improve for McKinnon in the next month. Carrick moved into Schools Commission territory again in June 1979 when he announced a $41.2 million budget cut for 1980 (mainly from capital works) across all education providers from school to university, instructing the Schools Commission that it would have to cut spending on government schools alone by $38 million. On the other hand, Category 6 (deprived) non-government school spending would rise by $3.3 million, an increase based on the Schools Commission reporting that needy non-government schools (mainly Catholic) were still well below government school resourcing standards for recurrent needs.

In line with Carrick's earlier statement that non-government school spending needed to catch up with spending on government school counterparts, these schools would receive a $14 million increase in total. To back his position on school funding Carrick published a justification in pamphlet form: *The Basic Facts*. Federal opposition education spokesman Senator John Button declared that 1980 would be 'a vintage year in the slide of real expenditure on education'.[24]

It was not just Carrick, however, who felt that there needed to be a reduction in expenditure when it came to school funding. A *Sydney Morning Herald* editorial on 8 June argued that the time had come

---

[23] 'New programs feeling the pinch', *Sydney Morning Herald*, 1 May 1979.

[24] 'Govt to cut education spending by $41.2 million', *Sydney Morning Herald*, 6 June 1979.

to pull back on funding schools which had benefited from 'a splurge of new building, the lavish ordering of new equipment and the ambitious development of new programs.'[25] The newspaper followed up this line of argument a month later when education correspondent Carolyn Parfitt published a feature article in which she suggested, 'the party is now over, and the 1980s are likely to see changes in education taking place within relatively stable levels of funding.'[26] Interestingly, the Bill Hayden-led ALP's response to the proposed cuts to government schools was low-key rather than furious.[27] It was almost as if the ALP did not disagree with Carrick's new policy direction because there may be adverse political consequences for them in bringing up the state aid issue yet again.

On 30 August 1979, the Schools Commission response to the Carrick stance was tabled in Parliament in the form of the Commission's financial report. This document pointed out, to the concern of some Commissioners, that while funding for government schools since 1976 had declined by 14 per cent in real terms, funding for non-government schools had risen by 24 per cent during the same period. Joan Kirner, who had recently left the Commission but was still committed to speaking up strongly in support of government schools, told the *Sydney Morning Herald* that if this trend continued, the non-government sector would be in receipt of all of the Commonwealth's school funding by 1985.[28]

---

[25] 'Cutting education', *Sydney Morning Herald*, 8 June 1979.

[26] 'Second look at education', *Sydney Morning Herald*, 16 July 1979.

[27] Whitlam had resigned as opposition leader in December 1977 after another election defeat. He was to resign from Parliament on 31 July 1979.

[28] 'Govt challenged on aid to schools', *Sydney Morning Herald*, 31 August 1979.

CHAPTER SEVEN

Carrick remained unmoved. He pointed out that the Schools Commission's role was simply to top up the 83 per cent state funds to government schools, implying that its job did not include getting caught up in arguments about who got what. He further pointed out that while it was true that the Commonwealth accepted more of the responsibility for non-government schools, only 3 per cent of the states' school funding went to a sector that accommodated 21 per cent of the nation's students.

Having clearly established the Fraser government's attitude to the Schools Commission and to school funding priorities, Carrick was rewarded by the prime minister. In December he received a promotion to the post of Minister for National Development and Energy. This was a so-called 'hot seat' ministry that included responsibility for petrol prices, a political flashpoint in a continental nation with high transport costs and rates of private vehicle ownership and usage. Carrick's first task was to announce a 20 per cent increase in petrol prices on 1 January 1980.

Wal Fife, an ambitious country Liberal from Wagga Wagga and Fraser's then Minister for Business and Consumer Affairs, took over the education portfolio from Carrick. Fife had started his ministerial career as assistant education minister in the New South Wales state parliament in 1965, but during the intervening years had occupied various state and federal ministerial posts. A convenor of New South Wales country Liberals, he was regarded as a loyal and congenial utility player rather than a star performer.[29] Ken Jones, still head of the education department, thought his latest minister a useful asset:

---

29   Fife, while a lifelong Anglican, had close connections with senior Catholic clergy in New South Wales, was a close friend of Archbishop Frank Carroll (see above) and was given a papal award towards the end of his career.

> I was still fortunate in that Fife was close to the Prime Minister. Fife was a Liberal in a country seat, and while [*sic*] the senior academic[s]/administrators tended to look down on Fife as not being really up to it in matters in the national level of education, which I thought was first a miscalculation on their part and second very stupid from their own point of view in the way they reacted to him. He didn't have the intellectual grasp that Carrick had about educational matters ... but Fife was a good grassroots politician, he had a very sound political nose and being the Senior Liberal Minister in a country seat he had Fraser's ear on those matters.[30]

During his term of office (1979–83), it was Fife's responsibility to persist with the policies and practices articulated by his predecessors Malcolm Fraser and John Carrick. These were an insistence that the states bear the major burden of funding government schools and that the Commonwealth would play a decreasing role in funding government schools and an increasing role in funding non-government schools. Such Commonwealth funding would be allocated according to ministerial guidelines on the advice of a variety of sources, with the advice of the Schools Commission progressively marginalised.

Fife seemed determined to keep a low profile during most of his official tenure and in that regard he certainly succeeded.[31] During the period January 1980-May 1982, even though there had been a general election in October 1980, he merited just three substantive mentions in the combined news and opinion columns of the *Sydney Morning Herald* and the *Sun-Herald*.

---

[30] Jones, 1985, TRC 1858/2/94. The reference to 'academics' is probably about McKinnon.

[31] 'Rating the Cabinet on a Scale of one to 10', *Sydney Morning Herald*, 16 August 1981. The bureaucratic allusion is almost certainly to a thinly-disguised Permanent Head Ken Jones.

CHAPTER SEVEN

The first of these Fife media allusions was, however, not to a low profile activity. Commissioner McKinnon had expected at least one renewal of his tenure, standard practice for such statutory appointments. By late 1980, however, he had clearly infuriated the Fraser government with his running commentary on the Coalition's education policy. During the post-election period, having brought in the new, three-category funding classification for non-government schools, Fife, without warning, declined to renew Ken McKinnon's contract as Commissioner.[32]

McKinnon had already been promised a renewal by Fife who, according to McKinnon, had remarked that 'as he respected the independence and quality of my advice he intended to re-appoint me'.[33] That being his belief, McKinnon had turned down in mid-year an unspecified high-status job in Paris. In this sudden turnaround, Fife sacked McKinnon in early December 1980, to the predictable fury of the unionists, government school parents' organisations and ALP shadow education spokesman John Dawkins.[34] McKinnon's replacement, announced immediately by Fife, was West Australian academic, footballer and committed Catholic educator Peter Tannock, a member of the Commission from its inception. Tannock was regarded with suspicion by government school supporters because of his Catholic background. Surprisingly, however, Teachers' Federation official David Widdup publicly stated that while the Commission's

---

[32] The three-category funding model was open to abuse. Wealthy Category One non-government schools could exploit the new system by diverting more income to capital works and less to recurrent costs, placing them in the more needy Category Two, with a concomitant increase in top-up Commonwealth funding.

[33] McKinnon, 2010, p.13.

[34] 'Parents, teachers angry as school chief is dumped', *Sydney Morning Herald*, 5 December 1980. McKinnon had asked six months prior for a confirmation that he would be reappointed but heard nothing.

Federation representative did not always agree with Tannock, the new appointee had always been a fair-minded chairman when, on occasions, he had taken over from McKinnon.[35]

And then it was Christmas and time for the summer holidays.

After Christmas, the DOGS case against funding denominational schools was moving towards a High Court resolution. Since May 1980, Fraser had been quietly preparing a constitutional amendment should the case succeed, and Fife's department had been preparing for any necessary temporary financial arrangements. But in February 1981 the DOGS case was thrown out, much to Fife's relief. A successful suit would have left the Australian education system in turmoil. One interesting feature of the High Court's decision was Whitlam-era Attorney General and now Justice Lionel Murphy's dissenting opinion that state aid for religious schools raised serious issues of church-state relations, a point of view that had previously brought Murphy into conflict with the New South Wales branch of the ALP.

In August 1981 political commentator Neil O'Reilly referred to Fife in a *Sun-Herald* article as 'a pleasant man who relies heavily on his department. Has shown weakness in dealing with bureaucrats who exceed their authority'. Fife scored a modest 4.5 on O'Reilly's ten-point scale.[36] But in the following month Fife would sponsor

---

[35] See n. 27.

[36] 'Rating the Cabinet on a scale of one to 10', *Sun-Herald*, 18 August 1981. Out of interest's sake, Deputy Prime Minister Doug Anthony came top with 8.5, Industry Minister Philip Lynch came second with 7.5, Finance Minister Margaret Guilfoyle was third with 7.5, Communications Minister Ian Sinclair came fourth with 6.7, John Howard was fifth scoring 7.0 as Treasurer and Carrick came seventh with 6.0. Authoritative political journalist Neil O'Reilly who had canvassed public servants and politicians before publishing his findings described Fraser's thirteen-person inner cabinet as a 'weak bunch'. The bureaucrat mentioned by O'Reilly was almost certainly Ken Jones.

CHAPTER SEVEN

an amendment to Commonwealth legislation which would allow new non-government schools to finance their operations through a Commonwealth loan guarantee. Opposed by ALP education spokesperson John Dawkins on the grounds that it would open the door to 'crackpot schools', the amendment was passed in October. Almost immediately, one of the smaller fundamentalist religious groups, the US-based Accelerated Christian Education group, began to expand its operations in Australia, at the vanguard of fundamentalist Christian school organisations.

In June 1982 Fraser transferred the amiable Fife from education to aviation to look after a contentious New South Wales issue: the proposed building of a third runway for Sydney's Kingsford Smith airport. Fife, who was pleased with what he had done as education minister, later commented: 'During the combined period of John Carrick and my occupancy of the Education Portfolio, more non-government schools were opened in Australia than in any other period in our history'.[37] As a moderate Anglican, he may later have been alarmed at what transpired in the non-government school sector when fundamentalist Christian and Islamic schools began to flourish in the 1990s: an unforeseen consequence of his and Carrick's actions.

Fraser's incoming education minister was New South Wales senator Peter Baume, a progressive Liberal with a reputation for speaking his mind to all comers. Baume, who had been in charge of Aboriginal affairs and (very briefly) health, was expected to carry on in education where Fife had left off, and he did. After Fife, Jones was taken aback by Baume's energy:

---

[37] Wal Fife, *Wal Fife: A Country Liberal*, Wagga Wagga, Peribo, p.193, 2008.

> He was a compulsive doer, a man who never sat still, always doing something. Wanted to get things done in a hurry, wanted to demonstrate that he was the Minister, as he said to me he had no sympathy [*sic*] with the "Yes Minister" programme [the first series of which] was being presented ... when I had Fife and then [second series] with Baume because it presented the Minister as an amiable fool and that was not Peter Baume's conception of himself as a Minister.[38]

Much more high profile than his predecessor, the new minister announced the government's school funding program for 1983, Fife's last ministerial gift to the Australian school system. In that 21 June 1982 announcement, the Carrick-Fife funding formula was changed again. The funding split was now to be even more in favour of the non-government school system, which was to receive $507 million, a 7.7 per cent increase on its 1982 allocation. Government school funding was cut to $463 million, a 2.2 per cent decrease from its 1982 allocation, not the 4.7 per cent increase requested by the Schools Commission earlier that year. Baume's defence of these figures was that school funding overall would go up by 3.8 per cent in 1983 and most of the increase in non-government funding would go to the poorer Catholic schools.

According to *Sydney Morning Herald* education reporter Andrew Casey, however, the likely victims of these cuts would be the Commission's special funding programs, for country, disadvantaged and 'ethnic' schools. Unsurprisingly, the by-now powerful, predominantly Catholic Australian Parents' Council (formed in the aftermath of the Goulburn closures), welcomed the new arrangements and the Australian Council of State Schools did not. The New South

---

[38] Jones, 1985, TRC 1858/2/109.

CHAPTER SEVEN

Wales ALP education minister, the highly capable and popular Ron Mulock, was also opposed to the changes. In a New South Wales education department with a budget close to $2 billion, and 60,000 staff, the Commonwealth cuts were going to hurt.[39]

Undeterred, Baume moved on, quickly developing his sought-after active public profile. Over the remaining period of his time in office (until March 1983) Baume suggested that, where practicable, government and non-government schools should share facilities. He further, and with some force, pointed out that aid to non-government schools was now a fixture in Australian society and any attempt to remove it would disadvantage both sectors. Baume also criticised the Teachers' Federation unionists for their unprecedented partisan involvement in a forthcoming March 1983 general election, announcing that federal Labor had a 'hit list' and would shut down 150 non-government schools if elected (the ALP said forty-one). The education minister then deflected the 'wealthy schools' criticism by indicating that grants to non-government schools were means tested. Moreover, he pointed out that prominent leading anti-state aiders had actually been educated at excellent non-government schools and went on to blame government teachers for their students' low retention rates. Some state schools, he suggested also, were just as wealthy as the better-endowed non-government schools the anti-state-aiders were attacking.

None of this saved the flagging Coalition government. On 5 March 1983, Bob Hawke, former Australian Council of Trade Unions president (1969–80), recently (1980) elected ALP member

---

[39] See obituary, 'Decent, high-performing Ron Mulock served as NSW deputy premier', *Sydney Morning Herald*, 20 October 2014.

for Wills and even more recently (February 1983) named ALP leader, took his party to a widely expected landslide victory over the Fraser government.

Hawke's election speech had contained twenty-one detailed references to schools. This sentence outlined his government's overarching view on funding: 'If all Australian children are to enjoy equal educational opportunities – the funding of all schools – government and non-government – must be based on fairness and need'.[40]

Fairness, too, had been mentioned in Fraser's election spiel, in which schools received four brief comments and this longer, vague mention, which could well have been drafted by Baume: 'Education needs to give all our children better opportunities to do the things they do well. The Schools Commission has pointed in the past to an over-reliance on academic curriculums. That suits academically-inclined students, but there are many other students who also deserve a fair go.'[41]

Fraser's reference to a fair go was really a diversion from what had happened to school funding during his term as prime minister. If we look at the changes in numbers of schools and students in the two major sectors over the Fraser years 1976–83, we can see a clear pattern. In 1976, there were 7306 government schools, 1698 Catholic schools and 440 mainly Anglican and other Protestant schools. By 1983 there were 7546 government schools, a percentage increase of 3.2 per cent. In 1983, Catholic schools numbered 1702, an increase of 0.2 percent. On the other hand, Anglican and other category

---

[40] See http://electionspeeches.moadoph.gov.au.

[41] See http://electionspeeches.moadoph.gov.au.

CHAPTER SEVEN

school numbers in 1983 had risen to 660, a 50 per cent increase.[42] Looking at student numbers, in 1976 there were 2,335,431 students in government schools, rising to 2,354,422 in 1983, a 0.8113 per cent increase. In 1976 there were 624,819 students in all non-government schools rising to 734,784 in 1983, a 17.59 per cent increase. Overall population increase during that period had been 9.5 per cent.

It comes as no surprise, therefore, to read in Wal Fife's memoirs that he was very pleased with his track record as education minister.

---

[42] *ABS Yearbooks* 1977–78 p.231 and 1985 p.231. The relative stability of Catholic schools despite growing Catholic numbers was almost certainly due to the closing down of smaller, older, inner city schools and the building of new, larger suburban schools.

Chapter Eight

THE HAWKE-RYAN YEARS

We Don't Want any Brawls

When Bob Hawke and the Labor Party took over from the Fraser-led Coalition government in March 1983, it was not the ALP's shadow education spokesperson John Dawkins who was given the education portfolio. Instead, Dawkins was given the finance ministry in Hawke's twelve-person outer ministry. Senator Susan Ryan was put in charge of the new department of education and youth affairs, becoming a member of the thirteen-person inner Cabinet, as well as minister assisting the prime minister for the status of women. Ryan was an outspoken, left-of-centre feminist who had been active in ACSSO and written a Labor policy essay on equality. She was to be the only woman in the inner and outer ministries during that first 1983–84 Hawke government.

Ryan was originally a Sydneysider from an Irish-descended working-class family in Maroubra. She had attended the local Brigidine convent before completing an Arts degree at Sydney University in 1962 and starting her professional career as a teacher.[1] After university, influenced by Germaine Greer (with whom she had sung in her university choir) and by US feminist Betty Friedan,

---

[1] Ryan later completed a master's degree at the Australian National University.

Ryan's life experiences led her towards a centrist but firm version of feminism and a leftish but not dogmatic form of socialism.

Ryan's political career began in 1969 when she founded the Belconnen branch of the ALP, becoming its president in 1971. In 1974 she became a member of the newly-founded Legislative Assembly and, during that early-mid 1970s period, also helped found the Women's Electoral Lobby (WEL). She was also one of the consultants recruited for the Schools Commission's 1975 *Girls and Schooling* report. Her rise through party ranks and her activist profile led to a September 1975 *Sydney Morning Herald* feature article by journalist Gwen Moseley, 'Political pin-up girl [sic] of International Women's Year'.[2]

In late 1975 Ryan was selected as ALP senator for the ACT and by 1982 she was (half in jest) being touted as Australia's first female prime minister by the *Sydney Morning Herald*'s influential 'Stay in Touch' columnist David Dale.[3] By now an ex-Catholic, Ryan was from the early 1980s the ALP's principal spokesperson on women's issues and its chief education specialist.

Ryan had endured the kinds of formative experiences common to many career-seeking women. As a working-class undergraduate at Sydney University she had been told that her preferred field of study, the law, was not for women. Taken aback, she took English literature instead. After university, and having married a diplomat, Ryan experienced the ancillary lifestyle of a diplomat's wife. As an ALP member, she also witnessed Bill Hayden's 1973 dinner party jibe that WEL was for middle-class housewives who had nothing better to do. Worse yet, on her first entry into the Senate, she and a

---

[2] 'A Woman on the Move', *Sydney Morning Herald*, 28 September 1975.

[3] 'Stay in Touch: People', *Sydney Morning Herald*, 29 April 1982.

CHAPTER EIGHT

female colleague were jeered as 'old boilers' by a would-be humorous ALP senator Mick Young. Even in March 1983, when in office as a Cabinet minister, a *Sydney Morning Herald* sub-editorial staff member felt it was appropriate to head a feature article on Ryan and other women in ALP politics 'Girls in the think-tank.'[4]

While Ryan was pleased to have been offered the position of minister assisting the prime minister for the status of women, she had really wanted education and canvassed Hawke for that ministry. According to Ryan, however, the prime minister was anxious about the possibility of her offending supposedly ALP-friendly Catholic bishops who were not used to dealing with women on equal terms.[5] More awkward would be her campaign against the ACT's 1978 Termination of Pregnancy Ordinance, which would have prohibited abortion clinics, instead referring pregnant women to public hospitals. Ryan lost that cause and gained the enmity of Catholic activists, many of whom were embedded in the Australian Parents' Council.[6]

Hawke surmised that were Ryan appointed to education, the Catholics would have to negotiate with a forthright minister who was a high-profile feminist, a vocal supporter of government schools, a divorced ex-Catholic and a pro-abortion crusader. Ryan was confident, however, that her Catholic upbringing and her already established close connections with the Catholic community,

---

[4] *Sydney Morning Herald*, 11 March 1983. The article was led by a crass banner headline, 'THE OTHER WOMAN BEHIND OUR PRIME MINISTER', a reference to the prime minister's personal assistant Jean Sinclair. It is possible that there may be a hidden punning message in the headline to those who knew about Hawke's reputation for philandering.

[5] Susan Ryan, *Catching the Waves*, Pymble, HarperCollins, pp.214–215, 1999.

[6] The Ordinance was repealed in 1992. Arguably, in some Catholic eyes, Ryan's pro-abortion stance was the greatest of her sins as a minister.

especially with Sydney's influential Archbishop James Carroll, would allow her to overcome any initial hostility.

Ryan's stated priority was to improve job opportunities for young people by encouraging school students either to stay on beyond the leaving age, return to school if they had already left, or enrol at a technical college. Retention rates were considered to be alarmingly low in the public education system and the new government's funding focus was to be on government schools and technical colleges, with an extra $45 million to be set aside over three years to help increase technical college enrolments. At the same time, Ryan was determined to pursue a clear, equal opportunity social justice agenda.

There were several obstacles in her way. The first of these was a complex group of political and bureaucratic difficulties, starting with Ryan having to deal with ideological divisions in the Cabinet's attitude to school education. Hawke and his ministers were anxious about the government's inherited budget deficit of $9.5 billion, an unwelcome and surprise legacy from the Fraser government. Additionally, in March 1983 Australia was dealing with double-digit inflation and unemployment. Funding priorities needed to be tied to economic recovery but ministers were split on how that recovery might be funded.

Hawke's first Cabinet was divided into factions, with New South Wales MP Stewart West the single Socialist-Left Cabinet member (he resigned on a matter of principle in November 1983), an initially non-aligned but incipient centre-Left faction to be led by Bill Hayden, as well as an economic rationalist Labor-Right faction led by the prime minister and Paul Keating.[7] Most of the Left and

---

[7] West became Immigration and Ethnic Affairs Minister. His anti-uranium stance led to his 1983 resignation. For the sake of explanatory convenience, these categories

CHAPTER EIGHT

what was to become the centre-Left wanted to maintain the ALP's traditional level of support for education, health and welfare despite the nation's budgetary problems. Labor-Right, on the other hand, wanted to curb spending. The Right and their allies within the centre-Left dominated both the Cabinet and the influential, tight-fisted Expenditure Review Committee.[8]

The Labor-Right members of Cabinet were wary of taking on big-spending education commitments so soon after the Whitlam government's 1975 demise, a downfall based in part on the Whitlam government's reputation for profligacy.[9] Hawke, Keating, Peter Walsh and Dawkins wanted to cut back on Ryan's department, which was in their view already overstaffed with 6000 public servants and running on a bloated annual budget of $5 billion.[10] Leftist ministers such as Brian Howe wanted to prioritise public spending, but in his case on social services rather than on education which, as Ryan put it in 1999, was seen by her rivals for funding as providing, 'the smallest [electoral] bang for bucks'.[11] Stuck in the middle sat centre-Left Ryan who, with assistance from ALP-aligned states, was keen to bring

---

are a simplified version of the ALP's 1980s factional groupings which were more complex and more shifting in nature and personnel than outlined here. The centre-Left faction firmed up in 1984.

[8] According to political journalist Glenn Milne there were six unaligned inner and outer Cabinet ministers in 1983 including John Dawkins and Peter Walsh. See 'These days it pays politicians to take sides in the ALP', *Sydney Morning Herald*, 8 January 1988.

[9] Journalist Milton Cockburn's advice to the ALP Caucus was a compulsory viewing of Peter Weir's television mini-series *The Dismissal*, which at the time was airing on ABC TV. Its first episode appeared the day after the ALP victory. See, '... but first, Caucus should watch The Dismissal', *Sydney Morning Herald*, 8 March 1983.

[10] Ryan, 1999, p.23.

[11] Ryan, 1999, p.25.

expensive and untested social justice programs into government and non-government schools.

In line with ALP policy, however, two education sectors were targeted for cutbacks by the Hawke government. The first of these was higher education, already heavily subsidised by the Commonwealth. Changes to the higher education sector were eventually to include a student contribution scheme, a move later opposed by Ryan, to her political cost. The second sector targeted for cuts was the wealthy non-Catholic element in the non-government school sector.

There was still some room for Ryan to manoeuvre, with funding allocated for government schools and colleges under the banner of her department's Participation and Equity Program (PEP), apparently a reworking of a Fraser-era policy, Transition to Employment.[12] Because of national youth unemployment issues, and despite the Cabinet's opposition to increasing education expenditure, in 1984 the PEP was given $74 million to encourage retention rates in schools and technical colleges by adapting the curriculum and improving the social environment of schools and colleges. The PEP's 'pull factor', combined with a high youth unemployment 'push factor', led to a sharp increase in retention rates.

Ryan was also keen to re-open the Whitlam-era, Canberra-based Curriculum Development Corporation (CDC), a low-cost multi-jurisdictional partnership organisation shut down during the Fraser years. The CDC's job had been to provide exemplary curriculum materials which jurisdictions could choose to adopt for classroom use at their discretion. The CDC, reincarnated in 1984 by Ryan, was a predecessor of the 1988 Commonwealth-instigated Curriculum

---

12   Ken Jones asserted in his 1985 interview that the PEP was a rebadged version of the 1979 Fraser-era program. Jones, 1985, TRC 1858 96-97.

CHAPTER EIGHT

Corporation, and was the first faltering step on a meandering road towards Australia's 2010 national curriculum.

In private, Ryan and her department were concerned about several non-government school phenomena. First, they were anxious about the growth in numbers of low-cost Christian fundamentalist schools, an expansion that had been encouraged by Wal Fife's Commonwealth loan scheme. Such schools counted as low-resource, needy establishments requiring expensive up-front recurrent and capital funding from the Commonwealth. Also, from a bureaucratic and political point of view, there had been an alarming rise in fringe religions and sects taking advantage of the Fife loans initiative.[13] Such schools were based on fundamentalist religious curricula and outmoded student disciplinary practices that were the antithesis of everything that the ALP and progressive educators stood for. There was an associated problem in the seemingly untrammelled growth in numbers of outer-suburban and regional Catholic schools, a development that had been spotted and publicly called out by Ken McKinnon as placing an increasingly unconscionable burden on Commonwealth funding.[14]

A related issue (already noted above) was a tendency among wealthier non-government schools to take advantage of the Fife-instigated three-tier funding system by diverting a disproportionate amount of privately-raised money to capital works, leaving their recurrent funding accounts looking relatively bare. Such schools then attracted high levels of Commonwealth money for recurrent expenses. Some wealthy schools could game the three-tier system

---

[13] The private nature of Ryan's concerns did not stop them being leaked to the press, see 'Education – Ryan Style', *Sydney Morning Herald*, 25 March 1983.

[14] See, 'State Aid drain: Catholic Schools blamed', *Sydney Morning Herald*, 23 July 1983.

further by deliberately creating such a poor set of recurrent figures that they were moved into the middle needs category as schools that were worse off than their actual circumstances indicated. In this way, the shrewder non-government schools could, perfectly legitimately, build superior facilities while leaving much of their salary and other fixed costs to the Commonwealth.

A second major obstacle to Ryan's reformist management of education was the Canberra bureaucratic system's continuing dislike of the Schools Commission, still regarded as a maverick organisation beyond departmental control. It was not only the public servants who loathed the Schools Commission. Cabinet members Hawke, Keating and Dawkins wanted it gone too. Bureaucrats and politicians were anxious about an open-ended, needs-based approach to school funding. Ryan, on the other hand, wanted the Commission kept on as an advisory council at least, this being also a goal of the previous government.

A third and less manageable obstacle to Ryan's school reform ambitions was the frenzied and divisive atmosphere within which school-funding policy was still being debated by various stakeholders and lobby groups. The new minister's aim on assuming office had been to avoid confrontation and sell her plans as rational measures that would benefit all. Ryan had no time for the militant Teachers' Federation nor for its ideological opponent the vocal Australian Parents' Council. As the new minister was to discover, however, there was little rationality about the state aid debate.

Ryan wanted to clear the ground before she commenced her real work. Within days of her Cabinet appointment she decided to sack the long-serving Ken Jones and replace him with Peter Wilenski, a former

CHAPTER EIGHT

Whitlam appointee who was still on the public service Division One (departmental head) unattached list. After the Whitlam dismissal, Wilenski had worked with the Wran government as a consultant, then moved to academia and later worked with Ryan and Gareth Evans and ALP staffer (and later public servant) Michael Costello on the ALP's 'Transition to Government' committee, where he had been told to avoid any hint of Whitlamesque urgency. Wilenski had excellent credentials but was a very divisive figure in the Canberra bureaucracy and even within the Hawke Cabinet.

A reformer with a zeal for gender equality, open government and Indigenous rights, Wilenski was disliked by many members of the traditionalist, male-dominated Commonwealth public service (the so-called 'Commonwealth Club'). Ken Jones, on the other hand, was a senior, middle-of-the-road member of the Commonwealth Club group who, in his almost decade long-year tenure as head of the education department had assisted Coalition ministers in devising education policies. These policies were regarded unfavourably by the ALP and Ken Jones had sat across the table from Ryan in her capacity as lobbyist for ACSSO. Jones was therefore regarded by the ALP education lobby as having been too close to previous Coalition governments. The Jones sacking came straight after Hawke's first Cabinet meeting on Wednesday 16 March. Before that date there had been a week of informal contacts between the Hawke government and the Canberra bureaucracy, but no official sign, not even unofficial gossip, suggesting that Jones, who believed he had served both sides of politics even-handedly, would be dumped as department head.

When offering the education and women's affairs posts to Ryan prior to his first Cabinet meeting, the prime minister had suggested that Wilenski should go directly to Ryan's department as head.[15]

Immediately following the conclusion of Hawke's first Cabinet meeting, in March, Jones received a telephone message to attend Ryan's office and in a tense encounter was told that 'the Cabinet' wanted Wilenski to replace him. Ryan's department head was then given a week's notice without cause. Jones quickly used his Canberra connections to negotiate a position for himself as head of Administrative Services. He stayed on there until he was appointed head of Local Government and Administrative Services in 1984. He retired in 1986 after thirteen years as a permanent secretary (later first secretary), bitter to the end about how he had been handled by Hawke and Ryan.[16]

Wilenski, who, as Treasury Secretary John Stone had remarked, had no background in education policy, was almost certainly parked in Education and Youth Affairs as a political favour and a prelude to filling a more important post. His significant job-to-be was the most senior post in the public service, chair of the Public Service Board. Wilenski's Cabinet supporters (Dawkins, Evans and Hawke) knew that the position was about to become vacant on 1 November 1983 when incumbent Sir William Cole's term of office expired. Accordingly, Wilenski stayed in Education for only seven months before leaving his temporary accommodation for a role that better suited his high-flying talents.

---

[15] Ryan described the sacking of an unnamed public servant who was 'competent and experienced' as a 'difficult and unwelcome one'. Ryan, 1999, p.220.

[16] Jones, 1985, TRC 1858/2/120-121, '... frankly I think the Hawke government treated me very badly ... a week's notice is what they used to give housemaids in Victorian times'.

CHAPTER EIGHT

As far as can be ascertained, Wilenski, constantly distracted by being on call as a policy consultant to other Cabinet ministers and their advisers, provided two lasting contributions of note during his brief time at Education and Youth Affairs. The first of these was an all-staff memorandum requiring the use of clear and succinct writing in departmental communications, including a precise use of the word 'decimate'.[17] His second contribution was, on the occasion of his departure, to recommend as his acting successor in Susan Ryan's ministry his outstanding deputy (and protégée) Helen Williams, who in January 1985 would become the first woman appointed to head a public service department.

As first steps go, Ryan's abrupt sacking of Ken Jones was a sign of an impending change of regime style in Education, from bureaucratic business as usual to the vigorous sweeping of a new broom.

Having replaced Jones, Ryan moved on to deal with schooling. When asked in late March about her plans for non-government schools, Ryan answered, 'We don't want any brawls. We want harmonious relations with private schools. The needs-based policy for funding private schools was clearly spelled out in the [election] campaign'.[18] Having made that firm comment, three days later Ryan announced that she was restructuring the Schools Commission by reducing its number of representatives. Five about-to-be vacated positions would now go to government school nominees leaving the Commission with only one guaranteed non-government representative in the person of Father John Williams, of the National

---

17   'Stay in Touch,' *Sydney Morning Herald*, 16 September 1983.
18   'Senator Susan's school-led recovery', *Sydney Morning Herald*, 20 March 1983. At first glance, the comment reads like a shot across the bows of the non-government school lobbyists but it is much more likely to have been Ryan's rationalism at work. In effect she was saying, 'The plan is out there, now I need to get on with the job'.

Catholic Education Commission. The Australian Parents' Council representative was also ousted and replaced by Lyndsay Connors, a former executive officer of ACSSO and a close friend of Ryan's. This was step two completed in Ryan's new broom policy.

In April 1983 Hawke convened a promised economic summit in Canberra at which Ryan, the only female speaker, outlined her major policy initiative, which was the uncontroversial but ambitious goal of raising school retention rates in order to deal with the serious problem of students leaving senior school to go on the dole. A month later, Ryan went back to new broom activity.

Ryan's step three came in late May when, having already declared that the APC would be dropped from the Schools Commission, she announced that non-government school parents would no longer be represented in any form on the reconstituted Schools Commission. The new part-time members were to be Van Davy, outspoken president of the Teachers' Federation; Joan Brown, a former president of ACSSO; Vincent Faulkner of the Catholic Education Office; and Victoria and Paul Hughes of the National Aboriginal Education Committee. Non-government schools were to be represented by Rev. DB Clarke, headmaster of Hutchins School in Hobart and Faulkner, while Peter Tannock, who had taken over from Ken McKinnon as chair, was to remain in his position. This meant that, Tannock aside, non-government schools had three representatives out of twelve members, a complete turnaround from the days of the 'Private Schools Commission'.

Step four came in August 1983, almost immediately after the July ALP national conference, in which the ALP centre-Left faction, including Ryan, had sided with the Left to vote (yet again) for a motion, astonishingly sponsored by Ryan herself, advocating

CHAPTER EIGHT

the complete phasing out of state aid to non-government schools. It was a case of poor timing since, in late July, the government's interim school funding guidelines for 1984 had been published. They recommended an immediate 25 per cent cut in recurrent funding to the wealthiest 41 non-government schools, followed by a policy of gradual reduction of Commonwealth support for these wealthier schools. This announcement came as no surprise, since it was a reworked version of the ALP's opposition policy that had led to education minister Peter Baume's previous use of the very effective 'hit list' jibe – although his list had contained a wildly exaggerated 150 schools. And it was no surprise that Ryan now found herself the object of 'hit list' criticism from the non-government school lobby.[19]

By the end of the year, when the guidelines for 1984 legislation were about to pass through the parliamentary process, the non-government school lobby groups in New South Wales, both Catholic and non-Catholic, had begun to organise their resistance, apparently having learned their tactics from the Teachers' Federation. Meetings had been convened in regional New South Wales and a major rally was scheduled by the APC for Sydney Town Hall on 7 November 1983. Susan Ryan, in Ireland on a speaking tour at the time, was targeted by the non-government lobby as the sponsor of the guidelines. Meanwhile, the Teachers' Federation promised to mobilise its own anti-state aid supporters.

In scenes reminiscent of emotional 1960s state aid demonstrations, an estimated 5000 Catholics, Protestants and others gathered at the Town Hall to listen to and cheer on a list of speakers that

---

[19] The New South Wales non-government school lobby began to prepare a 'Political Action Kit'. See, 'Private school parents plan their battle over funding', *Sydney Morning Herald*, 19 August 1983.

included Tasmanian Catholic senator Brian Harradine (he raised the Communist menace in the form of the Teachers' Federation), Monica Turner of the Catholic Parents and Friends' Association and New South Wales ALP education minister Ron Mulock (standing in for Ryan). Unsurprisingly, Mulock was jeered and slow-handclapped.

At the meeting, there was even some wild talk of 'Judas money', taken from Protestant schools to fund the Catholic education system. In the end, a motion was passed about the 'arbitrary' and 'discriminatory' actions of the state and Commonwealth Governments. Old-style protest meetings of the Sydney Town Hall kind, this time with Catholics and Protestants apparently side-by-side, worried the Hawke government, especially when the traditionally anti-ALP *Sydney Morning Herald* began to head up its larger state aid articles with photographs of a drawn and tense-looking Susan Ryan.

Back from her speaking tour, Ryan immediately issued a statement decrying the assertions of her critics, promising that state aid would remain for non-government schools and assuring parents that she intended to remove the term 'state aid' from the 'Australian political agenda'.[20] Not everybody was convinced by Ryan's statement. A long and pugnacious letter, 'Ready for a long fight', from Liberal Party official, a certain Mrs Bronwyn Bishop, slightly disingenuously writing primarily as a 'concerned parent', added her censure to the litany of complaints that Ryan was unfairly targeting non-government schools.[21]

---

[20] 'Ryan gives pledge on future of State aid for schools', *Sydney Morning Herald*, 14 November 1983.

[21] *Sydney Morning Herald*, 16 November 1983. After a long and controversial career as a Liberal politician, Bishop resigned in 2015 from her position as Speaker and left parliament following an expenses scandal. For more background on the 1983–84

CHAPTER EIGHT

Ryan, with her long, high-profile, pro-public education track record, had been an easy target for supporters of non-government schools. Distracted by her July-December oversight of a highly contentious Sex Discrimination Bill and taken aback by the irrationality and mendacity of her more extreme critics, she retaliated, dismissing the protest leaders as anti-ALP agitators. In doing so, she misjudged the intense nature of the debate and the capabilities of the non-government school lobby.[22] Ryan also misunderstood the power of popular and media opposition to her proposed funding changes. During this bitter 1983 campaign, Ryan's denials were all but drowned out by the media storm which adopted the non-government schools' social justice agenda in arguing for choice, an equitable redistribution of taxes and freedom to worship.

Hawke, who had promised cuts to spending in the non-government school sector, prior to the election, was now boxed in by the furore enveloping his education minister. Within Cabinet, Ryan's colleagues felt she was failing to sell the government's proposed funding changes, which were actually far less damaging to the non-government schools than the state aid lobby groups were suggesting.

To resolve the issue, early in the New Year the prime minister privately convened a successful conciliation meeting in the Cabinet room between Ryan and the members of the Central Commission of Catholic Bishops, the latter group chaired by ALP-friendly Archbishop James Carroll. This occasion, which would have been

---

campaign against Ryan see Jane Kenway's unpublished PhD dissertation, 'High Status Private Schooling and the Processes of an Educational Hegemony', Murdoch University, 1987, pp.163-178, and 'Letters to the Editor', *Sydney Morning Herald*, 16 November 1983.

[22] An excellent, concise account of the course of the Sex Discrimination legislation can be found in Frank Bongiorno's *The Eighties: The Decade that Transformed Australia*, Collingwood, Black Inc., 2015, pp.56–57, 2015.

awkward for most bishops, was unprecedented in terms of its nature and where it was held, with each of these decisions being designed to flatter and, through that, help to obtain consensus.[23]

From then on, Hawke kept abreast of Ryan's policy initiatives, making sure that suitably placatory messages were conveyed to a watchful non-government sector. At the same time, behind closed doors he demanded that a new plan had to be drawn up by the Schools Commission, still under Tannock's direction and still in the business of suggesting funding levels. Hawke then went public on his government's new direction in a keynote speech to the National Press Club in Canberra on 22 February 1984.

In his long (4600-word) address, Hawke outlined the achievements of the year just gone and the priorities of the year to come. One of those priorities was education, and when it came to schools, needy non-government schools (mainly Catholic) were to gain additional funding. This announcement was calculated to defuse the 1983 state aid argument, but Hawke's new strategy of increasing aid to non-government schools was a revocation of his party's 1983 state aid policy and it infuriated anti-state aid sentiment in the Party.[24]

While Hawke had temporarily blotted his ALP policy copybook he had also brought the ALP back into power after the 1975 trauma and was not too concerned about any internal opposition. Almost as

---

[23] The awkwardness was not just about state aid. It was also about Ryan's feminism and about the ALP's pro-abortion stance. For details of this undated meeting (but probably in early February 1984) see Ryan, 1999, pp.230–231. In dealing with the bishops directly, Hawke avoided going head-to-head with the tough-minded (and less susceptible to flattery) Father John Williams of the National Catholic Education Commission.

[24] ALP secularists, such as Schools Commissioner Van Davy, were certain that Catholic schools were already over-funded and the Commonwealth was paying them to instruct their students in Catholic dogma. See 'Church denies misuse of school funds', *Sydney Morning Herald*, 21 February 1984.

CHAPTER EIGHT

an aside he announced that he had given himself the task of keeping a close eye on Ryan. The education section of his speech is worth quoting in full:

> This year my Government is giving more money to non-government schools than any Government before it. The fact is that in 1984 the neediest non-government schools, and that includes more than 90 per cent of all non-government schools, will receive higher Commonwealth Grants in real terms than before. Arrangements for 1985 and beyond are not yet settled. The Government has asked the Schools Commission to provide advice and options on new arrangements for non-government school general resources funding. No new arrangements will be implemented without the fullest possible consultations with non-government schools, and I give a guarantee that I will be fully involved in this process. I will not only be interested in seeing that all views are heard but, with Senator Susan Ryan, will aim to ensure that the Government's objectives in this area are carried forward in so equitable a fashion that they have the full support of the interested parties.[25]

In response, and under pressure from Hawke and Ryan, the Schools Commission recommended in April 1984 an eight-year legislative guarantee for a new school funding system and a proposal that all schools would receive funding at existing levels, with many even receiving increases. The legislative guarantee, forced through Cabinet by Hawke and Ryan, was for four years in the first instance with an additional four to be negotiated later. It was a useful public relations stunt. The guarantee was combined with a reassuring promise to maintain funding levels for all schools, a policy turnaround that was

---

[25] Speech by the Prime Minister – Mr Bob Hawke National Press Club Canberra – 22 February 1984, PM Transcripts, Department of the Prime Minister and Cabinet, http://pmtranscripts.pmc.gov.au/release/transcript-6327.

to have long-term repercussions for both major political parties.[26] This 1984 funding promise later became a millstone around the ALP's neck when the Liberals exploited it to the advantage of non-government schools, with the ALP obliged to make similar promises in policy statements and in negotiations with the non-government sector.

The new needs-based funding model for non-government schools was to be based on an Education Resource Index (ERI), which decided its recurrent funding allocations on the difference between a non-government school's per capita income and the equivalent per capita resource level for government schools, a 'community standard'. The ERI consisted of twelve funding categories with Category One schools eligible for the lowest level of Commonwealth support and Category Twelve schools eligible for the highest level. Catholic systemic schools were all to be grouped in Category Ten. This arrangement attempted to ensure that non-government schools could not profit from Commonwealth funding (by switching internal funds to benefit from a recategorisation) while guaranteeing a generous level of support for systemic Catholic schools, thus defusing Catholic political agitation and splitting it away from other non-government school factions.

The Schools Commission proposals, which had included a financial transparency requirement for non-government schools (to deter manipulation of the system), encountered immediate criticism from the APC. The APC's spokeswoman Margaret Slattery disapproved of the proposed financial accountability as governmental intrusion, and criticised the twelve-tier system on the vague grounds that more

---

[26] While legislation cannot be guaranteed beyond a government's term, the eight-year promise was actually carried out.

CHAPTER EIGHT

schools that were on the 'hit list' would receive less funding. The government school lobby took a different tack. Shirley Berg of the New South Wales Federation of Parents and Citizens Organisations argued, equally vaguely, that the new proposals privileged non-government schools.

Whatever the case, an anti-Ryan political campaign ensued, led mainly by the Murdoch press. The campaign came shortly after Ryan's new departmental head Richard (Dick) Johnson started work at Education in April 1984. His appointment, following on from Wilenski's departure, constituted an example of an academic square peg being put into a bureaucratic round hole.

Johnson was a classicist and educational philosopher from the ANU with a background in higher education committee work and an interest in distance education. There is no clear indication why Johnson was appointed to run a department with a multibillion-dollar budget and thousands of staff scattered in offices throughout the nation. There is a strong possibility, however, that either or both of Ryan's confidants, Wilenski and Karmel, recommended him to Ryan's office, each holding Johnson in high academic regard. Presumably, if that was the case, they thought his skills were transferable. However, the Johnson appointment was soon to become an indicator of a fairly clueless Ryan ministry.

The former academic now found himself working for a besieged and inexperienced minister faced by a Murdoch press campaign which persistently employed scare tactics; for example citing battling parents struggling to send their children to non-government schools, socialist attacks on educational excellence and a threatened shutdown of the entire non-government school system. A feverish, seven-month public crusade in 1984 followed, incited by the major, and some minor, non-government school lobbies. These included local claques of anti-ALP Catholics such as the New South Wales, regionally-based Catholic Friends and Parents, led by the vociferous Monica Turner, the more sedate non-government school associations such as the Association of Independent Schools, and the APC led by the formidable Margaret Slattery.[27] Despite Ryan's avowals that non-government schools would not be cut off from state aid and that extra financial support would be made available, the protests from non-government school supporters continued with the ALP Left now anxious about yet more Ryan concessions to the non-government school lobby.[28]

Meanwhile, in August 1984, and on firmer ground, Ryan initiated a *Quality of Education Review* on how to improve the links between learning in schools and employment. The review was led by Peter Karmel, and its report was released in April 1985, advocating a back-to-basics approach for literacy and numeracy, less focus on funding issues and more emphasis on outcomes, conclusions that did not go down well with teacher unions.[29] Following on from that report, Ryan launched a new *Basic Learning in Primary Schools Program*, to prepare students for learning at the secondary school level.

In the broader political world, on 8 October 1984 Hawke announced that an early general election would take place on 1 December, an attempt to consolidate his government's position. Day-to-day parliamentary politics ground to a halt in late October and, as the

---

[27] See, 'Senator Ryan bites into the most poisonous debate in Australia', *Sydney Morning Herald*, 17 December 1983.

[28] See for example, 'Ryan defends funds for wealthy schools', *Sydney Morning Herald*, 16 August 1984, and '$156 million extra fails to placate public schools', *Sydney Morning Herald*, 18 August 1984.

[29] 'Get back to basics', *Sydney Morning Herald*, 19th June 1985.

CHAPTER EIGHT

December general election grew closer, anti-Ryan condemnations by the Opposition and non-government school supporters intensified. Things took a turn for the worse when Coalition senator Peter Baume began to speak up for the Catholic cause, still attempting to drive a wedge between Catholic supporters of state aid and the ALP.

The election was won by the Hawke government with a 1.4 per cent negative swing and a reduction in its lower house majority from 25 to 16 (in an enlarged House), a decrease that seemed to have little to do with state aid since the election had largely been fought on the Hawke government's economic policy. Ryan retained her ministry, but only just, in the newly sworn-in Cabinet.

In early 1985, the twinned Hawke-Ryan education policy process continued, but without Dick Johnson, who Ryan had by now let go.[30] The Hawke government moved on to dealing with the financial burden placed on the Commonwealth by the alarming expansion of new non-government schools. The government's remedy was its 1985 *New Schools Policy*, brought in under Susan Ryan's auspices but with Hawke as the great explainer and chief persuader. The policy focused on augmenting the capital resources of existing schools rather than subsidising new projects and it raised the threshold requirement for starting a new non-government school from an easily achievable 20 students to a far less attainable 50 beginners. In supporting the Commonwealth's strategy, the states came up with their own solution

---

[30] This dismissal was almost certainly a result of a blameless Johnson's inexperience in the role. Johnson himself quickly passes over the event in his chapter 'To wish and to will: reflections on policy formation and implementation in Australian distance education', in T. Evans and D. Nation, *Opening Education: Policies and Practices from Open and Distance Education*, London, Routledge, 1996, p.96. He does say, cryptically, 'It is salutary for historians to realise that such developments quite often occur for similarly random and pragmatic reasons, not as the outcome of high policy'. Johnson was found another job as Special Commissioner. His replacement at Education was Helen Williams. Things calmed down when Williams returned.

to the unlimited and deregulated school expansions problem. They decided on a tighter regulation of new fundamentalist schools, targeting inadequate curriculum, harsh discipline and isolation from broader communities as areas of concern.

On 10 March 1985, Hawke, by now the deliverer of good educational tidings, gave a strategically significant speech in launching the *New Schools Policy* at St Jerome's (Catholic) Primary School in Punchbowl, Sydney. The thrust of his carefully-framed talk was that, in his view, the non-government education system had reached its limit for the time being. From now on, the Commonwealth Government would support, allowing for regulatory provisos, a needs-based expansion of existing non-government schools, a public policy which was in line with the government's budgetary constraints:

> The new funding basis which is taking effect in 1985 will have the effect of reducing over time the resource gaps between different schools. Schools that are relatively disadvantaged will receive very considerable increases in resources over the next 8 years, based on a new assessment of needs and tied to a common measure of resources across both government and non-government schools.[31]

In giving his speech, Hawke referred to the drift away from government schools towards non-government schools in the following terms:

> As you know, over recent years there has been a great deal of debate over the future of [the government] system, and in particular the future of Commonwealth assistance for

---

[31] Speech by the prime minister, St Jerome's School – Sydney – 10 March 1985, PM Transcripts, Department of the Prime Minister and Cabinet. The Catholic hierarchy, anxious about out of control school development, were at that stage still in favour of the *New Schools Policy*. http://pmtranscripts.pmc.gov.au/release/transcript-6609.

CHAPTER EIGHT

non-government schools. Much of that debate stemmed from parents' concern over the way their children should be educated and the kind of values they wish to see associated with that education. The policy my Government announced last year [to end the divisiveness of the state-aid debate] recognised these concerns.[32]

However, while Hawke had originally promised that his government would resolve the state aid impasse, all that had happened since his accession to power in March 1983 had been the postponement of any firm action regarding Commonwealth funding to the wealthier schools. This lack of action left him wide open to criticism from the teacher unions and from the ALP's Left faction but still, to an ALP prime minister now with two consecutive election victories to his name, this was of little concern.

Indeed, Hawke had taken a step in quite a different direction from ALP policy by publicly recognising the importance to parents of schooling that had some kind of moral and ethical base, either religious or secular. As a Labor prime minister he was not in a position to support that kind of holistic approach to education within government schools which, in 1985, remained firmly under the curricular control of the states and Northern Territory governments. However, his Liberal rival and eventual successor John Howard was to go down that very track just over a decade later with his 'no values' critique of government schools and his associated school chaplaincy scheme as a solution to the alleged problem.

---

[32] Between 1982 and 1984 total government school numbers had fallen slightly from 2.28 million to 2.26 million, a percentage fall of just under 1 per cent but part of a long-term trend that continued. By 1987, the year when Ryan left office, the 1982–87 decline had reached 3.7 per cent. Non-government school numbers rose 13.5 per cent over the same period. *ABS Yearbook*, 1989, p.285.

Ryan was moved out of Education and Youth Affairs after a July 1987 general election. Her political failures had been stacking up. She had stumbled badly over the state-aid issue in 1983, she had publicly criticised the Hawke government's higher education tuition fees in 1985 and then, as Senate leader in February 1987, tabled a confidential and electorally-damaging briefing statement on home-interest rates, a briefing that directly contradicted the Hawke and Keating public position on finance.[33] For various reasons she had run through four department heads (sacking two) before Helen Williams settled back in the job in 1985. These were not good ministerial credentials and Hawke had run out of patience. In his third and final ministry, Hawke transferred her to the lower status post of Special Minister of State (a general factotum without a department).

The former minister's new jobs included handling the government's deeply unpopular (and ultimately failed) identity card policy, as well as the less fraught 1988 bicentennial commemorations. Her former department went to John Dawkins, who abolished the Schools Commission, folding it into the new National Board of Education, Employment and Training (NBEET), and reconstituting it as an advisory 'Schools Council', precisely what Ryan had wanted when still in Education and Youth Affairs. Dawkins then turned his attention towards reforming and revamping Australia's universities, before becoming Treasurer in 1991 and leaving politics altogether at the end of 1993. As for school funding, the ALP had announced with great confidence in its 1990 achievement report on education that, with the ERI in place, the nation was almost halfway through 'sixteen years of stability' [1984–2000].

---

[33] Ryan's error, gleefully seized on by the Opposition, was made after a celebratory lunch. See 'Oh! Susan! But it wasn't always so', *Sydney Morning Herald*, 27 February 1987.

CHAPTER EIGHT

By that time, to assist the Commonwealth in assessing the funding needs of non-government schools, an Average Government School Recurrent Costs scheme (AGSRC) had been designed for implementation in 1993. Under the AGSRC, funding was tied to a needs-based actual costs system, an improvement on its predecessor, a notional and vague 'basket of services' calculation.[34]

During what was to become two successive Keating governments (1991–96) Kim Beazley (Jnr) was appointed overall education minister with Ross Free as junior minister for Schools, Vocational Education and Training. Non-government school funding was managed without its customary controversy within the framework of the 1984 funding model and based on the AGSRC. Indeed, from 1993 to 1996, 'state aid' became a phrase more associated with flood relief and farming subsidies. It seemed as if the ALP's prophesy of sixteen years of stability was to be fulfilled.

Notwithstanding this, despite Hawke's political promises in the early 1980s to cut back on non-government school funding, and in the face of the *New Schools Policy*, there had been a remarkable growth in non-government schools. At a time when the general population of Australia grew by just over 19 per cent, the growth figures for the non-government sector during the Hawke and Keating governments revealed an interesting phenomenon. Anglican schools rose from 100 to 124 (a 24 per cent increase) and Other schools (a then ABS category of mainly non-Anglican Christian and fringe schools) rose from 560 to 724 (a 29 per cent increase), while Catholic schools fell in number from 1702 to 1696 (a 4.7 per cent decrease). The Catholic

---

[34] Cit. Wilkinson et al., 2006, p.149.

figures were almost certainly caused by a mix of old smaller schools being shut down while new bigger schools were being built.[35]

The Anglican figures, after decades of slow growth prior to 1983, showed that a demand was being met for parents looking for a different kind of mainstream education, and the Other category schools clearly benefited hugely from Fife's loan changes before Hawke's *New Schools Policy* could rein them in. During the Hawke and Keating years, the versions of educational social justice of the Catholic and the Protestant communities had clearly made impressive gains, thanks to the platform built by Carrick, Fraser and Fife, providing a foundation for an educational policy that was to be expanded and refined after John Howard's March 1996 general election victory.

As for Ryan, her achievements as education minister remain notable despite her inexperience, gaffes, management issues, combative dealings with critics and penchant for taking on senior colleagues. During her time in office, retention rates did rise, from 35 to 60 per cent at Year 12 level between 1982 and 1987. Disadvantage and class-based issues in schools were more directly addressed through the PEP, and she had focused on Indigenous education instead of just taking an interest in it, as had been the case with the more capable of her Liberal predecessors, Fraser and Baume. Additionally, Ryan played an important part in public service reform, in raising gender equity issues in schools and in establishing equal employment opportunities for women. Ryan's own view of her time as an education minister is that she was ill-prepared for a ministerial position.[36] With that

---

[35] *ABS Yearbook*, 1997 p.236.

[36] Susan Ryan, 'Rollers and Dumpers - Life as a Cabinet Minister', *The Sydney Papers*, Vol. 11, No. 3, pp.20–27, 1999.

CHAPTER EIGHT

comment in mind, and with the advantage of hindsight, it is possible that had Ryan kept Jones on as department head, some of her 1983–84 missteps might have been avoided. Such a supposition, however, discounts what seems to have been both an ideological and personal predisposition on Ryan's part to fight back.

Hawke seemed to remain unimpressed by her achievements. In his 1994 memoirs, most of the members of his first cabinet merited extended and very favourable mentions, superlatives even. His sole assessment of Ryan is a brief comment that comes after an encomium remarking that Dawkins was an 'outstanding', 'quick', 'formidable', 'adventurous' and reformist education minister who had built his achievements on the 'solid foundations laid by Susan Ryan'.[37]

It was Hawke himself who, in order to keep the state aid peace, set what was to become a disastrous negotiating precedent for the ALP, by promising that under an ALP government existing funding levels for all schools would be maintained. If we add that Hawke promise to Whitlam's 1969 state-aid policy reversal, still seen by many in the ALP as an opportunistic accession to Catholic interests, the Labor movement now seemed to be heading towards an irretrievable position of support for the Catholic Church.

Ryan announced her retirement from politics in January 1988, moving on to careers in publishing, business and finance, academia and social administration. Interestingly, after having fought for the education ministry in 1983 and made a difference in that role, in 1989 she cited her major achievements in office as the 1984 Sex Discrimination Act, the 1986 Affirmative Action Act and the

---

[37] R. Hawke, *The Hawke Memoirs*, Port Melbourne, William Heinemann, p.160, 1994.

1987 Family Package (financial support for a low-income families). Education did not merit a mention.[38]

As for signs of future trends in education and of 'sixteen years of stability', Paul Keating had unexpectedly and comfortably won his 1993 'unwinnable' general election, partly with the assistance of Liberal leader John Hewson's electorally unpopular *Fightback!* policy and partly with the help of the ALP's Catholic vote, which had led the Coalition's Catholic vote by nine percentage points.[39] The ALP's sixteen years of stability came to an end four years before their time, however, when in 1996 David Kemp was appointed education minister in the first Howard government.

---

[38] G. Little, *Speaking for Myself*, Melbourne, McPhee Gribble, p.131, 1989.

[39] C. Bean, 'The Coalition and the Electorate 1983-1993', in *For Better or For Worse: The Federal Coalition*, B. Costar, ed., Melbourne, Melbourne University Press, 1994.

Chapter Nine

MINISTER KEMP AND THE SOCIO-ECONOMIC STATUS SYSTEM

A Complete Corruption

In 1993, as Liberal Party politicians gloomily considered a decade's worth of successive general election losses and faced up to the prospect of yet another three years in opposition, an intense period of internal party bickering, leadership challenges and reflection was to follow. As part of that reflection, the party began the search for a possible route to victory in the next general election. Andrew Robb, the Liberal Party's National Director, was given the responsibility of conducting a review of 1993's disastrous election campaign.

Robb knew that there were several factors that had contributed to the Coalition's humiliating defeat. Principal among them was Opposition leader John Hewson's radical and unpopular, because deemed to be unfair, policy document, *Fightback!*. This may have been a free market economist's daydream, but it turned out to be a huge electoral nightmare for the Coalition. Robb identified several possible solutions to the Liberal Party's ten-year losing streak. These included more of a focus on Liberal grassroots support, a more efficient party organisation, obtaining an increase in party funding and taking a more pragmatic approach to targeting electoral sectors, including Catholic voters. This latter move had originally been suggested by Liberal Party political scientist David Kemp. As early as 1971, Kemp had pointed out that while non-churchgoing Catholics were more likely to be ALP supporters, more traditionally-inclined, regular Catholic church attenders preferred a conservative world of hierarchy and authority.[1]

By the early 1990s, Kemp's research might have been considered out of date since, as we have seen, the ALP Catholic vote in the 1993 general election was well ahead of the Coalition's Catholic vote. Among the debris of that 1993 campaign, however, the Catholic Robb discovered an interesting contradiction. While Catholic voters had indeed turned against the Coalition, fifteen of the seventeen new Coalition parliamentary representatives were Catholics, demonstrating changes in attitude within the party at a grassroots level.

The Liberal Party was regarded with suspicion by many Catholics, bishops and lay electors alike, and many Protestant Liberals remained cautious about reaching out to Catholics. The more reactionary of these Protestant Liberals had come from a tradition that had recently despised Catholics as déclassé, superstitious Irish-Australians who lived in a culture dominated by meddlesome priests and bishops.[2] But it became clear to Robb that Catholics had the potential to become an electoral asset for the Coalition, thanks to the improved

---

[1] Kemp became Liberal MP for Goldstein (1990–2004) and later education minister in the Howard administration.

[2] John Howard himself comments on this phenomenon in his political memoir, J. Howard, *Lazarus Rising: a personal and political autobiography*, Sydney, HarperCollins, pp.31–32, 2010.

CHAPTER NINE

status and rising social expectations of this community and some attitudinal changes within the Liberal Party. The implication for Coalition education policy was clear: traditionally-minded Catholics formed a huge voting bloc situated within a denomination that made up almost a quarter of the nation's population, a group which sent the vast majority of its children to fee-paying schools.

Robb's explanation for the majority of Catholics voting Labor in 1993 was that this derived from intense, issue-based, anti-Coalition lobbying by Catholic opinion formers. In Robb's view, an increasingly middle-class Catholic electorate had been influenced to vote Labor by key Catholic organisations opposed to *Fightback!*. These included the Bishops' Committee for Justice, Development and Peace, the Queensland and West Australian Catholic Social Justice Commissions, and the Canberra-based Catholic Social Welfare Commission led by David Cappo, a South Australian social activist and later parish priest (1996–2000). Indeed, Cappo had developed a close affinity with ALP Minister for Employment, Education and Training, Simon Crean, and with Brian Howe, Minister for Housing and Regional Development. He was regarded as a vital Catholic spokesman against economic rationalism and Hewson's economic and industrial relations policies.

Robb was convinced that good political liaison work with Catholics by ALP politicians, combined with consequent subtle politics-from-the-pulpit proselytising, had been at work during the 1993 general election campaign. Not old-style thundering denunciations from the pulpit, the kind of rant that Arthur Calwell had been forced to listen to in 1963, but gentle reminders that while the Church could not and would not direct votes, Catholics should use their consciences to decide which of the major parties was more Catholic-friendly.[3]

Robb also realised that, after ten years of successive Labor governments, all was not well within the Catholic community. In the early 1990s, the Catholic Church was exercised by several issues which affected the viability of its education system. First, there remained the continuing decline in recruitment into the lower-status religious orders that had once provided cheap teaching labour, particularly in Catholic primary schools. As recounted earlier, replacing brothers and nuns with lay teachers who were insistent on having salary equivalence with government teachers had increased the recurrent expenses of the Catholic education system's schools. In addition, school principals, once low-cost clerics, were now being replaced by high-cost lay teachers who, for historical reasons, came from a very small talent pool of possible candidates. Third, old and often dilapidated inner-urban Catholic schools were facing sharply declining student numbers, with parents increasingly placing their children in better-equipped government schools in areas where there was inadequate Catholic provision. Inner-urban flight too had led to a growing demand for Catholic school places in suburban areas, but any new development initiatives were hampered by the Commonwealth Government's 1985 *New Schools Policy* restrictions.[4]

---

[3] Australian National University academic John Warhurst's 2008 article 'The Catholic Lobby: Structures, Policy Styles and Religious Networks' is an excellent account and analysis of how an increasingly forceful Catholic Church presses for its various causes. See *The Australian Journal of Public Administration*, vol. 67, no. 2 pp.213–230.

[4] Having said that, all Catholic systemic schools still received high need Scale 10 (of 12) funding per student, calculated on the overall socio-economic background of a school's students, whereas non-systemic Catholic schools could only achieve Scale 6 funding at best.

CHAPTER NINE

Catholic schools in Sydney and elsewhere had also faced a major funding crisis during and after the Keating 1990–91 recession. Interest rates had risen as high as 17 per cent and disposable income fell. Private contributions from the low to middle-income Catholic communities dried up. School tuition fees charged to already struggling families had to increase to cover the gap and, bearing in mind that capital improvements in systemic schools were generally funded half by private donations and half by government subsidies (more or less), building programs were adversely affected precisely at a time when demand for places in newer schools was increasing.

In that context, the executive director of the Sydney Archdiocesan School Board, the energetic Brother Kelvin Canavan, had become an active social justice advocate for the Catholic education cause during the 1980s and 1990s. Canavan persistently lobbied State and Commonwealth politicians and blitzed media outlets, schools, parents and local politicians with pithy, one-page summary statements explaining the Catholic school system's funding plight (later called 'Fact Sheets'). He appeared regularly on television, radio and at carefully organised public meetings to spruik for increased funding for his schools.[5] Significantly, he plied his trade in John Howard's home state and in the city that housed the national headquarters of the Liberal Party.

In New South Wales, Canavan, as the public face of Catholic education, became an effective, high profile lobbyist and, according to

---

[5] In a celebratory summary of his achievements *Celebrating 40 years of government financial assistance to Catholic Schools in Sydney 1968–2008*, Sydney, Catholic Education Office, 2010, there are over 60 photographs 1987–2007 of Canavan with politicians, ranging from Bob Hawke (1987) to Paul Keating (1991) and on to John Howard (2000). Interestingly, there is no sign of Susan Ryan.

the NSW Catholic Education Office, even pressured politicians with the threat of a possible electoral backlash, speaking repeatedly of:

> ... the continuing financial sacrifice made by parents who choose to send their sons and daughters to a Catholic school. He considered it important to remind the parliamentarians present, and the wider community, of the cost to tax-paying parents of tuition fees, levies and other charges.[6]

By the mid-1990s, Canavan's argument had become clear. The Catholic system was in trouble yet again and needed a fairer deal from the state and Commonwealth governments.

The state of Victoria did not have a Kelvin Canavan but it did have the Catholic Andrew Robb, who came to regard the 1992–93 Catholic rejection of the Coalition's policies not as a continuation of an established trend, but rather as a trend reversal caused by a community's short term response to particular issues, especially *Fightback!*. His own figures showed that, prior to 1993, economically and socially aspirational Catholic voters had been abandoning the ALP, a change of direction that had become more noticeable during Susan Ryan's tenure as education minister. Robb's most up-to-date analysis was based largely on 1993 exit polls and was supported in a more methodical way by political sociologist Clive Bean. Among other things, Bean pointed out that Catholic support for the Liberal Party (not so much the Nationals) had slowly risen during the period 1983–90, only to plunge in 1993, mainly over *Fightback!*[7]

---

[6] Cit. *Celebrating 40 years of government financial assistance*, 2010, p.15. Behind the scenes lobbying was carried out by Brother John Taylor of the Catholic Education Commission who was to be succeeded as lobbyist and chair by Dr Brian Croke, administrator and historian.

[7] C. Bean, 'The Coalition and the Electorate 1983-1993', in B. Costar, 1994.

CHAPTER NINE

As a Catholic who wanted to expand Liberal Party membership, Robb's values and background were directly related to his political interest in targeting the Catholic community at a national level. Robb came from a large, rural working-class family; he had been successively educated in three Catholic schools before going on to agricultural college, and then on to La Trobe University where he studied economics while working full-time for the Victorian Department of Agriculture. It was at La Trobe, and alienated by the university's famously radical student activists of the 1970s, that Robb had turned towards conservative politics. It was at La Trobe, too, that one of his university economics lecturers, Laszlo Csapo, a refugee from Soviet-era Hungary, had helped turn him towards an anti-collectivist ideology.[8]

If we use Robb's personal and political autobiography as a guide, his overall social and political philosophy – classically liberal in its values – can be summarised as follows: first, his working class parents taught him the value of educational achievement; second, life on the land showed him that the world can be a tough and unreasoning place requiring firmness of mind and an ability to plan ahead; third, a deal is never done until it is signed, sealed and delivered; fourth, good leadership is not just about pointing the way, it is also about paying attention to those who follow; fifth, individual choice and enterprise will outdo a collectivist culture which assumes that the government knows best; last but not least, Robb's Catholicism was an important part of his world because it was, and remains, a dominant feature of his family life and of his community work, and because it lends authority, spirituality and stability to his life and life

---

[8] A. Robb, *Black dog daze: public life, private demons*, Carlton, Melbourne University Publishing, 2011.

in general. Having said that, Robb, who gained his negotiating skills running the National Farmers' Federation during tough anti-union campaigns of the 1980s, was a ruthless political operator with an unquenchable belief in the benefits of laissez-faire capitalism and in the value of competition and diversity in education.[9]

Clive Bean suggested in his post-1993 analysis that had the Liberal Party courted the favour of a range of electorally influential groups, the 1993 result might have been reversed. Looking back, in 1996, Robb remarked:

> I have felt strongly over the past decade that our positioning as a party, our values and priorities, meant that we should have much more in common with this group [Catholics], which to a large extent reflected the traditional labour base largely ignored by Labor. Once John Howard became leader I was convinced we had the opportunity to remove the barriers we erected for ourselves in 1993.[10]

Robb's optimism could have been strengthened in 1993 by the release of the morally traditionalist encyclical *Veritatis Splendor*, by Pope John Paul II. This document was much more in tune with the Coalition side of politics than that of the ALP. John Paul II's visit to Australia in January 1995 further shored up the morale of conservative elements in the Catholic community.

The appointment of George Pell as Archbishop of Melbourne in 1996 was a further indicator of the direction the Church was taking. From 2001 Pell would form a bond with Archbishop of Sydney Peter Jensen, an evangelical Anglican. They both became spokesmen

---

[9] A. Robb, 2011.

[10] Cit. Milton Cockburn's feature article 'A Leap of Faith', *Sydney Morning Herald*, 27 April 1996.

CHAPTER NINE

for conservative social and doctrinal values, and Pell, a highly controversial figure, famously became a mentor to a young Liberal politician, Tony Abbott, who described him as 'one of the greatest churchmen that Australia has seen'.[11] In April 2013 Pell, by then a cardinal, attended an invitation-only seventieth anniversary dinner given in honour of neo-conservative lobby 'think tank', the Institute of Public Affairs. Later that year Sydney's conservative tabloid, *The Daily Telegraph*, revealed Pell had recently spoken as guest of honour at a secret meeting of senior conservative figures in the Chartwell Society. Pell was there to give a political 'pep-talk' to Liberal MPs.[12]

Following Howard's return to the position of party leader in January 1995, Robb began a series of consultations with bishops and other Catholic leaders around Australia, working through local networks of Catholic Liberal MPs in each state. At the same time he developed a correspondence network with key Catholic organisations. He explained his strategy: 'We were determined to ensure that once we got into a campaign there would be no surprises, no problems. We discussed a range of issues, particularly education, but also health and industrial relations'.[13] Almost certainly among that range of issues was Susan Ryan's restrictive *New Schools Policy*, which had hit even carefully-managed Catholic school expansion. Robb extended the scope of his interest-group political discussions to include other religions and potential allies of convenience, for

---

[11] *ABC Lateline*, Interview with Tony Jones, 30 September 2004.

[12] 'Abbott, Bolt, Rinehart fawn in the IPA court of King Murdoch', *Crikey.com*, 5 April 2013. Pell was in the front row. See also, 'James Packer, John Howard and Cardinal George Pell part of secret Chartwell Society', *Daily Telegraph*, 2 June 2013.

[13] Cit. Cockburn, 1996.

example making preference overtures to environmental groups.[14] The party's education focus prior to the 1996 election, however, remained the Catholics and the Catholic school system.

On 16 February 1996, having adopted a small-target pre-election strategy for all of its policies during the run-up to the 2 March 1996 general election, the Coalition announced a modest school funding plan. Avoiding provocative measures by promising a 5 per cent increase for all schools, the Coalition committed an extra $150 million to government schools and TAFE colleges, and $49.5 million for non-government schools, with $19.5 million of that allocation assigned to the building of new schools. The Coalition's education spokesman, David Kemp, also promised that if elected the Coalition would abolish the contentious *New Schools Policy*. Howard was sending the Catholic bishops and leaders of the other major denominations a direct message that, if the Coalition were to be elected, not only would the ALP's *New Schools Policy* be killed off but the new government would set aside a large sum of money for new denominational schools.

As for the ALP's promises, Keating made nine references to education in his 14 February policy speech, strongly linking his policies on schooling to skills and training and promising to spend $1.5 billion on school education and training through the ALP's *Working Nation* program. There was no mention of state aid.

In his 18 February 1996 general policy speech, and in keeping with the Coalition's low-key strategy, Howard's address was mainly about the economy, industrial relations and social security. While he made no direct mention of education he did include a discourse on family values that targeted low- to middle-income families and

---

[14] Howard, 2010, p.222.

CHAPTER NINE

promised tax relief and 'choice', ideas that would have appealed to traditional Catholic opinion. His next promise was to safeguard Australia's natural heritage, committing $1 billion to the Wilderness Society, a nod to the environmentalists whose preferences Robb, by now a seasoned interest-group political operator, had so assiduously been courting.

On Election Day, 2 March 1996, the Coalition won a huge majority in the House of Representatives, winning ninety-four seats as against the ALP's forty-nine. The 1996 election saw Labor's lowest primary vote since 1934. Robb's strategy of pursuing interest group politics, rather than simply attempting to persuade voters as a whole, contributed in part to that victorious campaign against a seemingly out-of-touch prime minister and a tired and jaded ALP government. Robb was quick to point out in a television appearance that a preponderance of Catholic voters had backed the Coalition.

Indeed, exit polls showed that, while in the 1993 general election the ALP's Catholic vote had led the Coalition's Catholic vote by nine percentage points, the March 1996 election saw the Coalition's Catholic vote ahead of Labor's Catholic support by ten percentage points, a remarkable 19 per cent turnaround.[15] At the same time, the 1996 election success had introduced 'Howard's battlers' to the nation, a mix of blue and white collar aspirational voters, many of whom came from pro-ALP Catholic backgrounds. 'Howard's battlers' was a term first used, apparently, by *The Sydney Morning Herald*'s Canberra bureau chief Geoff Kitney on 5 March 1996, and it was consciously used again a week later by Robb himself in his 13 March address to the National Press

---

[15] Cockburn, 1996.

Club.¹⁶ Following the Coalition's landslide victory, Robb then pushed for his party to conduct regular polls as a way of testing the mood of the electorate between elections and of tracking the attitudes of the newly-recruited support from former ALP voters.

Four months after the Coalition's victory, Howard entered the public debate about education. During his Sir Thomas Playford Memorial Lecture in Adelaide Town Hall on 5 July, Howard expatiated not on school funding, but on history as a political issue. He commented: 'One of the more insidious developments in Australian political life over the past decade or so has been the attempt to re-write Australian history in the service of a partisan political cause … My predecessor as Prime Minister regarded the partisan re-interpretation of Australia's past as central to much of the agenda for the future that he sought to implement'.

And so began a Howard-led 1996–2007 Liberal Party culture-war for the school history curriculum to be altered to provide more 'balance', a campaign that was to include a 2005 classroom initiative featuring a patriotic version of Gallipoli's legacy, led by then education minister Brendan Nelson, and a mid-2006 history summit which, in the end, failed to meet Howard's cultural objectives. The culture-war ended in October 2007 with the publication of a Howard-auspiced guide to teaching Australian history, which was to be ditched by the Rudd ALP government in 2008 after Kevin Rudd's November 2007 general election victory.¹⁷ These attempts to bring conservative

---

[16]   'Battler Factor Key to Liberal Victory, *Sydney Morning Herald*, 5 March 1996.

[17]   See for example, '"Teach Australian Values or Clear Off" says Nelson'. ABC PM, 24 August 2005, http://www.abc.net.au/pm/content/2005/s1445262.htm, and T. Taylor, 'Under Siege from Right and Left: A Tale of the Australian History Wars', in T. Taylor & R. Guyver (eds) *History Wars in the Classroom: Global Perspectives*, Charlotte, Information Age Publishing, 2012, pp.25–50.

CHAPTER NINE

values into government school classes were reinforced by Howard's controversial 2006 $90 million voluntary school chaplaincy program for government and non-government schools.

On a more substantive note, the Howard government, in the person of new schools minister David Kemp, moved rapidly to deal with the school funding issue. Kemp, a free-market, small-government ideologue, had worked as a political science academic at Melbourne and Monash Universities (1975–90), and as speech writer and adviser to Malcolm Fraser briefly, becoming director of Fraser's prime ministerial office. Kemp's real political career however began in 1990 when he was elected Liberal member for the safe Melbourne seat of Goldstein, famously defeating the moderate Liberal Ian Macphee at the pre-selection stage. Kemp then became a shadow cabinet member during the Coalition's early 1990s leadership battles.

After the Coalition's 1996 triumph, Kemp, whose experience and track record within the party suggested he should have been given a Cabinet portfolio, was appointed (junior) Minister for Schools, Vocational Education and Training, Minister assisting the Prime Minister for the Public Service, and Minister assisting the Minister for Finance for Privatisation. In Cabinet, education as a single portfolio was represented by famously abrasive South Australian senator Amanda Vanstone in her capacity as Minister for Employment, Education, Training and Youth Affairs.[18]

Kemp moved quickly to announce a national 'back to basics' literacy testing initiative and his next step was to incorporate new

---

[18] The Vanstone appointment was seen as Howard's attempt to appoint a second female minister to Cabinet. Liberal Senator Jocelyn Newman was the other female Cabinet appointee, as Minister of Social Security. After a confrontational year in office, Vanstone was dropped from the Cabinet in October 1997 to be replaced by Kemp, who became Minister for Employment, Education, Training and Youth Affairs.

funding arrangements in Treasurer Peter Costello's August 1996 budget. A 5 per cent cross-sectoral increase in funding was to be accompanied by a $30 million allocation (over three years) to non-government schools for capital works. Kemp's forward estimates in his budget calculations allowed for what was by now a continuing drift from government to non-government schools, saving the states and territories an estimated $360 million during the 1997–2000 funding period. Kemp would attempt to recoup at least half of this sum through what later became known as the Enrolment Benchmark Adjustment scheme, or EBA.[19] The general response in the media and among educators was that the non-government sector had been the big winners in the Howard government's first budget.[20]

Overcoming his frustration at playing second fiddle to Vanstone, in May 1996 Kemp also announced that Labor's *New Schools Policy*, originally aimed at the untrammelled growth of Protestant schools, would be abolished. Parents wanting to set up a new school would no longer have to prove that their initiative would not adversely affect enrolments in nearby government schools. Furthermore, non-systemic schools (mainly the smaller Christian fundamentalist institutions) could now have access to increased funding, an entitlement denied them under Labor's guidelines. The three social justice explanations for the changes were, according to Kemp, choice, accountability and thrift.

Kemp's more detailed clarification of his three-word rationale was that because parents would now be able to send their children

---

19   At that stage 38 per cent of non-government schools' running costs were provided by the Commonwealth with an additional 18 per cent coming from states and territories. Government schools received 13 per cent of their funding from the Commonwealth.

20   See for example, 'Private Schools Winners as Funding Rises 5pc', *Sydney Morning Herald*, 21 August 1996.

CHAPTER NINE

to schools that reflected their values, schools would become more accountable to and directly funded by their communities. To critics of the Coalition approach to education, Kemp's policy was narrowly ideological, especially as parents could choose only if they could afford the options available, parents in regional and rural communities had few if any choices, parents had little or no say over their state's education policy, and benefits from lowering costs would be difficult to discern.[21]

One issue not mentioned in Kemp's strategy throughout his period in office was whether or not increased government funding for supposedly competitive non-government schools was in line with his free market philosophy. This was possibly because the long-term political value of the subsidies far outweighed any need to stick to a consistent free market script. The Liberals had already worked out that Coalition support for non-government schools generally would strengthen its electoral base among beneficiaries of that funding. The school funding tactic had been helpful in 1963 and very successful in 1996. Now that the Coalition had spread its generosity with taxpayers' funds well beyond the Catholic Church, the political effect, both short and long term, was bound to be increasingly beneficial.

Australian Education Union (AEU) spokesperson Sharan Burrow was unimpressed by the direction that Kemp was taking, pointing out that by giving more money to non-government schools, Kemp was taking it away from government schools.[22] Ann Morrow, chair

---

[21] Simon Marginson wrote extensively about the background to this 1990s approach in his book *Markets in Education*, St Leonards, Allen & Unwin, 1997.

[22] The AEU, a national umbrella union for government education employees, was founded in 1993 after a series of mergers involving what became affiliated state-based unions. For Burrow see 'Private Schools Set to Multiply', *Sydney Morning Herald*, 20 May 1996.

of the Dawkins-created Schools Council, agreed with Burrow in her criticisms of the Kemp plan, refining the point in arguing that by giving the socially, financially and denominationally selective non-government schools additional funding, families who had no choice were sending their children to increasingly disadvantaged government schools, thus compounding divisions of social class.[23]

It was not just Kemp's abolition or modification of programs that exasperated education professionals and other commentators during that May 1996 period of rapid educational change. Providing an open-ended increase of funding to start non-government schools, while the nation faced a large budget deficit, was also potentially financially damaging. This had been the very budgetary weakness pinpointed by the Hawke government when bringing in its *New Schools Policy*. Even the normally conservative *Australian Financial Review* was taken aback at Kemp's position of allowing consumer choice to determine a school student's educational destination whatever the overall budgetary consequences.[24]

Howard himself was very happy with the legislation that abolished the *New Schools Program*, as he reported in his memoirs: 'I remain intensely proud of this change as it has resulted in a rapid expansion in the number of low- to-moderate-fee-level independent schools.'[25] From Howard's point of view, Kemp was encouraging social aspir-

---

[23] 'Imbalance in Funding Hurts State Schools', *Sydney Morning Herald*, 24 May 1996, and 'Funding Race Leaves State Schools Behind', *The Age*, 25 May 1996. Kemp closed down the Schools Council and its umbrella organisation NBEET in June 1996.

[24] 'Private schools win Coalition's approval', *Australian Financial Review*, 22 May 1996.

[25] Howard, p.243. Interestingly, throughout his memoir he mentions freedom of choice several times when writing about education, without explaining exactly how this might apply to parents who were on low incomes and/or lived in rural or remote areas.

CHAPTER NINE

ation. From an ALP point of view, Kemp was discouraging social mobility. Not that the ALP could do much to prevent the Coalition from carrying out Kemp's schemes. During the Howard years (1996–2007) Labor lost three elections (1998, 2001 and 2004) and four leaders (Beazley, Crean, Latham, Beazley) before eventually settling on Kevin Rudd in 2006.

There were other reasons behind Kemp's decision. First, his aim was to, over time, continue the process of slowly edging the Commonwealth away from the business of funding state-managed government schools. He calculated that having more students in non-government schools that were only partially funded by the Commonwealth was an improvement on the expensive status quo in which both systems were funded by Canberra.

Kemp like Howard also claimed to believe that selective non-government schools were superior to state and territory comprehensive schools in educational terms. Howard made that quite clear in a June 1996 'First 100 Days in office' interview in which he commented that the continuing drift away from non-selective government schools was because they provided an education that was regarded by many parents as lacking in values and standards.[26] Howard's implication was that government schools were for those who did not aspire and who did not share Liberal values. Accordingly, government schools did not need increased Commonwealth funding over and above the minimum necessary to function at a basic level (literacy and numeracy). The states and territories could provide the rest. That was their duty.

---

[26] 'Academics cry foul', *Sydney Morning Herald*, 8 June 1996. The article's headline was a reference to Vanstone's already tumultuous dealings with Australia's higher education sector.

Finally, selective non-government schools (with high retention rates and noticeably better matriculation results) were in tune with individualistic and self-improving Coalition values. Accordingly, any increase in subsidising such a Liberal-friendly school-funding approach would work to the long-term advantage of Coalition politics. That was a perception commonly held by the more opportunistic members of the conservative political community at least.

These May 1996 decisions taken by Kemp marked the start of a new approach to Coalition education policy, a more overt and unapologetic preferencing of the values of non-government schools over government schools. This was the onset of a strategic Coalition government residualisation approach to school education in which all non-government schools would, over time, receive increasingly disproportionate funding benefits at the expense of government schools.

Residualisation as a concept was not a new idea. Indeed, then Victorian Secondary Education Association research officer Barbara Preston had written about it as a concealed policy strategy in 1984 when she categorised education systems in democracies as either universal (all schools are inclusive and all education has a social value) or residual (non-government schools are preferred socially, economically and politically while government schools are the schools of last resort).[27]

---

[27] Barbara Preston, 'Residualistion: what's that?' *The Australian Teacher*, No. 8, May 1984, pp.5–7. Preston's article was critical of what she describes as a (Tannock-led) Schools Commission view that discussion of how non-government schools should be funded was not a matter for the public education sector. The residualisation theme was later taken up by Melbourne University education researcher Richard Teese in his submission to the Gonski panel and in his paper, 'From opportunity to outcomes. The changing role of public schooling in Australia and national funding arrangements', University of Melbourne, September 2011. (Teese was assisted in writing the paper by Anne Walstab).

CHAPTER NINE

Kemp and Howard's initiative, which had already been prefaced by a steady growth in the favouring of non-government schools by Kemp's Coalition predecessors, was the creation of an explicit Coalition narrative that non-government schools were the better option and government schools needed to aspire to be more like their distinguished counterparts. From 1996 onwards, the Coalition's social justice rationale that had supported the expansion of non-government schooling during the Gorton and Fraser eras, mainly principled, was dropped. Kemp and Howard favoured a rationale based on free market forces, preferred cultural values, an expected Commonwealth financial benefit and an anticipated large-scale electoral gain. As far as Howard and Kemp were concerned, the major inequity in the disbursement of Commonwealth funds to schools flowed from the funding of government schools taking too much money out of the system. This was zero-sum politics reversed and it was an approach to be taken up again in 2013 by Howard's protégé Tony Abbott.

Controversy about the Howard government's favouritism of non-government schools intensified in October 1996, as Kemp's States Grants bill was introduced into parliament. Hostility to the bill, led by Opposition education spokesman Peter Baldwin, centred on the Commonwealth clawing back $1712 per student in recurrent funding if a student transferred from the government- to the non-government sector. Baldwin was joined in his criticism by the Democrats, the unions, the newly-formed Australian Schools Lobby and even by conservative states Queensland, South Australia and Western Australia. The states complained to a Senate inquiry that they had not been consulted about the clawback system and, as a matter of principle, they were opposed to parental choice determining how state education systems were to be funded. Despite the protests, the bill passed the Senate and became law on 1 January 1997. As a well-briefed, obdurate parliamentary performer, who seemed to relish political battles, Kemp brushed off these attacks and moved on to his next challenge.

Kemp's next major project in 1997–98 was to continue to defend the Howard government's controversial Work for the Dole scheme, which had attracted criticism from employers, training institutions and, unsurprisingly, from the Coalition's political opponents. The resilient Kemp survived that confrontation and began planning his next move in shifting students from government schools to non-government schools, a complete change in the funding model from the ERI scheme, now in its thirteenth year.[28]

In 1996, management consultants KPMG had been commissioned by Kemp to review the twelve-tier, needs-based ERI funding system which had been criticised on educational grounds because of its inflexibility and its complexity. The government asked KPMG particularly to canvass the views of the non-government school system in preparing their report *Evaluation of the Administration of the General Recurrent Grants for Schools Program*. As might have been expected, representatives of those mainly Protestant non-government schools placed in the highly-resourced and low-funded ERI tiers were opposed to the needs-based ERI, seeing it as a hostile ALP initiative favouring disadvantaged schools. Kemp agreed with them and portrayed the ERI as a partisan political plot aimed at the

---

[28] The author is grateful to Jim McMorrow and the authors of the I.R. Wilkinson et al (2006) report commissioned by the Department of Education, Science and Training for backgrounding this summary of how the SES system was introduced.

CHAPTER NINE

destruction of the non-government sector. Kemp decided that a new approach to funding was needed.

In February 1997, Kemp's department (now of Education, Employment, Training and Youth Affairs, or DEETYA) began a departmental inquiry into funding issues, setting up a small departmental and stakeholder review team to examine overseas and domestic funding models while between April and June offering a series of consultations with the non-government school sector. In October 1997, by which time Kemp had replaced Amanda Vanstone as Minister in Cabinet, DEETYA produced its report, outlining several funding options but declaring the government did not yet have a preferred system.

Broadly, Kemp and the non-government schools preferred a new socio-economic basis for a funding system that did not rely on assessment of a school's private income as the main funding criterion. As it happened, a funding model for dealing with socio-economic disadvantage, designed by Deakin University researcher Ken Ross and Victorian education department statistician Stephen Farish, was one of several already being used in various ways by different education systems, including Catholic schools. This SES (socio-economic status) system, as its DEETYA variant was to be known, was not based on assessment of a school's income or resources but of the income, parent occupation and education levels within a school's Census Collection Data district (CCD). The CCD, a small, ABS locational entity which, on average, contained about 250 households, was a much smaller district than a postcode area or any other local or regional zone used for statistical analysis. Its sample size carried the risk of anomalies which were to become one feature of the controversial SES model's failings.

Early in 1998 DETYA (having replaced 'DEETYA') set up an SES simulation project in which 90 per cent of all non-government schools participated. The project's conclusion was that, apart from a few minor problems in the Indigenous community schools, the proposed SES system was administratively straightforward and seemed to provide a reliable socio-economic ranking system. Then followed a validation study with its results released in May 1999. A clear connection was shown between selected SES scores and other statistical methodological approaches used by the Australian Council for Educational Research and the Commonwealth Government. The ensuing validation report was positive.

It appeared Kemp's department had carried out an efficient and careful consultative process in preparing the ground for the new funding system. Kemp announced on 11 May 1999 that the SES funding model would be introduced for non-government schools for a four-year period starting in January 2001.[29] Behind a facade of statistically-based even-handedness, however, there lay a carefully constructed system that used the SES modelling to favour non-government schools.

DETYA's SES model was based on students' parental residential addresses in each CCD, giving an averaged-out assessment of a school's SES score which then formed the basis of a school's per capita funding. Indexed funding was then based on the Average Government School Recurrent Costs (AGSRC). Non-government schools that appeared to have a high proportion of students from

---

[29] Kemp's Second Reading speech in the House of Representatives, 29 June 2000, referred to the proposed needs-based legislation as 'transparent, objective and equitable' commenting on its attention to accountability, choice and flexibility, and arguing that it would increase funding to 'schools serving the neediest communities [who] will receive the greatest financial support'.

CHAPTER NINE

low socio-economic communities could gain up to 70 per cent of the annually adjusted AGSRC contribution to running costs. Schools that reported a high proportion of students from wealthier CCDs could gain a maximum of 13.7 per cent only of the annually-adjusted AGSRC.

Before the system was introduced, Kemp had promised that the non-government schools would not lose any financial ground and he introduced a 'Funding Maintained' (FM) variation into the SES policy to carry out that promise. Funding Maintained meant that those schools due to have reduced funding during the 2001–04 SES funding period kept their pre-SES funding levels, which were still tied to annual ASGRC indexation. This meant they received an annual increase that was in step with funding to government schools while keeping their FM bonus.

In 2005, a 'Funding Guaranteed' (FG) policy was introduced by Kemp for schools transitioning into the SES's second funding period 2005–08. This was a similar arrangement to the FM approach but without indexation. The idea was that once an FG school's notional SES funding amount was equal to or greater than its frozen (2008) amount, the school moved into full SES mode. What this meant was that wealthy and middling non-government schools could carry over into their SES funding any financial advantage they might have gained from the ERI system even if it did not tally with the SES model.

The Catholic schools regarded DETYA's SES as a narrow and inflexible arrangement and had opted out during that first period, cautious about replacing their internally-operated funding approach, which took into account broader historical and current resource influences as well as socio-economic factors. In 2004, to help persuade the Catholic schools to switch to SES during the second 2005–08 SES funding period, the government gave them an interim 'deemed' SES score known in-house as the 'FC' (Funding Catholic) grant, which would act as a basis for providing an extra $362 million in funding for 40 per cent of Catholic schools across 2005–08, and any remaining late-starters would be given a start-up SES score based on their indexed 2004 funding status. The FC was launched by Cardinal Pell and John Howard on Sunday 29 February 2004. In an election year, it was politically advantageous for Howard to have a single Catholic, Protestant and other non-government bloc on board to counter any ALP attempts to undermine this new system.[30] At the launch, Pell gave Howard an enthusiastic vote of thanks.

By 2004, therefore, there were six different SES arrangements. They were the original indexed SES model (which had its already described flaws), the Catholic opt-out SES model, the indexed Funding Maintained 2000 model, the indexed Funding Maintained 2004 model, the non-indexed Funding Guaranteed model and the FC 2004 model. According to Kemp's successor as education minister, Brendan Nelson, the plan had been to 'wean' Catholic schools off these supplementary bonuses. But that never happened.[31]

---

[30] 'PM dangles $362m for Catholic schools', *The Australian*, 29 February 2004.

[31] 'Howard wanted to wean schools off funds deal', *The Australian*, 7 May 2011. This was Brendan Nelson's interpretation. In 2006 he publicly stated his views about gradual reduction in the FC arrangement being wound down during the 2008-12 funding period. His suggestion was not followed up. In April 2011, the Coalition's shadow education minister Christopher Pyne told a National Press Club luncheon that a Coalition government would keep the funding arrangements despite the inconsistency of similar schools in the same system receiving different amounts of government funding. See, 'Pyne backs status quo on schools', *The Australian*, 7 April 2011. Significantly, Pyne also announced at that luncheon he would remove the financial details of non-government schools from the My School website.

CHAPTER NINE

There was another problem with the government's SES system. The Ross-Farish Index had been designed to assess the socio-economic status of *in situ* populations for *in situ* services; this worked well for local health authorities and for systemic Catholic schools, but did not take into account service provision for school students attending boarding schools that could be hundreds of kilometres away from their parents' CCD. Accordingly, boarding and part-boarding schools benefited from the SES model because they almost invariably took relatively wealthy rural/regional/remote students who came from pockets of high asset/highly educated/high status families that were situated in CCDs where low-income wage earners and modest-income small business operators were the norm, thus giving an exaggeratedly low SES reading.

There was a second, associated, SES anomaly. Older non-government schools, which had been based for historic reasons in inner-city areas, benefited from a low SES reading. In this case, a wealthy and well-established school might find itself serving students who came from affluent middle-class pockets within neighbouring CCDs that had predominantly low-income residents.

And there was a third anomaly. Suburban students as well as students from regional/rural areas that contained predominantly artisan-level, aspirational residents who were cashed up but with tax-minimised income, low educational qualifications and low status jobs, brought high levels of SES funding to their non-government schools.

Consequently, from 2001 onwards a large proportion of wealthy and middling non-government schools were funded well above what should have been their SES rate. As far as these non-government schools were concerned, it was a win-win. With the FM, FG and FC amendments to the SES process in place, 60.3 per cent of non-government schools were nominally within the Commonwealth's SES scheme but actually in their own sub-schemes, benefiting inordinately.[32] Education expert Jim McMorrow has calculated that Commonwealth support for non-government school funding in real terms increased 137.4 per cent during the 1995–2008 period of the Howard government while Commonwealth funding for government schools during the same period increased by 68 per cent.[33] Using McMorrow's adjusted figures, the greater number of government schools were allocated $2.104 billion in 1995–96 and $3.541 billion in 1997–98. The lesser number of non-government schools received $2.778 billion in 1995–96 and $3.819 billion in 1997–98. McMorrow, a former teacher later attached to the University of Sydney as an adjunct associate professor, had worked in senior policy and administration roles at Commonwealth and state level for three decades. His professional background and grasp of the figures made him a powerful authority in school funding debates. His analysis of the SES funding scheme is as yet unchallenged by the scheme's supporters.

The ALP Opposition, which had voted for the new system in 2000 and maintained a wait-and-see approach, under Kim Beazley Jnr's leadership, changed their position as the first year of the SES system unfolded and as political and professional resistance to the SES became more vocal. Opposition to the SES was strengthened by

---

[32] Based on figures provided by Social Policy Section report *Australian Government funding for schools explained: 2013*, written by Marilyn Harrington and published 8 March 2013 for Parliamentary Library, http://www.aph.gov.au/About_Parliament/Parliamentary_Departments/Parliamentary_Library/pubs/BN/2012-2013/schoolfunding.

[33] J. McMorrow, 'Reviewing the evidence: Issues in Commonwealth funding of government and non-government schools in the Howard and Rudd years', August 2008, p.4, Sydney, Australian Education Union.

CHAPTER NINE

the September 2001 leaking of a report provided to the government by Ken Ross, one of the SES's two designers. The report, marked 'Confidential not for Circulation', cited major technical errors in the new system's operations and argued that factors such as accommodation (rental or owned), family stability and unemployment should bear more weight in the formula.

Ross, at that time working for UNESCO in Paris, suggested the SES model was actually 'not suitable for the purpose of guiding large-scale resource allocation decisions among Australia's non-government schools' and 'a complete corruption of the intended standardisation process'. Ross concluded that a fundamental design requirement, dating back to 1950, had been ignored in the SES model and it was now impossible to use the wealth of parental neighbourhoods 'to conclude the wealth of fee-paying parents at each school'. He continued, 'It is quite significant to note here that the sole source of technical advice for the construction of the SES index was a university faculty of medicine and not a faculty of education'.

Kemp, whose department had been sitting on the report, quickly brushed off the suggestion that the SES system was flawed, arguing that these issues were 'tiny' and made little difference.[34] The Ross report, released two weeks after the 9/11 Al-Qaeda terrorist attacks on the United States, was then forgotten after Howard's announcement of a November general election. Howard would lead the Coalition to victory largely on the back of security and migration fears. Any sustained impact that the Ross report might have had was lost in the election process and in Australia's post 9/11 sense of shock. The

---

[34] This section is based on two media reports, 'Schools Funding Formula "Flawed"', *The Age*, 27 September 2001, and 'Private school funding flaws', *The Australian*, 27 September 2001.

unyielding Kemp, having completed his task of setting up an opaque, biased and inequitable funding system, instead of the transparent, objective and equitable system that was promised, moved on to take over the Environment and Energy portfolio after the Coalition's election victory.[35]

Just before Christmas, a more seemingly emollient Brendan Nelson commenced as Minister, announcing he was prepared to fix the SES's 'teething problems'.[36] After the Christmas break, however, Nelson made no attempt to fix the so-called teething problems. Rather, in February 2002 Nelson wrote to *The Canberra Times* defending the SES as 'the fairest way'.[37]

Whatever the level of sincerity in Nelson's late 2001 commitment to fix 'teething problems', the case for any further preferential funding of non-government schools was compromised early in 2002 when the wealthy non-government schools increased their fees by as much as 10 per cent, notwithstanding their SES dividend. There was more to come. In May 2002, the Howard government announced a $1 billion budget figure for non-government school funding, rising to an estimated $5 billion over the 2003–06 funding period. In contrast, Commonwealth funding levels for government schools during the same period were set to rise from $400 million to $2.55 billion.

The enactment of the SES system from 2001 onwards gave rise to a cycle of responses to each successive government announcement about school funding. First, government school parents' organisations were dismayed, government school teacher unions were enraged,

---

[35] The promise was contained within Kemp's second reading speech in the House of Representatives on 29 July 2000.

[36] Cit. 'Teachers urged to end fight on funds', *The Courier Mail*, 6 December 2001.

[37] 'SES funding is the fairest way', Letters column, *The Canberra Times*, 13 February 2002.

CHAPTER NINE

non-government school representatives were contented (apart from the low-fee Christian schools who wanted yet more money), professional observers were frustrated and the government remained unblushingly adamant that SES was both fair and transparent, that it met the needs of an education system geared to parental choice and that it saved the taxpayers money.

Matters came to a head during the run-up to the 9 October 2004 general election, a campaign fought by the Coalition largely on trust, global terror, conservation issues and education funding. John Howard slowly edged ahead of his volatile rival Mark Latham who, on 14 September 2004, had announced in mid-campaign that he would cut Commonwealth funding to sixty-seven wealthy non-government schools and freeze funding for 111 other non-government schools. This immediately provoked a new 'hit list' media campaign by the pro-Coalition press, mainly *The Australian*, and an unprecedented denunciation of ALP policy by Cardinal Pell, who joined with archbishops Jensen, Hart (Catholic, Melbourne) and Watson (Anglican Melbourne). The tone of their attack, published on the eve of Latham's campaign launch in Brisbane, was alarmist and potentially very damaging:

> We express our concern at the lack of clarity in Labor's proposal and the potentially divisive mechanism for redistributing funds within the non-government schools sector. It is also regrettable that the government funding for particular non-government schools with greater need is to be taken from other schools within the non-government schools sector, which is likely to benefit schools of one faith background largely at the expense of another.[38]

---

[38] 'Churches savage Latham - Archbishops Jensen and Pell unite over schools policy', *The Australian*, 29 September 2004.

In the event, Latham and the ALP lost and Howard won a third term as prime minister, in part because of increasing support from Catholic voters. According to the post-election research of academics Clive Bean and Ian McAllister, by 2004 the Coalition was ahead of the ALP among Catholics by 9 points, and when it came to regular churchgoers (most of whom were Catholics) the Coalition led the ALP by 22 points.[39] ANU academic John Warhurst concurred. This increasing support for the Howard approach from regular churchgoers between 1996–2004 was instrumental in keeping the Coalition in power.

After 2004, the SES system continued in unaltered fashion. Over the six years that followed the implementation of the SES system in 2001, the Coalition's school funding policy became arguably the most contentious and unjust school funding system since the introduction of Commonwealth schools' funding. SES was loathed by supporters of government schools as a politically partisan and class-based attempt to undermine public education, and was disparaged in newspaper editorials in both the centrist and the conservative press as unfair and divisive. It even elicited public comments of dismay and guilt among a small number of head teachers of wealthy secondary schools about these boom times for their (and other) elite schools, some of which were accused of having spent the SES bonus money as windfall profits.[40]

On the other hand, looking at the effects of SES as a measure of the strategic success of the Kemp-Howard initiative 1996–2007,

---

[39] Cit. by John Warhurst in 'Religion in 21st century Australian National Politics', *Papers on Parliament*, No 46, December 2006, p.2.

[40] See for example, 'Elite Schools enjoy a boom with a view to expand', *The Age*, 9 June 2007, and 'Principal slams massive edifices', *The Age*, 9 June 2007.

CHAPTER NINE

their plan worked. In the section of the 1997 *ABS Yearbook* that deals with numbers and types of schools operating in Australia, there were 7366 government schools, 1969 Catholic schools and 804 other non-government schools. The *ABS Yearbook 2008* records the same group of figures for 2006 as 6902 government schools, 1703 Catholic schools and 1007 other non-government schools, with the other non-government category providing the largest percentage rise, at 25.2 percent.[41]

As for transparency, objectivity and equitability, as we have seen, the SES's original designer Ken Ross, together with those few guilt-ridden principals of wealthy non-government schools, had found it wanting. By 2007, even that steadfast defender of Liberal Party policy *The Australian* had turned against the SES system, declaring its position in an August 2007 feature piece arguing that the ALP had a better education policy than the Coalition's. In a remarkable turn of events, this article, which would have had to be approved by the newspaper's combatively conservative editor Chris Mitchell, was written by *The Australian*'s long standing and professional education correspondent Justine Ferrari, who based her report on an interview with Kevin Donnelly – *The Australian*'s pro-Liberal education columnist.[42]

In the lead-up to the October 2007 general election, the ALP was led by a confident Kevin Rudd, a relatively new centrist figure in national politics. Rudd had, in 2006, prepared for office by channelling Bob Hawke, as it were: announcing he was not a socialist

---

[41] *ABS Yearbook* 1997, p.236 and *ABS Yearbook* 2008, p.379.

[42] 'Labor "on top" in education debate', *The Australian*, 18 August 2007. Mitchell had a friendly relationship with fellow Queenslander Rudd until they fell out in 2008 over an *Australian* article critical of Rudd, 'Captain Chaos and the workings of the inner circle', 21 June 2008. See Chris Mitchell's wonderfully self-regarding memoir, *Making Headlines*, Carlton, Melbourne University Press, pp.33–55, 2016.

and promising to continue with the SES. This move gave rise to cries of betrayal by government school supporters.[43] Notwithstanding this disappointment for supporters of government schools, Rudd and the ALP won in a landslide and Howard lost his own seat to former ABC news presenter and journalist Maxine McKew. Julia Gillard was appointed deputy prime minister and minister of Education, Employment and Workplace Relations, a so-called 'super-ministry'.

---

[43] 'Rudd Rejects Socialism', *The Age*, 14 December 2006, and '"Pseudo Libs": Labor accused on schools funding', *The Age*, 10 October 2007. The move to keep the SES for the time disappointed government school supporters but came as no surprise. To avoid a 'hit list' campaign, in the absence of any other option and bearing in mind that major changes in school funding models require a long lead-in period, Rudd and his then shadow education spokesman Stephen Smith had been flagging the short-term retention of the SES for most of 2007.

Chapter Ten

JULIA GILLARD AND IRRESPONSIBLE, UNTRUTHFUL FEAR CAMPAIGNS

Kevin Rudd's accession to prime ministerial authority after his party's 24 November 2007 general election victory had been remarkably quick by ALP standards. Queenslander Rudd, formerly a public servant and diplomat, had been elected as federal member for Griffith in 1998, becoming shadow foreign minister in 2001 and then leader of the ALP opposition in 2006, just ten months before his party's victory over a jaded and spent Howard government.

There was something of Tony Blair about Rudd, who was a young, vigorous, clean-cut and persuasive ALP leader, seemingly more contemporary than his immediate predecessors, who had for more than a decade been involved in backstabbing and musical chairs. Prior to Rudd's accession as ALP leader, the party had been obliged to choose between a possibly unwell Kim Beazley, an accomplished but unexciting Simon Crean, and a hot-blooded and ailing Mark Latham. Rudd, a new man on a mission, got the call.[1] By his side

---

[1] In 2004, Beazley had suffered from a brain condition, Schaltenbrand's syndrome. Although he'd made a full recovery, rumours circulated in 2006 that he was still suffering from health issues.

was his deputy leader, Julia Gillard, member for the Victorian seat of Lalor.

Rudd had plans for 2008 and beyond. Climate change was to be tackled. Howard-era 'reckless' spending was to stop. Indigenous wrongs were to be righted. Industrial relations were to be reformed in favour of fairness. And school students and teachers were to take part in an 'Education Revolution', a term borrowed from Blair government adviser Michael Barber.

When Tony Blair became the UK's prime minister in 1997, after eighteen years of Conservative Party rule, he had decided that his novice New Labour government needed, among other things, an education expert to work on recasting education policy with the then Secretary of State for Education David Blunkett. Blair had been impressed by former teacher union official Michael Barber's exhortatory 1996 book, *The Learning Game: Arguments for an Education Revolution*. Barber was appointed Chief Adviser to Blunkett and, in 2001, Chief Adviser on Delivery.

Barber's main point was that when an education system is failing, as it was in the UK, it will not save itself. Intervention is needed. Beyond that he argued that teachers needed to be regularly tested for competence, that high expectations of students are the *sine qua non* of a good school education, the basics are necessary and lifelong learning is as much a part of 'education' as is school learning. Effectively it was a mix of old-fashioned remedies and new catchphrases wrapped up in a 'revolutionary' package. Brian Caldwell, the experienced observer of Australian politics and policy outcomes at the University of Melbourne, thought the Rudd Revolution discussion paper *The Australian Economy Needs An Education Revolution*, of January 2007,

CHAPTER TEN

less a solution than a borrowed slogan.[2]

Julia Gillard, new Deputy Prime Minister and minister in charge of Education, Employment and Workplace Relations, and Social Inclusion, was born in South Wales in 1961, of parents who were to become 'Ten pound Poms' in 1966. The Gillards lived in the then declining South Wales port of Barry and migrated to Australia partly to look for a better life in a new country and partly to move to the warm, dry state of South Australia, to remedy young Julia's bronchial pneumonia, a condition exacerbated by the cold, damp South Welsh climate.[3] In Adelaide, Gillard's parents worked in the caring professions, with father John a psychiatric nurse and mother Moira a worker at a Salvation Army aged-care hostel. Gillard's parents had experienced and respected hard work, appreciated educational and cultural achievement and expected their two daughters, Alison and Julia, to have careers of their own.

Julia Gillard studied Arts and Law at the University of Adelaide and in her second year became involved in Labor Club student politics, going on to become President of the Australian Union of Students (1983–84), a period in her life which she relished as a valuable, if over-idealistic (a self-judgement), preparation for the real world of parliamentary politics. Having completed her Arts/Law degree at the University of Melbourne in 1989, Gillard then began work as a lawyer in the industrial relations section of Melbourne

---

[2] 'Rudd has a long way to go to become the education prime minister', *Sydney Morning Herald*, 6 December 2007. Caldwell is former Dean of the Faculty of Education and a highly regarded education consultant.

[3] The Gillard family thought that their GP was recommending Australia. After they had decided to migrate, they found that that he was thinking more of Cornwall.

lawyers Slater and Gordon, becoming within three years their youngest partner.[4]

A political career seemed inevitable and, after several false starts and a mid-1990s apprenticeship as chief of staff to Victorian ALP Opposition leader John Brumby, Gillard successfully contested the safe Victorian seat of Lalor in the 1998 general election. As with Rudd, Gillard then experienced an express run to Cabinet status. In 2001, with Simon Crean as ALP leader, she entered the shadow cabinet to look after the Population and Immigration portfolio. Early in 2003 she was handed the additional responsibilities of Reconciliation and Indigenous Affairs as well as Health. In late 2006, with Rudd having edged out Beazley as Opposition leader, she became his deputy. A mere year later Gillard became Deputy Prime Minister and a minister with three portfolios.[5]

What had been clear throughout Gillard's rapid rise to power was her intellect, sense of inclusiveness, great capacity for hard work and her impressive legal talents, including an aptitude for negotiation. What was not clear when she became a politician was that she would have to endure sustained misogynistic hostility from the Coalition side of politics prior to and during her time in office as minister and prime minister. Long before the November 2007 election, that campaign had already begun when, in May 2006, Liberal senator and provocateur Bill Heffernan had claimed that Gillard was unfit for leadership because, 'anyone who chooses to remain deliberately barren

---

[4] Slater and Gordon were an ALP and union-linked social justice law firm.

[5] Much of this biographical section is gleaned from Julia Gillard's 2014 political memoir *My Story*, North Sydney, Random House, as well as excerpts from a 6 March 2006 interview Gillard gave for *Australian Story*, ABC Television.

CHAPTER TEN

... they've got no idea what life's about'.[6] Coalition Health Minister Tony Abbott took up the refrain in October 2007, announcing that Gillard 'lacked broader life experience'.[7] Media observers, as well as the public generally, took this as code for her status as a single woman with no children.[8] Media commentators also believed that the Coalition was targeting Gillard as a (female) weak link in the Rudd Shadow Cabinet. In an unsavoury series of incidents, a small number of Coalition politicians, a few Coalition-supporting radio shock jocks, a number of conservative newspaper columnists as well as larger numbers of Coalition supporters were later to follow Heffernan and Abbott's lead, as a thwarted Opposition became increasingly frustrated at Gillard's ability to remain in power as prime minister (2010–13) of a minority government. As a consequence of the campaign against her, a furious 'weakest link' gave a memorably excoriating parliamentary speech on 9 October 2012, chastising Abbott for his misogyny that, thanks to social media, became a global phenomenon. In a television interview one year later, Abbott, by now Opposition leader, asserted that her misogyny speech had been unfair.[9]

As an education minister Gillard had one overarching objective: to ensure that all Australian children had an equal level of access to

---

[6] 27 May 2006, 'Hard Man on the Hill', *Good Weekend*. Heffernan stood by his comment a year later in *The Bulletin*, 1 May 2007.

[7] 'Abbott in new Gillard attack', *The Advertiser*, 6 October 2007. Abbott denied that was what he meant.

[8] Feminist writer and policymaker Anne Summers dealt with the misogyny issue in a 31 August 2012 human rights and social justice lecture at Newcastle University. http://www.annesummers.com.au/speeches/her-rights-at-work-r-rated-version/.

[9] *Kitchen Cabinet*, 4 September 2013, ABC Television, Season 3. Episode 7. See also Kerry-Anne Walsh, *The Stalking of Julia Gillard*, Sydney, Allen & Unwin, 2013, an anti-Rudd philippic regarding Gillard's 'stalking' and unseating by Rudd in 2013.

what she termed 'educational excellence'. This is how she expressed her views in her 1998 maiden parliamentary speech as member for Lalor:

> The students from my electorate are not any less intelligent than those from Higgins or Kooyong [wealthy Liberal-voting constituencies] but their educational opportunities are not the same. Certainly this massive discrepancy would be lessened if we as a nation were prepared to seriously tackle the inequality of opportunity that exists in our education system and create a high-class state school system.[10]

As Gillard saw it, redressing that socially crippling imbalance entailed moving away from what she termed 'ruthless dogfights' about the relative value of two major education systems that were closed to Commonwealth scrutiny.[11] Gillard wanted to progress towards policymaking and dealing with the 'brutal' legacy of the Howard years when, she argued, Coalition prejudices that the non-government schools were more successful than their public counterparts prevailed, and where questions about what actually went on in the classrooms of Australia were ignored.

For Gillard, transparency was the starting point for serious policy discussion and parental understanding. In March 2008, after having been briefed by the education department officials and meeting with stakeholders, she began her own education revolution by mapping out her My School initiative, a school-by-school online information system using NAPLAN (the National Assessment Program – Literacy and Numeracy) data as well as other information, including what later became an Index of Community Socio-educational

---

[10] Cit. Gillard, 2014, p.239.
[11] Gillard, 2014, p.247.

CHAPTER TEN

Advantage (ICSEA), in a way that would be accessible to all, providing Australian parents, policymakers, media and researchers alike with detailed year-by-year information on all Australian schools.

During the preparatory period for My School, in November 2008, Gillard invited Joel Klein, controversial New York School Chancellor, to Australia. This was a Gillard attempt to gain a policy advantage over embedded systemic attitudes by picking the brains of an outside expert. Klein, a former lawyer and a back-to-basics favourite of US conservative think tanks and local Australian media (especially *The Australian*), had just introduced an innovative $US95 million computer-based Achievement Reporting and Innovation System (ARIS) in New York, but he was seen by teachers there as a punitive, anti-teacher Chancellor with a reputation for shutting down schools.[12] The Klein visit to Australia turned out to be a public relations disaster. Gillard's comment that 'As a nation we have to say we will no longer tolerate an education system that underachieves' was regarded by the AEU as a possible prelude to Klein-like teacher sackings and school closures.[13] The Klein episode was regarded as yet another policy-borrowing stunt – one of a succession of such borrowings common in the 1990s.

Part of Gillard's strategic aim for Australia's classrooms was to use My School to increase teacher expectations and improve teacher

---

[12] ARIS made available to parents current and past student scores in reading, maths, social studies, and science tests as well as other test scores, high school credits earned; enrolment history; family contact information; English Language Learner and special education status; data on course grades, attendance, and other biographical information. See http://sinergiany.org/parents-center/aris-achievement-reporting-and-innovation-system.

[13] 'Education gets an F Grade', *The Advertiser*, 28 November 2008. Klein was fired by New York's Mayor Bloomberg in 2010 after stirring up controversy on both sides of US politics while gaining little headway in the city's campaign to improve educational standards. In 2014 ARIS was dumped.

accountability. Another move in that direction was to support the controversial Teach for Australia program, a 2010-initiated six-week crash course for high-flying graduates that was to be run by selected universities and operate in a limited number of jurisdictions.[14] The purpose of the program was to induct highly-motivated prospective teachers into the profession without their going through what was about to become the national standard, a two-year pre-service teacher education program.[15] The Teach for Australia model, another policy-borrowing idea, was based on privately-funded US and Canadian precursors. In Australia it aroused controversy because it side-stepped and by implication snubbed traditional university courses and because it avoided traditional state-level registration requirements, annoying the AEU. Gillard's support for what was widely regarded by teachers and the AEU as another public relations manoeuvre further reduced her popularity among teachers.[16]

As for My School, in a customary Commonwealth ploy, Gillard tied ongoing Commonwealth funding to state and territory participation in the My School project and then successfully negotiated her way through that jurisdictional minefield. My School still drew fire from the AEU, anxious that My School data might lead to league tables,

---

[14]   Teach for Australia's mission statement, 'Our vision is of an Australia where all children, regardless of background, attain an excellent education' was aligned exactly with Gillard's own vision.

[15]   This was the Master of Teaching, a program that was quickly taking over from the long-standing, one-year Graduate Diploma of Education.

[16]   An Australian Council for Education Research evaluation showed that Teach for Australia (TFA) was popular with principals who employed the TFA 'associates' but had been expensive to run and numbers (fewer than 225 p.a.) had been too small to calculate any national educational improvement. See Paul Weldon, Phillip McKenzie, Elizabeth Kleinhenz and Kate Reid, *Teach for Australia Pathway: Evaluation Report Phase 3 of 3*, 2013, Australian Council for Educational Research, http://research.acer.edu.au/cgi/viewcontent.cgi?article=1013&context=teacher_education. The Teach for Australia program still exists at the time of writing.

CHAPTER TEN

which it did, thanks to a media that was outside government control.[17] Scheduled to be implemented early in 2010, the My School website crashed on its 20 January debut and had to be revamped in 2010–11. Since its launch however, My School has gradually become accepted by both sides of politics, by parents, by researchers, by teachers and even by the AEU as a valuable educational resource.[18]

Gillard's next project was a national curriculum. In 2006 John Howard had attempted to produce a personalised version of a national curriculum in Australian history, intended to be a prelude to national curriculum frameworks in English, mathematics and science. The Howard project foundered, however, because of its blatantly ideological objectives.[19] Learning from that debacle, in 2008 Gillard set up an independent statutory authority, the National Curriculum Board (later the Australian Curriculum and Assessment Authority) chaired by the professionally-eminent and politically-astute educator Barry McGaw. In December 2010, a complex design began with an extended consultation process followed by the introductory section of a staged implementation which received general endorsement from states and territories.[20]

---

[17] School league tables in the Australian media generally produce little in the way of controversy unlike in the UK, where media-produced tables are an annual source of media discussion and debate. The UK's GOV.UK produces locality comparison tables for schools in England. Scotland, Northern Ireland and Wales have their own sites.

[18] For AEU's use of My School to gather data see for example 'State schools funding in retreat', *The Sunday Age*, 6 April 2014.

[19] See T. Taylor, 'Howard's End: a narrative memoir of political contrivance, neo-conservative ideology and the Australian history curriculum', *Curriculum Journal* (UK) Vol. 20 No. 4, 2009, pp.317–329.

[20] In English, mathematics, science and history. See T. Taylor, 'Scarcely an Immaculate Conception: New Professionalism Encounters Old Politics in the Formation of the Australian National History Curriculum', *International Journal of Historical Learning, Teaching and Research* (UK), Vol. No. 2 May 2013. www.history.org.uk/secondary/resource/6445/the-international-journal-volume-11-number-2.

By this time the Rudd government, and Gillard in particular, had been coming under increasing criticism from the conservative media, particularly *The Australian*, for the $16.2 billion Building the Education Revolution program, hastily introduced from 2007. This initiative was designed to provide publicly-funded employment and economic stability during the aftermath of the 2008 Global Financial Crisis through a national array of capital works and infrastructure projects.[21] Unfortunately, some BER projects were badly handled at the local level, with accusations of feather-bedded contracts, dangerous work practices and unwanted building works.[22]

While dealing with these unrelenting attacks from the conservative media as well as an AEU anti-NAPLAN industrial campaign (dropped in May 2010), Gillard announced in Sydney, on 14 April 2010, that there would be a review of the school funding system, a development that caught the media and the education community by surprise. The timing was perhaps a diversionary tactic.

In her detailed announcement, described as a prelude to an even more comprehensive statement to come, Gillard was quite outspoken about the need for a change to the funding system, arguing that under

---

21 *The Australian*, led by hard-nosed editor-in-chief Chris Mitchell, had turned on the Rudd government after its editor discovered that the new prime minister was not, as Mitchell had first thought, a John Howard redux. As for *The Australian*'s attack on Building the Education Revolution (BER), on one day alone, 1 April 2010, it carried seven articles attacking BER. There was also a daily 'Schools Watch' feature to keep Gillard on the defensive. Despite a relatively positive series of evaluations, *The Australian* was still pursuing its campaign as late as 2014.

22 *The Australian* seemed to be obsessed with Gillard. In 2010 the newspaper mentioned her in 5916 articles while *The Age* published 2003 mentions and the *Sydney Morning Herald* published a mere 1715. During the same period and apparently hanging on to the past, *The Australian* published 1680 mentions of ex-prime minister John Howard, compared with *The Age*'s 553. Looking to the future perhaps, *The Australian* mentioned Opposition leader Tony Abbott 5035 times during 2010 (Dow Jones Factiva database, global.factiva.com, accessed January 2017).

CHAPTER TEN

the SES/AGSRC arrangement, privileged non-government schools were piggy-backing off annual rises in school government funding, keeping already over-funded non-government schools constantly ahead of their government counterparts. Gillard promised that she would release a discussion paper at the end of April 2010 which would contain draft terms of reference for the review. The paper was then to be followed by a month of consultations leading to finalised terms of reference.

Interestingly, Gillard mentioned two political matters in her April speech, matters which related to the state of party politics in 2010. First, she commented, 'I also believe this review should be conducted in an atmosphere without fear'. Her second set of remarks, in a key passage, was more direct:

> There will be those who seek to misrepresent what I have set out here today, to distort the implications of my argument, to seek premature restriction and closure of this review's conclusions. I fully expect the Opposition led by Mr Abbott to start an irresponsible untruthful fear campaign trying to scare schools by saying they will lose money ... But [her hoped for] spirited and open exchange and consideration is not the same as seeking to close off debate. We will not allow our opponents to misrepresent the nature of this review, and we will seek community support for a process which is open, thorough and balanced. I urge all Australians not to see threats from this review but opportunities.[23]

On 30 May, in the midst of a growing prime ministerial leadership crisis in which Gillard was being touted by the conservative press as a replacement for a failing Rudd, the review panel was named and the

---

[23] Julia Gillard, 'A future fair for all – School funding in Australia', 15 April 2010, Minister's Media Centre, https://ministers.employment.gov.au/node/67/6521.

discussion paper was released. The panel was to be chaired by David Gonski, chair of the Australian Stock Exchange and a community-minded businessman with a great deal of experience in chairing high level committees. The other panel members were Peter Tannock (at that stage Vice-Chancellor of Notre Dame University; Ken Boston, former Director-General of the New South Wales Education Department (1992–2002) and more recently Chief Executive Officer of the UK's Qualifications and Curriculum Authority; Kathryn Greiner, chancellor of the private Bond University and a prominent Liberal Party member with a background in issues of educational disadvantage; and Carmen Lawrence, former ALP premier of Western Australia, a former federal MP and a government schools advocate. In 2011, Bill Scales, a prominent economist and business adviser, chancellor of Swinburne University and member of the Bradley review of higher education, also joined the panel.

On paper, the composition of the panel was a tactical and strategic masterstroke. Gonski was almost universally liked and respected on the Liberal side of politics, and his appointment would help reassure the non-government sector that the review was not a hostile Whitlamesque manoeuvre. And although a businessman, as far as Labor was concerned Gonski was not political operator. Tannock represented the Catholic interest, and his experience as Schools Commissioner gave him the kind of technical background that would be valuable to the panel's discussions and decisions. Boston had been a high profile New South Wales education administrator who, apart from his professional and political expertise, unofficially represented Australia's most politically troublesome state. Greiner was a prominent New South Wales Liberal and her appointment would disarm that side of politics, especially in her home state. Lawrence

CHAPTER TEN

was an experienced ALP politician who would be able to steer the discussion into practical areas of policymaking. Scales was there to help the panel deal with the relationship between schooling and productivity. Of the panel members only Carmen Lawrence could clearly be identified as a Labor Party supporter and / or government school advocate.

At first, the responses from the two principal education stakeholders were guardedly welcoming, though divided in expectations. The executive director of the Independent Schools Council of Australia (ISCA), Bill Daniels, said 'the panel members brought a wide range of experience and expertise to the review … We will reinforce the case that independent schools make significant social, educational contributions and value their direct and sustained partnership with the commonwealth government'. The AEU's president, Angelo Gavrielatos, was slightly more pointed, announcing that the review provided an opportunity to get rid of the 'discredited' initiatives of the Howard era. The AEU, he commented, would continue to insist on three core principles: that equity in education exists only when government schools set the nation's educational standards; that the primary obligation of all government was to fund government schools adequately and properly; and that parents have the right to send their children to a government school of the 'highest quality' in their communities.[24]

---

[24] 'Gillard puts funding on notice — OUT TOP SCHOOLS', *The Australian*, 1 May 2010. It is unclear why the article's heading included the alarmist phrase 'out top schools' in capitals. Written by the normally well-informed and balanced education correspondent Justine Ferrari, the article makes no mention of getting rid of 'top schools'. A possible explanation is that Ferrari's headline was edited by hands-on editor-in-chief Chris Mitchell or by a sub-editor under Mitchell's direction as a premature but telling first shot in what became a prolonged anti-Gonski campaign by *The Australian*.

Remarkably, considering their rivalries for Commonwealth resources, the two education sectors were in harmony about the necessity for an improved, needs-based funding system for all schools. At the time, the commissioning of the Gonski report was greeted with only mild interest in the media. There was however one loud dissenting voice: that of Trevor Cobbold, spokesperson for the Save Our Schools advocacy group. Cobbold attacked the composition of the panel which, he claimed, was biased because a majority of its members had attended private school.[25] Gonski had attended a selective high school, four other panel members had attended at least one Catholic school during their educational progress and a fifth had attended a high-fee private school.

Probably still trying to work out how to respond to the composition of the Gonski panel and its terms of reference, the normally irrepressible shadow education minister, Christopher Pyne, was uncharacteristically silent on the matter, if not silent on the Gillard-commissioned BER review, which he thought 'propaganda', or the national curriculum: a 'disaster' with too much Aboriginal history.[26] Following Pyne's example, the Opposition's response in general to Gonski was non-existent throughout May 2010 and it was not until July, when Gillard had taken over from Rudd as prime minister, that Pyne took time out from his anti-BER campaign to reassure his fellow Catholics of the Bishops Commission for Catholic Education that the Coalition would support the Gonski panel's findings as long as the SES remained in place:

---

[25] See 'Public schools advocate slams Gonski review appointments', *Australian Associated Press*, 2 May 2010.

[26] 'School building review "propaganda"', *The Age*, 5 May 2010, and 'The new history wars', *Sunday Herald Sun*, 30 May 2010.

CHAPTER TEN

But we are fully committed to the SES funding model. We are fully committed to funding maintained and guaranteed and to the ... indexation of non-government schools. There's no reason why the SES funding model shouldn't be reviewed just like other aspects of government policy is constantly reviewed. The difference is that the Coalition introduced the SES funding model, we are committed to it, we think it's an objective way of funding non-government schools, whereas the Labor Party, including Julia Gillard, is on the record saying it is one of the most heinous things that's ever been created.[27]

In other words, while the government's discussion paper had called for a funding system that was transparent, fair, financially sustainable and not dominated by political arguments, the Coalition would not support any major changes to an SES model by now almost universally regarded as partisan, opaque and unfair.

Gillard, as prime minister, chose Peter Garrett to handle the schools portfolio, a courageous appointment considering that Garrett was still under intense fire from the Coalition as well as *The Australian* for his handling of the troublesome Home Insulation Program, another Rudd infrastructure initiative (2009–10) more commonly known as the Pink Batts Scheme.[28] Gillard's view was that Garrett, who had been a relatively young and inexperienced minister for the environment, needed a different ministry to get away from the Pink Batts imbroglio.

---

27 'Coalition may adopt Labor review findings', *The Australian*, 8 July 2010.
28 Four young electricians died and 224 houses caught fire as a consequence of poor administration and bungled local implementation. No adverse findings were made against Garrett in a 2013-14 Royal Commission report. I. Hangar, *Report of the Royal Commission into the Home Insulation Program*, Commonwealth of Australia, www.homeinsultaitonroyalcommission.gov.au/documentation/documents/reportoftheroyalcommisionintothehomeinsulationprogram.pdf.

CLASS WARS

As an incoming prime minister who had auspiced so much educational policy change at ministerial level in just over two years, Gillard kept a close interest in education matters, especially when it came to funding, even building her 21 August 2010 election campaign speech around education policy.[29] Indeed, much of the election commentary about education during that campaign came from Gillard's office while Garrett was quietly negotiating the final details of the first stage of the national curriculum with his State and Territory equivalents. An agreed version was due towards the end of the year. Gillard's recollection of this unusual dual control arrangement was that 'Peter wore well my interventionist approach to the school-funding work. I think he knew on accepting the ministry that I would not be letting go of work I loved and cared about so much.'[30]

On the funding front, however, all was not well. During the run up to the August 2010 general election, Gillard had noticed that after the Christopher Pyne letter of 8 July, funding negotiations between the Commonwealth and the Catholic sector had suddenly become 'inexplicably difficult'.[31] Towards the end of July, and in order to deal with that issue, Gillard, a self-described atheist, met a delegation of Catholic bishops that included the self-assured George Pell. During the previous year, as noted above, Pell had been closely in touch with the Opposition.[32] The delegation's view was that, despite Gillard's reassurances that no school would lose out because of any Gonski

---

[29] Announced on 17 July 2010.

[30] Gillard, 2014, p.259.

[31] Gillard, 2014, p.258. A hint that Pyne might have been stirring up the bishops.

[32] Pell, who had strong connections with the Liberal Party and whose national authority within the Catholic Church was about to be enhanced by his imminent appointment as cardinal but was eventually to be eroded by 2017 charges of sexual abuse, was still in the middle of an authority-draining and drawn-out public

CHAPTER TEN

changes, alterations to the funding system would mean a loss of funding for their schools.

Gillard was boxed in and decided that, in the middle of a very tight election campaign, it was too risky to continue with her insistence on a rapid implementation of the panel's findings. In doing so, she would draw the ire of a powerful Pell-led Catholic lobby that, in previous incarnations, had helped bring Mark Latham down in 2004 and John Howard become prime minister in 1996. Very reluctantly, Gillard agreed to put off changes to the non-government funding system until the end of 2013, by which time another general election would have taken place. What this meant was that unlike preceding education ministers Malcolm Fraser in 1970, and David Kemp in 2000, Gillard would not be in a position to fully embed any new system before the next election. The Catholic Church had used its political clout and its connections to gain its own ends, and the Church, under George Pell's Liberal-leaning control, came dangerously close to infringing on the constitutional proprieties regarding separation of church and state.

The more immediate 21 August 2010 election was virtually a tie, with the ALP hanging on as a minority government with the help of crossbenchers in both houses. During her second period of government as prime minister, Gillard, together with Senate leader Chris Evans and Leader of the House Anthony Albanese, became preoccupied with keeping the government afloat. Meanwhile the Gonski panel continued with its work in unobtrusive fashion. Gonski's report was submitted to the government in December

---

controversy regarding his alleged inaction over child sexual abuse by Catholic clergymen. See David Marr's censorious essay, *The Prince: Faith, Abuse and George Pell*, Quarterly Essay 51, Collingwood, Black Inc., 2013.

2011, with the prime minister announcing that she would read it during the Christmas break and then make her decision about how to respond to the report's findings. Before Christmas, Gillard reshuffled her cabinet in a tricky and divisive factional readjustment, but the unaligned Garrett managed to keep his place.[33] With the national curriculum agreement having been reached on 8 December 2010, it would now be Garrett's job, with the assistance of close Gillard ally Brendan O'Connor, to sell the Gonski report's findings.[34] In effect this meant that, in an unusual arrangement, the prelude to the Gonski legislation was being handled by three Cabinet members, Gillard, Garrett and O'Connor.

Having had two months to read over and develop an official response to the report, the government released the Gonski panel's deliberations on 20 February 2012, just a week before caucus was due to meet and vote on the ALP leadership, a fallout from the December 2011 reshuffle. Gillard won the 27 February spill 71 votes to 31, but this electorally-damaging leadership conflict, a precursor of the Gillard/Rudd reversal in June 2013, when Rudd would take back the leadership, dominated the headlines during late February, at the expense of any positive publicity for the government regarding the Gonski initiative.[35]

---

[33] The reshuffle, which nearly unseated Gillard, is not mentioned in her memoir.

[34] O'Connor, a versatile and successful minister with several Rudd/Gillard ministerial portfolios already under his belt, was to be Minister for Human Services and Minister Assisting For School Education. The implication was clear. O'Connor was to mentor Garrett. Interestingly, Gillard mentions Garrett's achievements in the national curriculum agreement and teacher professional standards but not in selling school funding reform.

[35] Over and above its normal political reporting and feature articles, *The Australian* ran a series of 176 articles across 20–28 February, headlined 'Labor in Crisis'. This debilitating February 2011 ALP dispute is not mentioned in Gillard's political memoir.

CHAPTER TEN

The Gonski report itself had found that Australia's overall school education system, while scoring relatively satisfactorily in the major international league tables, had been in relative global decline over the previous ten years.[36] The report also pointed out that there was a growing gap between highest and lowest performing students in Australian schools, with too many students not reaching minimum educational standards, and that there was an unacceptable link between low achievement and educational disadvantage.

As for funding, the panel noted that there were systemic inconsistencies: in dealing with disadvantaged students, reporting on educational outcomes and in the effectiveness of the funding regimes. The existing approach to funding, the panel found, was unnecessarily complex, lacking in coherence, involved duplication of effort and was based on an inaccurate and obscure AGSRC index that was limited in scope. Moreover, there were imbalances and overlaps between Commonwealth and state/territory funding responsibilities. The panel further noted that not all states and territories were in a position to fund their schools adequately, either because of economic issues or because some jurisdictions contained a high proportion of disadvantaged students.[37] There was also a simplistic and inaccurate perception that the Commonwealth Government funded non-government schools while states and territories funded government schools. As for capital works programs, they lacked planning and

---

[36] The two major benchmark assessments were the triennial OECD annual reports on 15-year olds' educational achievement known as the PISA (The Programme for International Student Assessment) and TIMMS (The International Association for the Evaluation of Educational Achievement or IEA's cyclical Trends in International Mathematics and Science Studies).

[37] A gentle indication of resourcing and achievement issues in Tasmania, the Northern Territory and remote regions in New South Wales and Western Australia.

were uncoordinated, with government schools particularly lacking in capital investment. In other words, the Australian education system was an organisational and funding mess.

The solution advocated by the Gonski report was to increase education spending by $5 billion per annum across all sectors, money which was to be allocated in a balanced fashion within a revised system to be overseen by an independent National Schools Resourcing Body. The new funding regime would be based upon a commonly-agreed and universally-applied schooling resource standard which would form a basis for recurrent funding across all school sectors. The per capita amount suggested for the schooling resource standard was $8000 per primary student and $10,500 per secondary student. There would be additional loadings for particular needs including disadvantaged students, Indigenous students, students with English language learning difficulties, disabled students, school size and school location. The Gonski approach further insisted that all schools with similar student populations, government or non-government, needed the same level of resourcing. The new system would be reviewed every four years and realistically indexed within those four years to ensure it continued to meet community aspirations.[38]

As to the vexed question of private contributions to non-government schools, that would be addressed by assessing a school community's historical capacity to raise contributions over time, with an SES formula as the starting point before any subsequent modifications began. In other words, there would be a gradual

---

[38] This is a rather naïve suggestion since there exist across Australia communities that, for a variety of reasons, have low educational aspirations or, even worse, are anti-school.

CHAPTER TEN

transition to a new scheme that would not penalise schools for raising too much money privately.

Overall, the wealthiest 25 per cent of non-government schools could expect a 10 per cent per capita Gonski funding contribution based on the new schooling resource standard. On a sliding scale, the least wealthy schools would receive up to 80 per cent of the schooling resource standard. This is the crucial private funding section of the report:

> For most non-government schools the public contribution would be reduced as the capacity of the school and parents to contribute to the cost of schooling increases. If the actual private contribution exceeded that which is anticipated in the funding formula, a non-government school would have total resources in excess of the resource standard. Non-government schools would not be required to raise private income or fees equivalent to the anticipated private contribution.[39]

In that part of the report, the panel indicated that its proposed scheme would take into account the government's promise that not a dollar in Commonwealth contributions would be lost by any non-government school.

The initial response from major stakeholders was positive, if guarded. 'Show us the money' was the common refrain. Bill Daniels, executive director of ISCA, was pleased that a complex solution was being offered for a complex problem but was taken aback by a promised additional period of consultation and argued that schools needed a detailed dollar figure, not just a framework. 'Without the money it's not going to work', he added, later firming up ISCA's

---

[39] *Review of Funding for Schooling: Final Report*, Canberra, Department of Education, Employment and Workplace Relations, 2011, p.173.

doubts with an August announcement of a 'hit list' campaign.[40] AEU president Angelo Gavrielatos wanted legislation for the money and the changes to take place in 2012 not 2013. Chris Watt, federal secretary of the Independent (Catholic) Education Union, asserted that unless the federal government put the recommended $5 billion into the scheme, Catholic systemic schools would suffer. Business Council of Australia chief executive Jennifer Westacott supported the idea of a basic resource funding level.[41] The common issue that non-government schools had with the report was that the panel had not provided any detailed recommendations about money.

At this stage, Gillard (and Garrett), beset by other budgetary problems, were weakening the Gonski cause by not putting a detailed forward estimates figure on the proposed reforms during that initial period. By now, Gillard and Garrett faced three major Gonski problems. First, in meeting the not-a-dollar-less criterion (voiced by Kemp and Howard in 1996 as a trap for the ALP) Gillard had created a continuing level of expectation, tying the government to maintaining favourable funding levels to non-government schools at existing levels, whatever their needs might or might not be. Second, not outlining how the money would be allocated gave the impression that the proposed changes were not fully costed and the government was hiding something, perhaps a cut to non-government funding. This led to damaging media speculation. The third issue was the enforced implementation delay caused by pressure from the powerful Catholic lobby. This hesitation gave the states and territories, as well as the major stakeholders, enough time to press for individual

---

[40] '300 schools face funding cuts ... but Gillard stands firm on pledge', *Sunday Herald Sun*, 19 August 2011.

[41] Educators back broad direction of findings', *Canberra Times*, 21 February 2012.

CHAPTER TEN

deals, time for the Opposition to build a negative image of what was a generally well-received set of proposals, and time for Gonski supporters to become discontented.

The Opposition's approach to the Gonski report was both precipitate and contradictory. Originally the Opposition had declared in July 2011 it would support the Gonski model as long as Gillard kept the SES, an oxymoronic position at best and a devious declaration at worst. Education spokesman Christopher Pyne, whose electorate of Sturt contained eight non-government schools, then rejected the 286-page report out of hand. This rejection apparently came before he had read it and certainly before Gillard had even had the chance to respond to it. Pyne characterised the report's findings as a class-based assault, an ALP attempt to 'attack middle Australia'.[42] In denouncing the report, Pyne declared that a Coalition government would retain the existing SES model in which non-government schools would receive an additional $4.2 billion over the next funding period 2014–17.

Pyne's illogical and brazen approach was apparently based on three premises. First, the Gonski plan was an ALP initiative and had to be opposed on partisan political grounds. Second, the Coalition's relentless personal and political campaign against Gillard as an 'illegitimate' prime minister, especially after her minority government took power in the 2010 election, had to be continued. Finally, the original Gonski plan, Gillard's pet project, must be resisted on personal grounds.[43] More important than any of these motivations

---

[42] 'Coalition rejects Gonski plan', *Australian Financial Review*, 21 February 2012. Attacks on 'middle Australia' were quite a theme with Pyne. See his ABC Lateline interview 13 May 2011, http://www.abc.net.au/lateline/content/2011/s3216780.htm.

[43] 'I think it's fair to say that Julia Gillard has never been elected by the Australian public to be Prime Minister. She took over eight weeks ago because of faction

– 241 –

for a Coalition rejection of the well-received report was Gonski's attempt from the outset to bring in a funding system that was fair to all schools. Clearly Pyne wanted to retain a system that was unfair to the majority of schools. That angle was to become the basis of his and Tony Abbott's response to Gonski: the desire to preserve favouritism instead of offering fairness.[44] Accordingly, their intention was that the original Gonski would never get past the Opposition. Pyne had written the script and set up the stage and whatever came afterwards was merely political play-acting on the Coalition's part, with Pyne a consummate political actor.

Following on from Pyne's rejection of the Gonski report there ensued a period of educational skirmishing during 2012–13 while the already scheduled additional period of national funding consultations took place. Pyne's approach throughout the rest of 2012 varied from scare campaigns (school fees would go up), to diversion (the money should go to improving teacher quality), hyperbole (Gonski would cost $113 billion), falsehoods (Australia had one of the most equitable education systems in the world), obfuscation (the Left worry too much about class sizes), prevarication (if elected the Opposition would delay starting the reforms for two years), and more diversion (Australia needs a different reform agenda for schools). The point that all of Pyne's assertions had in common was that Gillard's version of the proposed Gonski reforms, whatever it might be, would undoubtedly damage the non-government school system.

---

leaders giving her the job and now two country independents have given her the job, so it's fair to say this government doesn't have any legitimacy', Christopher Pyne, SBS program *Lateline*, 8 September 2010.

44   Abbott was quite blatant about it. See his speech at the August ISCA conference.

CHAPTER TEN

As 2012 progressed, demands increased from all the major stakeholders, including the states and territories, non-government school lobbyists and government school lobbyists, for a detailed statement about funding from the government. Disappointingly for the education community as a whole, the May budget figures for proposed education spending included money for a 'Schoolkids Bonus' and some additional funding for a laptop program, but no mention of a commitment to Gonski, which had been expected to be funded within the framework of the former Howard government's National Plan for School Improvement. While the government's lack of commitment at that stage was unsurprising, since Gillard had already put any reform package off until 2013, it left an impression that the Gonski reforms, now estimated to cost $6.5 billion, might be unattainable. And the lack of a detailed plan left a gap in the government's defences

Jumping in to fill the gap, Opposition leader Tony Abbott decided to raise the redistribution issue in speaking to the mid-year 2012 ISCA conference in Canberra. Reviving the Coalition's inverted social justice and reverse zero-sum arguments, Abbott claimed that public education received too much government funding, taking money away from the non-government sector. His conclusion was simply expressed: 'So there is no question of injustice to public schools here. If anything, the injustice is the other way'.[45]

Gillard met the Opposition criticisms by giving some impetus to her flagging education campaign in her September speech at the National Press Club, with a much-delayed response to Gonski. Gillard outlined a 'national crusade' for 2013, which would include

---

[45] Cit. 'Public schools get too much', *The Sydney Morning Herald*. 21 August 2012.

scrapping the SES model and introducing the Schooling Resource Standard. The prime minister forecast that the forthcoming 2013 election would be fought over education issues and that electors could expect, 'Big controversy, big headlines, big criticism', but the reform package was, 'the right thing to do, the Labor thing to do. And you'll see more of it.'[46]

By the end of the year, the government brought in the first reading of the Australian Education Bill on 28 November 2012. It was an aspirational statement rather than a detailed account of how Gonski would be implemented. Sought-after details of the proposed split between public education and non-government funding remained missing.[47] On 29 January 2013 Gillard then called a surprise general election for 14 September that year, supposedly to give the ALP time to prepare for a huge battle over education and welfare. Perhaps inadvertently, Gillard also gave the Abbott-led opposition yet more time to continue to wreck her political ambitions.

In the New Year, Coalition-led jurisdictions Queensland, Victoria, Western Australia and the Northern Territory, as well as the Catholic and non-government school sectors, expressed continuing anxieties about their schools losing out to needier government schools and, on that basis, objections to any specific Gonski-style changes if and when they were announced. The remaining jurisdictions of Tasmania, New South Wales, ACT and South Australia continued their negotiations with the Gillard government. These and other talks then led to a government safeguarding of the funding positions of

---

[46]   Cit., 'Big earners to be hit by education "crusade"', *The Sydney Morning Herald*, 4 September 2012.

[47]   Gillard's reason for the 2012-13 delay was that the states and territories were not yet ready to enter detailed negotiations.

CHAPTER TEN

Catholic and other non-government schools, an electorally cautious stance which was to be later also taken up by Victoria's incoming ALP government.[48]

In April 2013, the Commonwealth Government's reform plan was labelled the National Education Reform Agreement within which the Gillard government's extra $9.4 billion over six years (later known as 'the full Gonski') was to be based in part on controversial higher education cuts, a move that provoked yet more heat from the Opposition.[49] The Gonski plan still needed an implementation agreement from all the states and territories, and Gillard's biggest jurisdictional obstacles were New South Wales, Western Australia and Queensland. In New South Wales, experienced and amenable Liberal premier Barry O'Farrell had encountered a problem with the Gonski-style plan's indexation. New South Wales had been hit particularly hard by the 2008–09 Global Financial Crisis, and although he was open to the Gillard plan his position was that he was unable to meet the 5 per cent AGSRC-style annual increase in funding that would allow New South Wales schools to reach the proposed Schooling Resource Standard.

With a Council of Australian Governments (COAG) meeting due on 19 April 2013 and Pyne having labelled the government's model a 'Conski', Gillard needed to get O'Farrell's agreement prior to COAG to bolster her case, if only because New South Wales was the most populous and most politically influential state in Australia. To help, the Commonwealth's Treasury and Finance departments came

---

[48] In March 2015, a Victorian ALP government allocated a flat (as in neither sector-blind nor needs-based) 25 per cent of its own education budget to Catholic and other private schools, to howls of protests from Victoria's government school lobby.

[49] Pyne actually favoured reducing Commonwealth funding for universities and deregulating higher education but that policy was to come later.

up with a lower indexation figure for O'Farrell. Commonwealth funding for New South Wales was now to be indexed at 4.7 per cent while state funding was cut back to 3 per cent.

Meanwhile, the inexperienced and confrontational Liberal National Party state premier of Queensland, Campbell Newman (2012–15), having already shown his disposition by describing Gonski as a 'bucket of custard' [slang for vomit] and banning Peter Garret from Queensland government schools, turned up at COAG, according to Gillard, 'looking for a fight'.[50] Campbell found an ally in the long serving, parochial Liberal premier of Western Australia, Colin Barnett, who had just won a second term of office (9 March). Barnett was planning state-wide education cuts and had originally been opposed to an 'Over East' imposition of an interventionist national funding solution by any Commonwealth Government. Gillard's anxieties about the prospects of a common agreement proved accurate. COAG ended with no Commonwealth agreement with any jurisdiction. On 23 April, however, and after further Canberra-Sydney phone negotiations, O'Farrell accepted the revamped indexation model and, over time, brought the less recalcitrant of his conservative colleagues along with him. Gillard's reforms had passed the jurisdictional test even if not all states had signed off on the deal straight away.[51]

There was another trial that Gillard had to deal with, one from within Cabinet, where the champions of the new and costly National Disability Insurance Scheme (NDIS) were competing with education

---

[50] 'Queensland Premier Campbell Newman slams Gonski deal as a "bucket of custard"', *Courier Mail*, 26 June 2013; Gillard. p.265.

[51] The states that had not signed the agreement by year's end were Queensland, Western Australia and the Northern Territory.

CHAPTER TEN

for money. There were also challenges from education stakeholders, from the knife-edge parliamentary process, from still discontented state and territory malcontents, but more immediately from the ALP caucus itself. On 26 June 2013, with a string of negative opinion polls affecting ALP morale, Gillard became the second sitting prime minister to be ousted during a first term of office, in this case by her once banished predecessor Kevin Rudd.[52] On the very day that the prime minister lost her job, the third reading of her and Garrett's Australian Education bill passed through the Senate.

In summary, the legislation established goals for Australian schooling, provided grants of financial assistance to states and territories for their schools, gave recurrent funding for participating and non-participating schools as well as capital funding and other standard forms of support. Crucially, the legislation contained controversial provisos regarding ministerial oversight that included a requirement to refund money spent on resources or activities not approved by Canberra.[53] The Gillard compromises had also led to an abandonment of uniformity of provision, a crucial aim of the original Gonski panel's report. Furthermore, there was no mention of the Gonski Report's National Schools Resourcing Board, the collective jurisdictional body that, it was hoped, would oversee the distributive process. What Australia had instead was a system that still left space for long-established and deleterious political dogfights about education resources between states and territories, and between the jurisdictions and the Commonwealth. Gillard, while pushing

---

[52] Rudd had been the first. In a remarkable chain of events, Abbott was to become the third in September 2015.

[53] Parliamentary Business: Australian Education Bill 2013, Parliament of Australia, http://www.aph.gov.au/Parliamentary_Business/Bills_Legislation/Bills_Search_Results/Result?bId=r4945.

through the full Gonski in terms of funding, had abandoned the original Gonski in terms of process. And Australia was left with multiple Gonskis instead of a single national scheme.[54]

---

[54] There were eight state and territory agreements, eight Catholic agreements and a single non-Catholic agreement. Beyond that figure there were separate agreement for the minor denominations. Out of the seventeen major agreements, only the 900 ISCA schools (out of 9000 nationally) had agreed to the full Gonski. The 2013 onwards Coalition government claimed that there were twenty-seven Gonski agreements in all.

Chapter Eleven

CHRISTOPHER PYNE

Blowing Himself and the Gonski Reforms to Pieces

With Rudd now back in charge, Bill Shorten, Minister for Workplace Relations and skilled union negotiator, took over education from a discontented and bitter Garrett who, like Gillard, left politics altogether.[1] A revitalised Rudd now proposed to make changes to the Gillard education strategy by reconceptualising it as a six-year, $14.5 billion *Better Schools* program. This would include self-management (already established in several states), a coordinated national curriculum (already underway since 2010), and more testing of students (already tested at years three, five, seven and nine).

With a revitalised but vulnerable prime minister in The Lodge and a new education minister in office there then followed a protracted and highly publicised series of post-COAG stand-offs between Canberra and the more intractable conservative jurisdictions of Victoria, Northern Territory, Western Australia, Tasmania and Queensland. The main issue was the well-worn complaint about whether or not the Commonwealth's promise of extra money gave Canberra a statutory right to intervene in local education matters.

---

[1] Shorten had been Minister for Workplace Relations since 2011. He kept his position in that portfolio while dealing with education.

These more stubborn jurisdictions wanted legislated safeguards against such an eventuality.[2] After much blustering and haggling, all but three of the recalcitrants caved-in, with Victoria crucially falling into line in early August. The interventionist section of the legislation remained intact.

As for other major stakeholders, ISCA had already accepted the *Better Schools* plan in July 2013, while the National Catholic Education Commission had wrangled a special deal from Shorten and Rudd, allowing them to be exempt from the Schooling Resource Standard. The systemic Catholic schools were to keep the old socio-economic model. The Catholic systemic schools were also to retain their existing internal redistribution system, effectively giving the Catholics special state-within-a-state privileges.

The consequence was that the original Gonski intention of providing a sector-blind and equitable funding basis for all schools – based on the Schooling Resource Standard – had been reshaped by negotiated deals with the jurisdictions, with the Catholic system and with the smaller denominational groups of schools. In the non-government sector, only the ISCA schools would be bound to the original Gonski model, bearing in mind Gillard's assurance about their not losing a dollar. The upshot was that the principles of the original Gonski had by now been thoroughly compromised by these individual deals, some of them negotiated in secret, contrary to the Gonski panel's call for transparency. This turn of events exasperated supporters of the original Gonski and delighted the Opposition, which later plucked

---

[2] The concern was about three sections in the Australian Education Act. They were Section 105, which allowed the federal minister to issue directives which must be obeyed without any other recourse, and Sections 24 and 77, which made funding conditional on the states abiding by regulations that can be amended by Commonwealth directive.

CHAPTER ELEVEN

the figure of twenty-seven individual Gonski deals out of the air to attack the Rudd government's version of Gonski as a chaotic failure, bargained away by Gillard's caving in to stakeholders.

The next major development in the Gonski saga came in mid-winter 2013. To the surprise of media and education observers, Abbott and Pyne suddenly announced at a 2 August press conference that under the banner of its 'Students First' election platform, the Coalition would now be supporting the ALP's funding position in full. Having vehemently opposed Gonski for the first half of the year, Abbott explained his point of view:

> We will make sure that no school is worse off. The essential difference between Labor and the Coalition going into the coming election is not over funding, it's over the amount of control that the Commonwealth Government should have. Under the Coalition, you'll get the funding but you won't get the strings attached so what I want to say today is that as far as school funding is concerned, Kevin Rudd and I are on a unity ticket. There is no difference between Kevin Rudd and myself when it comes to school funding.[3]

Pyne, who had publicly announced on the previous day that Gonski was a 'great con' and a 'mirage', immediately changed tack and now supported his leader. 'You can vote Liberal or Labor and you'll get exactly the same amount of funding for your *school*' [author's italics]:

> ... we will adopt exactly the same funding envelope as Labor over the forward estimates so that school principals and parents, that school systems, states and territories can plan from 2014 and onwards knowing that they will attract exactly the same

---

[3] Cit. *Senate Committee on School Funding Report*, 2014, pp.87–88. http://www.aph.gov.au/Parliamentary_Business/Committees/Senate/School_Funding/School_Funding. The Coalition also promised to remove the contentious Commonwealth control Sections.

funds whether they are in the new model or out of the new model that Labor would have given them if the school system had gone ahead as planned.⁴

The Coalition then went into the 7 September 2013 general election ostensibly having promised a bipartisan, Gonski-style approach to needs-based funding, with $15 billion extra over six years with $10 billion coming from Canberra and the rest from states and territories.⁵

Why the August backflip? Prior to the September election, the Opposition was suddenly facing a resurgent Rudd-led ALP and found itself hamstrung in devising its anti-Gonski education platform because of a 2011 much-quoted comment of Abbott's: 'It is an absolute principle of democracy that governments should not and must not say one thing before an election and do the opposite afterwards'.⁶ Realising that a pre-election rejection of the popular Gonski model could diminish his election chances, and aware that accepting the model would lessen Commonwealth funding for the wealthier non-government schools, Abbott chose to take an unusual

---

4   Cit. *Senate Committee on School Funding Report*, 2014, pp.87–88. The 'con' statement was on ABC radio on 1 August. See 'School switch has taught us a lot about Abbott', *Herald-Sun*, 9 August 2013. Abbott must have directed Pyne into the new line of thinking overnight. None of the major media outlets saw it as anything other than Coalition support for the Gonski-model. See, for example, 'Gillard's gone, but Gonski reforms are here to stay', *Australian Financial Review*, 5 August 2013.

5   The other funding features were that all schools would now be funded on the same per-student school resource basis ($9,271 for primary students and $12,193 for secondary students) plus additional loadings for special resource needs (low-income families, students with disabilities, students from non-English speaking backgrounds and students living in rural and remote areas).

6   *Hansard*, 22 May 2011, http://parlinfo.aph.gov.au/parlInfo/search/display/display.w3p;query=Id%3A%22chamber%2Fhansardr%2Fc98fcd9b-9e94-4cb9-b317-af35f8e25267%2F0103%22. In July, after the Rudd takeover, the previously disastrous ALP polls now began to pick up to a point where the two parties were neck and neck.

CHAPTER ELEVEN

route in formulating the Coalition's new education policy, taking a loyal Pyne along with him.[7]

Their carefully-constructed joint promise in August 2013 to support the ALP's funding commitment did not directly mention Gonski nor the *Better Schools* program. Indeed, Abbott's use of the deliberately imprecise expression 'you'll get the funding', and Pyne's equally vague mention of a 'funding envelope' were intended to suggest that the Coalition had accepted Gonski, while actually forming the basis of a different position altogether. This was a cynical promise designed to neutralise the ALP's electoral advantage from supporting Gonski.

After a resounding general electoral triumph based largely on anti-asylum seeker/refugee issues, the Coalition quickly changed its mind about education, to the fury of Gonski supporters. Newly-installed education minister Pyne announced on 27 November that the Abbott government would maintain existing commitments to funding for 2014 but, after that, the government would renegotiate funding arrangements with the states and territories. The Gonski model was an 'utter shambles'.[8] This was to be a foreshortened version of Gonski. Now Australia had three versions of Gonski: the original, the full and the short, not to mention the alleged twenty-seven special deals.

---

[7] In June 2017, Pyne revealed in controversial circumstances that while he had been loyal to Abbott as party leader, he was a firm supporter of Abbott's party rival, Malcolm Turnbull. See, 'Christopher goes the Full Pyne as moderates' roast gives conservatives indigestion', *Guardian Australia*, 26 June 2017. For Abbott quote, see Parliamentary speech, *Hansard*, 22 August 2011, http://parlinfo.aph.gov.au/parlInfo/search/display/display.w3p;query=Id%3A%22chamber%2Fhansardr%2Fc98fcd9b-9e94-4cb9-b317-af35f8e25267%2F0103%22.

[8] Cit. 'Coalition to ditch Gonski model and renegotiate school funding agreements, says Education Minister Christopher Pyne', ABC News, 27 November 2017, http://www.abc.net.au/news/2013-11-26/pyne-adamant-gonski-school-funding-needs-overhaul2c-despite-st/5116978.

Abbott explained the sudden *volte face* to conservative columnist and television presenter Andrew Bolt during an odd interview in which, while each seemed to be talking at cross purposes, the mid-year tactic was made clear. The total amount of funding might be the same in the short term but no promises had been made about distribution:

> TONY ABBOTT: I think Christopher said 'schools' – plural – will get the same amount of money. The quantum will be the same.
>
> ANDREW BOLT: I hear that. 'Schools', plural. People just saw the [TV] grab. They heard 'school', your 'school', singular, and I don't understand why that promise was made. I would go a billion dollars into debt just to keep your promise. I don't know why you don't commit to it.
>
> TONY ABBOTT: But Andrew, we are going to keep our promise. We are going to keep the promise that we actually made, not the promise that some people thought that we made or the promise that some people might have liked us to make. We're going to keep the promise that we actually made.[9]

However, despite post-election feelings of euphoria and even triumphalism, as evinced in the above exchange, the Abbott government was soon to be a troubled affair. Despite a thirty-five-seat majority in the House of Representatives, the Coalition had to face a potentially tumultuous Senate with eight independently-minded crossbenchers who held the balance of power, and who would cause the Coalition considerable grief over the next two years.

---

[9] Ten Network, *The Bolt Report*, 1 December 2013, cit. Russell Marks, What Abbott Said… *The Monthly*, 27 May 2014, https://www.themonthly.com.au/blog/russell-marks/2014/05/27/1401138538/tony-abbott-said.

CHAPTER ELEVEN

Shortly after the 2013 election campaign, the prime minister quickly lost almost all of the political capital he had gained. His initial electoral approval and his capacity to act were adversely affected by several unexpected factors. First, there was the increasing unpopularity within the Coalition of his micro-managing chief of staff Peta Credlin. Then came his party's failure to deal successfully with the independently-minded Senate crossbenchers who blocked much of treasurer Joe Hockey's inequitable and hugely unpopular May 2014 budget. The government was further affected by Abbott's own idiosyncratic decision-making technique and, in a broader context, his failure to observe his promises of no cuts to health and the ABC and, notwithstanding his pre-election sophistry, no cuts to education.

According to University of Melbourne political scientist Sally Young, by mid-2015 Abbott had been the least effective legislative prime minister since the late 1960s and was being touted as a worse prime minister than the unfortunate William McMahon (1971–72), previous holder of that dismal record.[10] In September 2015, after a succession of poor polls and with a general election due in 2016, Abbott was ousted from the leadership of the Liberal party by his urbane and, at that time, political centrist rival Malcolm Turnbull.

Christopher Pyne's term in office as education minister had been almost as fraught and unsuccessful as that of his immediate superior. Pyne arrived in office having been appointed shadow education

---

[10] 'Is Tony Abbott's regime the worst federal government ever?' *Sydney Morning Herald*, 4 August 2015. See, among others, 'Kicking the Abbott', *The Saturday Paper*, 13 February, 2017, and 'Australian PM Tony Abbott labelled 'most incompetent' Western leader by US think tank expert', *The Independent*, 12 February 2015. An 11 March 2016 poll published by *The Australian* in 'John Howard retains voter standing as best PM of modern era' had Abbott as 'least best [sic]' prime minister.

– 255 –

spokesman in September 2008 by Turnbull. He kept that position throughout the Coalition's opposition period 2008–13, adding to his tasks the onerous and time-consuming job of manager of opposition business in the House of Representatives, in February 2009.

Pyne, a brash parliamentary character, was a much more active manager of opposition business than he was an education spokesman. Indeed, Pyne gave the impression of having spent much more of his time harassing the Rudd/Gillard/Rudd governments than of concentrating on his nominal position as education minister-in-waiting. As one measure of his public profile during his 2008–13 tenure as shadow education spokesman, he received a mere 66 mentions as schools specialist in the *Sydney Morning Herald* compared with his 478 general political mentions, an average of fewer than one school education mention per month, and this during the BER, My School, and the Gonski controversies.[11] In contrast, his immediate predecessor as education shadow minister, the ALP's Jenny Macklin, a less flamboyant and much more measured parliamentarian, averaged three times that number of mentions across 2001–06 while simultaneously holding down the position of deputy party leader.[12] In other words, as a potential education minister, Pyne made a good manager of parliamentary business. Nevertheless, he was appointed to a senior Cabinet job in education.[13]

---

[11] Factiva database search for mentions in the *Sydney Morning Herald* for 'Christopher Pyne and school' and 'Christopher Pyne', 16 September 2008-13 November 2013.

[12] Factiva database search for mentions in the *Sydney Morning Herald* for 'Jenny Macklin and school', 25 November 2001 to 12 October 2006.

[13] Tellingly, in his political memoir (Christopher Pyne, *A Letter to my Children*, Carlton, Melbourne University Press, 2015) Pyne refers only to his the 2009-13 Opposition house business role when commenting on that section of his career p.205.

CHAPTER ELEVEN

While appearing to be a hard-nosed and relentless warrior for the Liberal cause, Pyne's politics are actually quite progressive.[14] He was a prominent supporter of Indigenous land rights, history and culture in the 1990s when this was an unfashionable position on his side of politics. Pyne is also a republican in a largely monarchist party and a supporter of gay rights and same sex marriage, again unfashionable views in his own party. Pyne supports mental health reform also and has a strong personal social justice agenda based on, in his words, 'a society in which all individuals equally have access to the greatest and fairest possible opportunities'.[15]

This character appraisal seems inconsistent with his actions as a politician, considering his track record as a fairly lax opposition education spokesman and bearing in mind his almost hyperactively negative attitude and activities as an education minister in the Abbott government. But Pyne's own words and actions as well as media reports seem to suggest there are at least four Christopher Pynes. There is the private Pyne, a thoughtful Catholic family man with a progressive worldview, revealed in his engaging, if self-enhancing and frothy, memoir. There is the occasionally-glimpsed congenial and cheerful politician Pyne who has friends on both sides of politics, that include self-described fighter of Tories Anthony Albanese and the redoubtable ALP Senator Penny Wong.[16] There is Pyne the exasperating and irrepressible parliamentary attack dog who very effectively carried out his partisan duty to harass the ALP (and the Greens) at every

---

[14] A contradiction that is explained by his 26 June 2017 revelation of where his personal loyalty lay as opposed to his organisational loyalty.

[15] Pyne, p.192.

[16] Albanese is MP for the New South Wales seat of Grayndler. South Australian Wong is the intimidating ALP leader in the Senate and a relentless interrogator of the conservative side of politics.

turn. Finally, there is Pyne the foppish bourgeois South Australian who is distrusted by the more conservative elements among his party's ranks as an ambitious and self-serving leaker.[17]

Pyne also held to the kind of traditional Liberal outlook that preferred individual effort, as opposed to governmental direction, as the basis for a good life, asserting that denominationally-based schools were superior to the purportedly functional and collectivist government schools. In other words, Pyne was an out-and-out supporter of non-government schools and he believed that his job as education minister was to shift public expectation of what constituted good public educational provision from the not-quite-good-enough government school sector to the non-government sector. He played a part in creating this dynamic by blocking Gonski and ensuring that non-government schools continued to receive a disproportionate amount of Commonwealth funding. Professedly, an educational avenue for individual achievement within aspirational families of all classes, would be provided. The reality was a little different.

Once in office, Pyne announced three major initiatives which were to become the key policy goals of his ministry. Pyne's first proclamation in late September was a deregulation of university fees, a move that would disadvantage students from lower socio-economic backgrounds. He combined that proposal with planned cuts to student services, and the reintroduction of capped places, overturning a Gillard open door admissions policy.[18] Pyne even advocated collecting fees from dead students who still owed the government money

---

[17] See for example, 'Poodle or attack dog, Pyne shakes off critics on both sides', *The Sydney Morning Herald*, 15 March 2009. Gillard had described him as a 'mincing poodle'.

[18] Pyne had announced prior to the election that he would not cap places.

CHAPTER ELEVEN

under the Higher Education Contribution scheme or HECS. These higher education policy announcements of measures guaranteed to provoke ALP, union, parent and student outrage, alarmed the Prime Minister's Office (PMO). Abbott, locking the stable door after the horse had bolted, immediately issued a directive banning ministers from giving interviews without clearance from the PMO.[19] After a long and bitter struggle, Pyne's university deregulation plan, labelled a '$100,000 degree' policy in an alarmist campaign orchestrated by the new leader of the Opposition, Bill Shorten, was to be defeated; blocked by the Senate in March 2015.

Pyne's second major initiative was a controversial declaration that he would instigate a 2014 review of the national curriculum, initially proposed by Tony Abbott in early September 2013.[20] The first four-subject phase of the national curriculum had been agreed to by the states and territories and partially introduced in December 2010, with two more phases to follow.[21] There were three unusual aspects of this review. First, the critique was to take place before the national curriculum had been fully implemented. Second, one of the key features of the review was to be a search for left-wing bias, especially in the history curriculum. Third, the two reviewers named by Pyne to head the inquiry were freelance education consultant Kevin Donnelly

---

[19] 'Coalition to scrap uni fees, targets', *The Age*, 25 September 2013 and 'Abbott gags ministers on media interviews', *The Age*, 26 September 2013.

[20] 'New broom Pyne ready to reshape curriculum', *Sydney Morning Herald*, 28 September 2013, and 'Abbott to right what's left of school history', *The Advertiser*, 3 September 2013.

[21] This section on the national curriculum review draws on the author's article, 'Resisting the Regime: an insider's view of the politics of Australian history education 2006–2014', published in *The International Journal of Historical Learning Teaching and Research*, 14.1, Autumn, 2016, pp.16–27.

and business academic Ken Wiltshire, both Liberal Party supporters with strongly-held anti-progressive views about modern curriculum.

The review was greeted with dismay by most educators, who regarded it as an ideological investigation inspired by the ideas of the Institute of Public Affairs, a neo-conservative, self-described 'independent, non-profit public policy think tank'.[22] As it turned out, Pyne's national curriculum review, already under fire because of its ideological origins, became more of a farce than an aggressive politicised inquisition. In July 2014, Donnelly announced during a radio interview that he was in favour of corporal punishment 'if it's done properly', citing a personal experience of the benefits of corporal punishment, it emerged, was a confabulation.[23] Outrage ensued and education minister Pyne was forced to disown Donnelly's views while still hanging on to him as a reviewer. The credibility of the curriculum review, already trending downwards, was by now in steep decline.

The Donnelly-Wiltshire review's final report, published on 10 October 2014, made thirty recommendations overall, that included the IPA's demand for a greater focus on Western civilisation and Australia's 'Judeo-Christian' heritage in the history curriculum. The review also demanded reducing content in an overcrowded history curriculum, improving parental engagement generally, dealing with students with a disability, and 'rebalancing the curriculum' – code for reducing Indigenous and Asian content.

---

[22] The IPA wanted the national curriculum scrapped altogether because of its alleged left-wing bias. The 2013 version of the IPA was descendant of the original Adam Smith-style free market think tank founded in 1943. By 2013 the IPA had turned into a lobby group that represented corporate interests. It was staffed by a mix of young neo-conservative and libertarian ideologues who seemed to regard the IPA as a stepping stone to a parliamentary career.

[23] Corporal punishment is banned in Australian government schools and it is rarely if ever used in private schools.

CHAPTER ELEVEN

In late October, just over a week after the review's report was released, the office emails of Barry Spurr, review team member and Sydney University's poetry professor, were leaked to the media. Spurr had been appointed by Donnelly and Wiltshire to investigate the English literature component of the review's work. The emails in question, sent to colleagues and friends, were an offensive mix of homophobic, sexist and racist rants. Controversy ensued and Spurr was suspended by his university. He then left the curriculum review team and resigned from his university in December 2014. Once again, in the face of a media storm and public ridicule, education minister Pyne was forced to disown the views of a senior member of his hand-picked review team.

Nevertheless, Pyne steadfastly pressed on (he had little choice in the matter) and was ready to present a by-now discredited review's findings to the education ministers' council meeting in December 2014. This review being all about politics, Pyne cheerfully announced that the report was, 'a valuable, well researched, and well considered piece of work'.[24]

At that time, the Abbott government was in deep trouble, from a series of policy gaffes going back to that almost universally panned May 2014 budget. State Nationals MP Adrian Piccoli, the then New South Wales minister of education, took advantage of the weakness of the out-of-favour Abbott government and announced that his state would not necessarily implement any Pyne-initiated changes to the national curriculum. If New South Wales was not going to accept the review's findings, the other states and territories would almost certainly follow suit.

---

[24] Pyne media centre release 12 October 2014, 'Curriculum review and initial Government response released', https://ministers.education.gov.au/pyne/curriculum-review-and-initial-government-response-released.

The Education Council (of state and territory education ministers) met with Pyne in December 2014, discussed possible changes to the curriculum and referred them to ACARA. The curriculum authority then referred them on to a small number of their own specialist experts, absorbed their feedback and issued an anodyne response. ACARA recommended reducing some content, improving parental engagement and dealing with students with disabilities. The consequence was that the states and territories thought they might get round to the changes in content sometime in the future, or perhaps not. Pyne's review turned out to be a political flop because of its partisan nature and the ineptitude of the reviewers, only reaffirming in the minds of a majority of the education community that the Abbott government, over-reaching wildly on ideological grounds, was not just politically predisposed when it came to education policy, it was also manifestly incompetent.

Pyne's third major policy initiative was described on 25 November 2013 in *The Australian* as a 'back to the drawing board' exercise with the Gonski model. 'Everything needs to be examined fresh, because the model that Labor came up with is a shambles and quite unimplementable', remarked Pyne.'[25] This announcement, made without consulting the states and territories, aroused an immediate public furore that included an uncharacteristic revolt against a Coalition-led Commonwealth Government by the conservative states.[26] Andrew Piccoli, still the New South Wales education minister, was furious with Pyne, telling the media that, 'He's still fighting that [private

---

[25] 'ALP PLAN A SHAMBLES: PYNE Back to drawing board for Gonski'. The other major newspapers published the story the following day. One of Pyne's criticisms was that the Catholics, Tasmania and Victoria and not yet formally signed up for the Better Schools program even though they had planned to do so.

[26] 'Pyne sparks states' revolt on Gonski reversal', *The Australian*, 26 November 2013.

CHAPTER ELEVEN

versus public] war. But that war is over. That war was going on for 20 years, but what Gonski did was end it.'[27]

The general tenor of professional opposition to Pyne's November 2013 review plan was that the actual or proposed nature of the Gonski deals had by now been settled within the *Better Schools* program and was scheduled for introduction in 2014, in just one month's time. Any proposed non-consultative changes would lead to more financial uncertainty for government and non-government school systems alike, that had been preparing for some time for a long-term Gonski-style funding model. The general perception of mainstream, non-News Corp media commentary on the anti-Gonski move was that the government was being damaged by Pyne's latest attack on the Gonski initiative. As an article by experienced political editor Bernard Keane put it, 'Pyne blows himself, and the Gonski reform to pieces'.[28]

Just before Christmas 2013, and under pressure from all sides for being in such an ideologically-inspired muddle, Abbott and Pyne found an extra $2.8 billion to fund all schools and temporarily buy off criticism.[29] Their latest, short version of Gonski would take place during a four-year period, rather than during the *Better Schools* six-year period. The disbursement system, however, would retain all the inconsistencies of the Gillard negotiations.

---

[27] 'Surprise, Coalition backflip infuriates', *Sydney Morning Herald*, 29 November 2013.

[28] 'Pyne blows himself, and the Gonski reform to pieces', *Crikey.com*, 3 December 2013, https://www.crikey.com.au/2013/12/03/pyne-blows-himself-and-the-gonski-reforms-to-pieces/.

[29] In his 3 December article, Keane also pointed out that allocating a lump sum with no state-level accountability was yet another Pyne policy backflip in what he described as 'a complete stuff-up'.

These included two contentious elements. First, the Gillard promise to keep existing SES funding levels that would allow the wealthier non-government schools to receive additional windfall money on top of the Schooling Resource Standard. And second, there was the Gillard promise of allowing the Catholic education system to distribute the funding to systemic schools by using internal SES criteria rather than the supposedly universally-applied Schooling Resource Standard.

In the event, with government schools arguing that they were still inadequately funded under Gonski because of rising costs, and with wealthier non-government schools urging Pyne to abandon the needs-based Gonski model altogether, the Abbott government used a National Audit Commission report and a purported deficit and debt crisis as justifications to cut $1.5 billion from school funding in the government's notorious May 2014 budget.[30] Pyne then continued with his plan to terminate the Gonski model in 2017.[31] On 22 May, David Gonski himself, normally a reticent public figure, publicly attacked the Abbott school funding cuts and argued for retention of the full Gonski:

> We [the Gonski panel] advocated a transparent method for determining funding based on aspirational educational outcomes (rather than last year's costs) and recognising the importance of assisting those suffering disadvantage with the suggestion of five disadvantaged groups with a need for funding loadings. We felt strongly that any funding system

---

[30] Total school funding was expected to reach $25 billion by 2024–25, approximately $5 billion less than under the Better Schools version of the full Gonski deal.

[31] 'Extra funds inadequate for schools', *The Age*, 3 January 2014; 'Private schools say Gonski funding plan "unachievable"', *Sydney Morning Herald*, 14 March 2014; 'Fairer schools for all remains a dream', *Australian Financial Review*, 19 May 2014.

CHAPTER ELEVEN

must ensure differences in educational outcomes were not the result of differences in wealth.[32]

By now, the political argument was heating up even more, with Tony Abbott dismissing the ALP's support for the Gonski model as 'pie-in-the-sky'.[33] Shorten responded to Abbott and Pyne's plans with 'What a lazy, reckless, indifferent mob of swindlers this government are when they say we're not going to have anything more to do with the funding of [government] schools.'[34] Pyne, still assuming that he could get crossbench Senate support to push the education cuts through, announced to Christian school principals that the government had an 'emotional commitment' to non-government schools.[35]

Pyne's assumption that his education amendment bill would be passed was correct. The measure became law on 18 November 2014, stirring up a frenzy of criticism from a wide group of critics including the Australian Education Union, the states and territories (some claiming that they would now lose money) and the Catholic system, anxious about the survival of its regional schools under a new indexation arrangement. Meanwhile, a disarrayed Abbott government, foundering badly in the polls, tried to placate its detractors with a 2014 internal departmental review of school funding and was

---

[32] 'Disappointing direction for school funding', *The Age*, 22 May 2014. Gonksi gave the 2014 Jean Blackburn Memorial Lecture at the University of Melbourne and adapted it into this opinion editorial.

[33] 'Pyne banks on Senate support', *The Australian Financial Review*, 23 May 2015. The Abbott quote is cited in the 23 May article.

[34] 'Budget hostility sad, says auditor; Protesters "too narrow"', *The Canberra Times*, 23 May 2014. Shorten's colourful comment referred to Pyne's support for the privatisation of government schools by turning 1500 government schools into quasi private schools by 2017.

[35] 'Pyne sparks class war', *Sydney Morning Herald*, 31 May 2014.

still attempting to lure government schools into their quasi non-government model with funding promises. In 2015, Abbott and Pyne went further, flagging that it was considering a green paper that argued that the Commonwealth Government should get out of funding public education altogether, a radical proposal that infuriated, among others, former education bureaucrat and Gonski panel member Ken Boston.[36]

After a succession of deteriorating polls the prime minister was fired by his own party in September 2015, to be replaced as prime minister by Malcolm Turnbull. Pyne, whose partisan and inadequate management of his education portfolio (cutting Gonski; deregulating university fees; overseeing a farcical curriculum review) had contributed to the Coalition's poor polling, was shifted out of education. He became Minister of Industry, Innovation and Science and later Minister for Defence Industry, keeping his key position as Leader of the House of Representatives.[37]

If Pyne's term as education minister is judged on his achievement of personal policy ambitions, his contribution to his party's success and his contribution to the national good, unlike most of his predecessors he failed on all three counts. His declared policy ambitions in school education, for example, were to protect non-government schools, privatise public education and review the national curriculum. His behaviour as a minister stirred up such a storm of controversy in

---

[36] 'Gonski architect slams suggested public-private funding split', *The Canberra Times*, 23 June 2015. Boston was, however, in favour of giving full responsibility for public schools to the states and territories within a national Gonski-style funding model.

[37] Pyne moved to Defence after the July 2016 general election, a move almost certainly linked to South Australia's interest in its shipyards gaining contract work from Australia's submarine upgrade program.

CHAPTER ELEVEN

all three areas that the role of non-government schools came under increasingly hostile scrutiny.[38]

As for contributing to the success of his party, there is little doubt that the Abbott government's already dire polling in 2014–15 was adversely affected by Pyne's apparent negativity and cynicism about Gonski as well as by the hip pocket effect of his proposed privatisation of the universities.

When it comes to national good, Pyne did nothing to close the educational gap between disadvantage and privilege in the school education system. Indeed, if he achieved anything at all, he made it clear that he was keen to increase that chasm by supporting wealthy non-government schools at the expense of public education. Bernard Keane summed up Pyne's attitude and role as education minister in damning terms:

> Unlike most issues of government, education is not an esoteric mater for voters. It is persistently one of the most important issues in determining how people will vote, just below the economy and health. And it's an issue where voters don't trust the Coalition as much as Labor. So the first lesson should perhaps be not to wander, smirking, into a shed full of political dynamite and start lighting matches.[39]

On the other hand, Pyne was a very effective manager of the Coalition's parliamentary business in the lower house and outwardly

---

[38] Western Australia had introduced in 2009 its own Independent Public Schools (IPS) education program which was really a devolutionary initiative not a privatization scheme. Queensland had done much the same in 2013. Victoria had devolved its schools in the 1990s, putting increased workplace pressure on principals with a consequent increase in attrition rates and reduction in recruitment applications at the school leadership level. See for example '"This is not something anyone should go through, especially over a job": the sickness plaguing our principals', *The Age*, 23 October 2016.

[39] Keane, 2013.

seemed to have carried out Abbott's IPA-inspired radical education agenda with a strong sense of commitment.[40] As for Gonski, one unnamed Coalition federal Cabinet minister went directly to Pyne's motivation, telling the *Sydney Morning Herald* national affairs editor Tom Allard, 'Pyne has always hated it'.[41]

In September 2015, Pyne was succeeded in education and training by the much more staid and more reflective Simon Birmingham, a South Australian Liberal senator, former assistant education and training minister and a leading anti-Abbott coup plotter. Birmingham's first public comment on taking up the position was an announcement that he was looking forward to 'building on Christopher Pyne's unstinting efforts to ensure Australia has the highest standards of education at all levels, and to working collaboratively with education stakeholders to develop policy and to build broad support for any future reforms'.[42] There was no mention of school funding.

---

[40] Bearing in mind Pyne's later confession in June 2017 that he had been a Turnbull-style moderate in Abbott's clothing.

[41] 'Surprise, Coalition backflip infuriates', *Sydney Morning Herald*, 29 November 2013. If accurate, and there is no reason to suppose it is not, this quote by a Cabinet colleague explains a great deal about Pyne's actions, first as shadow education minister and then as education minister during 2011-15.

[42] 'Birmingham eager to break the deadlock', *The Australian*, 21 September 2015.

Chapter Twelve

SIMON BIRMINGHAM

Still on a Path to Nowhere?

After the antic behaviour of Christopher Pyne, Simon Birmingham's promotion to head the Commonwealth Ministry of Education and Training came to many in the sector as a relief.[1] The new appointee, a self-styled pragmatist who had gained media kudos as assistant minister to Pyne, was faced with three immediate policy concerns.[2] These were expanding childcare provision (including more early years emphasis on the basics), continuing his task of cleaning up the vocational education and training mess (local rorts and low educational standards) caused by a combination of state mismanagement and privatisation, and mending fences with a higher education sector that was looking for more funding certainty (deregulation was now off the table). School funding, not due for a close look until 2017, was put to one side for the time being, although Birmingham did announce in late 2015 that while there were indeed funding issues yet to be

---

[1] Not to Adrian Piccoli in New South Wales, who had publicly berated Birmingham for inadvisedly announcing that Gonski money had not brought educational improvement. 'Piccoli slams new federal counterpart over Gonski', *Sydney Morning Herald*, 24 September 2015. This was a fairly typical Piccoli/New South Wales negotiating shot across the bows at a new federal minister.

[2] See for example, 'Meet Simon Birmingham, a minister doing it right', *Australian Financial Review*, 14 September 2015.

resolved, the Turnbull government had no intention of implementing the full Gonski after 2017.³

During the early months of 2016, Birmingham's approach to school funding policy began with an accountability argument (extra money must bring improved test and examination results) and attacks on the ALP and the teacher unions for continuing to prosecute the Gonski model. The May 2016 budget preliminaries saw an upsurge in school funding policy debates but with no substantive decision yet to be made on changes to the school funding formula for the next funding period 2018–2020, there was still no governmental rush to commit to a new system. This was unsurprising since Turnbull and Birmingham faced seemingly intractable difficulties in attempting to devise a workable and generally acceptable funding model.

The government's first limitation was the continuing popularity of the Gonski model. Even though the full scheme had been rescinded by Pyne and later again by Birmingham, there had been that point in late 2013 when Pyne, in announcing that Gonski was to be dumped, had aroused the hostility of commentators across the political spectrum. Gonski, for all its imperfections, seemed to have gone a long way to solving a public versus private school funding conundrum that had exercised modern Australian public opinion since the Menzies years. From 2013 onwards, needs-based school funding seemed to have become the *sine qua non* of school education funding.

The second of the Turnbull government's problems in this area was over-funding in an estimated 150 non-government schools, a legacy of the SES transition into ERI and the ERI's transition into Gonski. There were also the special deals done by Gillard to get her needs-

---

3 'Coalition backs out of Gonski cash deal', *Sydney Morning Herald*, 29 December 2015.

CHAPTER TWELVE

based reforms through. At the same time, however, hanging around the necks of any needs-based funding reforms like dead albatrosses were the promises by Kemp in 1996, and Gillard in 2013, that no school would lose money moving into any new Commonwealth scheme.[4] These guarantees were now seen by non-government stakeholders, who had benefited from previous promises, as an essential and irrevocable commitment by any reformist government. As for government school supporters, the Kemp and Gillard promises were seen as a fairness issue.

The fairness issue here was that under the 2014–17 Gonski no-loss system, non-government schools' income – even those with the lowest level of private income – plus the schooling resource standard income, plus local state or territory non-government top-ups, exceeded the total income available to any individual government school. Education commentator Trevor Cobbold estimated in early 2016 that because of these variations, the non-government sector, as measured against the schooling resource standard, was being overfunded by $3 billion per annum, a point of view borne out later that year in a discussion during a Senate Estimates Committee hearing. An investigation by Fairfax media then revealed that over 150 non-government schools were overfunded, with some wealthy non-government schools receiving almost 300 per cent of their supposed entitlement, an astonishing figure.[5] What this meant was, for the ISCA schools at least, the Commonwealth funding was more of a surplus than a top-up. In these circumstances, and having done

---

[4] Ken Boston's imagery.

[5] 'Private schools benefit from more than $2 billion in government funding', *The Age*, 30 December 2015, and 'Poor schools fund gap', *The Sydney Morning Herald*, 12 October 2012.

their arithmetic in 2013, it is unsurprising that the ISCA schools signed up for Gonski so quickly.

Turning off the tap of a such a huge and firmly established bonus for the wealthier end of the non-government school sector would raise cries of 'hit lists', with possible floor-crossing in the House of Representatives and the Senate. This could be an electorally damaging development for a Coalition government facing a split between right and left, very poor poll ratings, an unruly Senate and a lower house majority of just one MP. To make matters even more difficult for the government, a surprisingly frank Birmingham announced that, using the current Gonski model, it might take as long as 100 years for some over-endowed non-government schools to get to their actual schooling resource standard funding level, an announcement that seemed to push the education minister firmly and inevitably in the direction of swingeing cuts to non-government school funding.[6]

A third problem was Catholic systemic schools managing their funding distribution within their closed SES-style system. Within that supposedly needs-based model, some wealthy Catholic schools were also overfunded, with, for example, Our Lady of Lourdes Catholic Primary School in Prahran (Melbourne), receiving $11,875 per student compared with neighbouring government primary school South Yarra Primary, whose per student schooling resource standard allocation was $7754 per annum. Not only that, but the

---

[6] 'More than 150 private schools over-funded by hundreds of millions of dollars each year', *Sydney Morning Herald*, 1 October 2016. Fairfax Media had done their own research for this article, which included their list of 150 over-funded schools and the 100 years comment by Birmingham. Turnbull and Birmingham did not help the politics of the education debate by attacking states and territories that allegedly had failed to pass on the benefits of Gonski funding to schools. Embarrassingly for the Liberal prime minister, in Victoria's case, it had been a former Liberal/National state government that had been responsible for that tactic. See 'Funding fails Victoria's schools', *The Age*, 3 February 2017.

CHAPTER TWELVE

Rudd government had struck a last-minute pre-election deal in 2013 with the Catholic schools in the ACT by giving them all a notional carry-over low-resource SES score of 101, when the actual average SES score of ACT Catholic schools was a high resource 118 (in some cases it rose to 128). This meant that ACT Catholic schools attracted much more funding than was their entitlement. Cobbold's figure for Catholic overfunding in the ACT alone was $50 million per annum.[7]

A fourth problem with replacing the Gonski model was to do with arguments about the variations in Commonwealth funding for the states and territories negotiated by successive ALP and Coalition governments in 2013. The most vocal jurisdictional opponent of the modified Gonski agreement was the conservative Western Australian government, which pleaded poverty and unfairness. South Australia too was identified as an underprivileged state while Tasmania and New South Wales were regarded by other jurisdictions as having been especially favoured.[8]

To meet immediate funding issues, in late 2016 the Turnbull government allocated an extra needs-based $1.2 billion to schools for the 2018–2020 funding period. In late March 2017, Birmingham, continuing his policy of non-commitment while announcing short-term funding increases, announced that school funding increases 2017–2020 would now be $3 billion, a revised funding period that allowed 2017's money to be added to what seemed a miserly $1.2 billion and a figure that was closer to the ALP's $4.5 billion.

The amount set aside was nonetheless still far short of the $4.5 billion in Gonski funding promised by the ALP for the same period.

---

[7] 'Sweetheart deals exposed: wealthy Catholic schools benefit from "corruption" of Gonski', *Sydney Morning Herald*, 12 October 2016.

[8] 'States flag "war about fairness" on Gonski changes', *The Australian*, 23 September 2016.

And Birmingham had tied the extra money to performance while indicating that he would discuss funding details with the jurisdictions over the next few months, prior to an Education Council meeting due in April 2017.

This decision to allocate extra funds suggested that the Turnbull government was still trying to work out where it stood on school funding policy. For example, Birmingham argued that funding did not matter anyway when it came to educational achievement. In April 2016 Turnbull suggested the Commonwealth should get out of funding public education altogether. Then, in May 2016, the Treasurer Scott Morrison allocated sizeable funding increases to all schools, a policy announcement that Turnbull took to a July 2016 general election that he hoped would resolve his numbers difficulties in the Senate. The election result was, however, not what Turnbull wanted. His new government faced a still-unmanageable Senate and a diminished Coalition majority in the House of Representatives (one seat, down from the 2013 majority figure of thirty).

After the election, the government still seemed to be baffled about school funding and was clearly putting off the evil day when a hard decision about a new funding model had to be negotiated, a process scheduled for that first 2017 Education Council meeting in Hobart.

In the meantime, Birmingham sat down on Friday 23 September 2016 in Adelaide at an Education Council meeting to begin what would inevitably be a bruising process of setting up such a new deal to replace Gonski. All the jurisdictions, bar Western Australia, wanted the Gonski-style model to continue. Birmingham, borrowing the 'corrupt' turn of phrase from educator Ken Boston (see below), declared that Gonski was gone and he needed a new model, with Commonwealth strings attached. It might need to be based on regulation rather than legislation because of the government's problems in the Senate, he commented.⁹

To the astonishment of educators and politicians alike (including many from his own side of politics) Birmingham then declared on ABC television on the following Monday 26 September that, yes indeed, some non-government schools were overfunded and this anomaly needed to be corrected.¹⁰ This seemingly indiscreet admission, made as part of an argument that Gonski was just not working, came as a break from Liberal Party tradition, directly contradicting the Abbott/Pyne approach and seeming to offer some hope that the Turnbull government was contemplating drawing the two education systems together rather than taking sides in the education debate. Unfortunately, any optimism that politicians were entering new territory was soon to be dispelled.

In response, Tanya Plibersek, ALP education spokesperson, tried to wedge Birmingham by demanding to see the Coalition's 'hit list'. ISCA turned on the Turnbull government, protesting that any cuts would be harmful, while the Catholic school system, preferring to do its protesting behind closed doors, argued that Birmingham should focus on standards rather than just on funding.¹¹

Plibersek, in an attempt to keep the Gonski approach alive, then threw a startlingly un-ALP comment into the mix by announcing that there was no compelling case to cut grants to overfunded non-

---

9   'Birmingham pushes deal on schools', *The Age*, 26 September 2016.
10 ABC program *Q&A*, 26 September 2016.
11 'Private schools turn on Turnbull', *The Sydney Morning Herald*, 28 September 2016 and 'Plibersek no to private school cuts', *The Sunday Age*, 4 December 2016. Plibersek's case (Birmingham's argument too) was that it was a minority of schools who were overfunded and the argument was merely a distraction from Gonski (not Birmingham's point of view).

government schools. In other words, Birmingham and Plibersek, in their desperate attempt to push the anti-Gonski and the pro-Gonski case respectively, were prepared to alarm their own colleagues by advocating the views of the other side. That was new at least. This political posturing, however, seemed at first to be just old-fashioned bluster and partisan hostility.

On 16 December 2016, Birmingham sat down again with the education ministers in another Education Council meeting in Melbourne. The contentious funding issue was put aside temporarily to focus on teacher quality as well as on reading and writing. With funding policy still unresolved and with education ministers arguing in familiar fashion about which jurisdiction should get what, if and when a funding policy was agreed upon, the next Education Council meeting was scheduled for April 2017, just one month before the 2017 budget. It was almost as if nothing had changed. Framing of school funding policy was back in the quarrelsome pre-Gonski era.

Meanwhile, the changing nature of the Australian political landscape following the Coalition's July 2016 narrow election victory provided Turnbull and Birmingham with an additional problem. Thanks to a series of state and territory elections during 2016–17, the Commonwealth Government was now obliged to face an array of ALP jurisdictions (five states and the two territories) administered by pro-Gonski governments.[12] The only state jurisdiction in Coalition hands was New South Wales, with its long and fractious history

---

[12] To demonstrate how strong the pro-Gonski-sentiment was in Australia's two most populous states, News South Wales Nationals' education minister Adrian Piccoli and his ALP Victorian counterpart James Merlino held a joint media conference in Melbourne. Merlino estimated that if the full Gonski was not implemented, Victoria's government schools would lose almost $1 billion per annum and Piccoli estimated that NSW schools would lose $400 million per annum. 'Unholy alliance fights school funding', *The Age*, 19 November 2016.

CHAPTER TWELVE

of conflict with Canberra and now its own concerns about possible Commonwealth non-implementation of Gonski and any possible non-Gonski replacement. Indeed, on the point of being selected as new Liberal state premier, in January 2017, Gladys Berejiklian warned Turnbull and Birmingham:

> It's not just about the money, it's about making sure the money that is available goes to where it is needed most. Quality public education is fundamental to giving everyone in this state equality of opportunity, which I believe is fundamental to a fair go. That's why I will be the strongest advocate for the Gonski reforms.[13]

By this time, the use of the term 'Gonski' had assumed a fixed meaning, implying a fully-funded, needs-based, sector-blind model as the starting point for negotiation. New South Wales and Victoria were taking the lead in demanding a needs-based equitable solution at a time when the Turnbull government was still floundering badly in the polls. To help disarm opposition from a powerful New South Wales political lobby, Birmingham began consulting with Adrian Piccoli.

While the states and territories wanted to keep Gonski as a headline demand, dealing with the real school funding issues would mean that the Commonwealth, states and territories, as Birmingham had suggested, would now have to negotiate a new funding model rather than mend Gonski. There was a consensus that too much tinkering with Gonski had already taken place, giving rise to a sensational September 2016 'corruption' accusation levelled at the Gonski

---

[13] 'Berejiklian gung-ho for Gonski', *The Australian*, 23 January 2017. Berejiklian was following Adrian Piccoli's line. Piccoli had been dumped as education minister in late 2016 because of his controversial approach to educational politics, not because of his point of view.

implementation process by Ken Boston, one of Gonski's principal designers and supporters. Boston, an influential and respected figure in the Australian education community, had found himself in the unexpected position of agreeing with Pyne about the corrupt character of the modified Gonski.[14] Boston argued that the funding of school education was a social justice issue and should be based on providing a public good (for all) and a positional good (for those who can achieve enhanced social or economic status). He was pessimistic about the future of schooling in Australia after the damage done to the Gonski model by both the ALP and the Coalition since 2013. In his view, the fairness, sector-blind, equality of opportunity, financial sustainability and transparency principles that were the original basis of Gonski had gradually been negotiated away during the Gillard and Rudd government discussion with major stakeholders during 2013.

From 2013 onwards Boston had become increasingly unhappy about the fate of Gonski. Indeed, having helped form a post-Gonski educational pressure group, 'The Need to Succeed', in November 2013, Boston publicly intervened several times during 2013–16 in favour of the original Gonski model. By late 2016, with no sign of the Turnbull government wanting to proceed with a modified Gonski, Boston reluctantly admitted that the Gonski initiative had been disastrously botched. In an early September 2016 meeting of educators in Sydney, Boston outlined the failures of the Gillard/ Rudd modified Gonski (including the overfunding problem) and

---

[14] Boston had been Director-General of Education in South Australia and New South Wales as well as Chief Executive of the UK's Qualifications and Curriculum Authority. Birmingham seized on his 'corruption' remark late in 2016 as a justification for new model negotiations.

CHAPTER TWELVE

announced, 'Gonski is history' and that it was not just the Coalition's fault. As Boston put it, 'Kevin Rudd and education minister Bill Shorten hawked this corruption of the Gonski report around the country, doing deals with premiers, bishops and various lobbies'.[15]

Speaking at the same meeting, Chris Bonnor, education researcher from the Centre for Policy Development think tank, concurred: 'Gonski had a solution but now that chance is gone'. Peter Goss, schools education director from the Grattan Institute fell into step: 'Something needs to happen, some new deal needs to be done'. This was the kind of talk that, in late 2016, gave rise in the media to the use of 'post-Gonski' as an adjective.

After the Christmas break, Boston delivered a talk in Brisbane, 'Gonski Review – Vision or Hallucination?', a detailed and pessimistic review of recent funding developments that seemed to be an epitaph for Gonski. He spoke scathingly of the lack of political progress in solving such an important national problem, and declared that because the ALP still saw educational progress in terms of lump sums of money, and the Coalition saw educational progress in terms of maintaining the entitlements of the non-government sector, nothing had changed for the better. His telling conclusion was that when it came to post-Gonski school funding, Australia was still 'on a path to nowhere'.[16]

During that first quarter of 2017, Birmingham, Turnbull and the various education ministers stayed away from funding issues.

---

[15] 'What Gonski really meant, and how that's been forgotten almost everywhere', *Inside Story*, 6 September 2016, http://insidestory.org.au/what-gonski-really-meant-and-how-thats-been-forgotten-almost-everywhere. He was less critical of Gillard.

[16] The text and video of Boston's trenchant speech given at the T.J. Ryan Foundation on 14 February 2017 can be accessed in full at http://www.tjryanfoundation.org.au/cms/page.asp?ID=2707.

Birmingham himself was tied up pushing his child care package through parliament but did have time to launch yet another back-to-basics (phonics) initiative late in January. In early February, he took time to criticise the states for cutting school funding out of their budgets while relying on the Gonski supplement to meet their bills. Malcolm Turnbull's contribution to the schooling debate was a mid-January education intervention in which he extolled the virtues of the teaching profession as a rebuke to ill-advised comments by Coalition backbencher Andrew Laming (Turnbull's daughter Daisy is a teacher). The state and territory ministers remained suspiciously restrained, almost as if there had been an agreement between Canberra and the eight other jurisdictions to pursue discreet avenues of professional and political consultation before the April Education Council meeting.[17]

As the policy silence lengthened and the media began to carry stories that the Turnbull government was about to make major cuts to overfunded non-government schools, ISCA and the Catholic sector became increasingly anxious about what lay ahead. By March the terms 'considerable uncertainty', 'increasingly alarmed', 'hit list' and [to be] 'aggressively stripped' had entered media reports strongly suggesting that Birmingham was not contemplating any special backroom deals with the non-government schools who were, at this preliminary stage, clearly out of the planning loop.[18]

---

[17] If mentioned at all, the ministers Rob Stokes (New South Wales), Kate Jones (Queensland), James Merlino (Victoria), Susan Close (South Australia), Jeremy Rockcliff (Tasmania), Meegan Fitzharris (ACT) and Eva Dina Lawler (NT), were reported as going about their normal state or territory-based business.

[18] 'Private schools targeted', *Canberra Times*, 5 February 2017; 'Private schools "increasingly alarmed" over government funding plans', *Sydney Morning Herald*,

CHAPTER TWELVE

Inconveniently for ISCA's public relations status, a Fairfax Media analysis of school fees in major non-government schools showed that they had risen by as much 20 per cent over the previous four years. Some schools were even charging 2017 tuition fees that had pushed beyond the $35,000 per annum mark, a figure that comprised 43 per cent of the national average wage (of $79,721).[19]

In what was the by-now customary pre-Budget announcement to the formal 9 May Budget statement, the Coalition government revealed its hand. At a press conference on 1 May, Malcolm Turnbull, Simon Birmingham and David Gonski (a personal friend of Turnbull's) held a joint press conference in which Turnbull and Birmingham announced that under the Coalition's *Quality Schools* program there would be another education review led by Gonski, funding would remain needs-based, there would be no special deals, a number of non-government schools (twenty-four) would have their funding cut, a process of equalising funding arrangements across all sectors would take ten years and the Turnbull government would commit itself to an extra $30.6 billion for school funding by 2027 (totalling $242.2 billion) with an extra $2.2 billion to be provided during 2018–2021.[20]

General reaction in the media was supportive. Public opinion was supportive. Not unexpectedly, the ALP's reaction to their

---

11 February 2017'; 'School sector calls for urgent answers on funding model', *The Age*, 11 February 2017; 'Overfunded private schools next on "hit list"', *Courier Mail*, 25 March 2017, and 'Plea for private school funding', *The Australian*, 30 March 2017.

[19] 'Top private school fees soar to $35,000', *Sydney Morning Herald*, 17 January 2017. Figures based on comparison of $35,000 as a percentage of ABS 'Average Weekly Earnings', November 2016: Full-time adult average weekly ordinary time earnings of $1533.10, http://www.abs.gov.au/ausstats/abs@.nsf/mf/6302.0.

[20] See for example, 'Malcolm Turnbull announces new post-Gonski national school funding package', *Sydney Morning Herald*, 2 May 2017. All the major media outlets carried the story.

(needs-based) policy clothes being stolen was not supportive, calling the announcement an 'act of political bastardry' and accusing Turnbull and Birmingham of outlining funding figures that were $22 billion below ALP proposed funding over the same period.[21] Predictably the AEU attacked the Gonski 2.0. process (as non-consultative) and content (not containing enough money), arguing that what was, in effect, Gonski 1.0 should not be scrapped. At first, more politically mainstream Greens were open to Gonski 2.0 but pressure from the AEU, many of whose members were Greens, led to a Green backflip with internal Green opposition to Gonski led by controversial Greens Senator Lee Rhiannon.[22] The Catholic Church too was horrified but for different reasons. Many of those Catholic schools that had benefited from the successive windfall funding increases would now be adversely affected by the mooted Gonski 2.0 cuts and the 'no special deals' announcement. Coming from Turnbull and Birmingham, who were both Catholics, this seemed to mark the end of the Catholic political ascendancy, in education policy at least.[23]

In spite of Turnbull and Birmingham's confident performance during the Gonski 2.0 announcements, notwithstanding the moral support derived from Gonski's presence and despite a generally favourable 'about time' response in the media, implementation of the government's Gonski 2.0 model still faced a range of opponents.

---

[21] 'Turnbull co-opts Gonski, costs Labor', *Australian Financial Review*, 2 May 2017.

[22] See 'The Greens are Being Torn Apart Over a School Funding Fight: Senator Lee Rhiannon could be in a lot of trouble'. *Huffington Post*, 26 June 2017. Rhiannon was temporarily expelled from the Greens' party room and lost party support for first place on the New South Wales Senate ticket.

[23] 'Catholics to "bear brunt" of Gonski 2.0, says Archbishop Fisher', *Sydney Morning Herald*, 8 May 2017. A small and troubling (for Turnbull) Catholic group remained in the party room.

CHAPTER TWELVE

These included supporters of Catholic schools running a heated scare campaign, a troublesome Senate, the Greens alliance with the AEU, an Education Council displeased, among other matters, with Canberra's insistence that the states and territories must increase their share of school funding, a hostile News Corp opposed to any funding changes that might adversely affect non-government schools and which saw Gonski 2.0 as part of a 'Labor-lite' Budget, a furious Abbott-led pro-Catholic enclave within the Coalition party room, a watchful ISCA sector that would be unhappy about any concessions to the Catholic system and an ALP fuming that Turnbull and Birmingham had apparently stolen their clothes.[24]

Of all the hostile forces lined up against Gonski 2.0 it was the Catholics who needed serious attention. When it came to the Greens-AEU position, there was a chance that the government could negotiate a way around that Senate impasse by going to the independent crossbenchers, which is what eventually happened, after the usual posturing and bluffing. With the states and territories, the government's attitude was that they should just shut up and take the Gonski 2.0 money. As for Abbott and his allies, the former prime minister spoke out against the new policy proposal at a packed party meeting on 8 May 2017 but to no avail. Gonski 2.0, seen by many Coalition politicians and by political commentators as a cleverly pre-emptive anti-ALP measure by Turnbull, was a rejection of the Coalition's previous hard-line neo-conservative position and a pointed rebuff of the Abbott camp.

Gonski 2.0 still had three other major political hurdles to overcome. As it happened, News Corp's anti-Gonski media campaign

---

[24] See for example, 'Alan Moran: 'Labor lite' Budget undermining a nation's wealth', *Herald Sun*, 11 May 2017.

– 283 –

was vitiated by popular support for the new funding model media. The ALP's opposition was based on a lame campaign that attacked the government's alleged $17 billion cuts to the original Gonski funding model and compared the government's (bird-in-the hand) scheduled school funding increase of $18.6 billion with its promised (two-birds-in-the-bush) $40 billion increase over ten years. The Catholics, however, were a different story.

Anxiety among Catholics focused on the view that because of accumulated ERI and SES overfunding concessions, some Catholic schools would experience cuts and these would be followed by fee hikes. Under Gonski 2.0, there would be no Catholic-administered SES model disbursement. A vociferous Catholic campaign against Gonski 2.0 was temporarily embarrassed by a 4 May revelation that the NSW Catholic education system was shifting money away from needy rural schools to urban schools within the Sydney archdiocese, but the anti-Gonski 2.0 forces continued to press their case.[25]

Birmingham and Turnbull pushed back against the hyperbolic rhetoric of Gonski 2.0's Catholic critics, with the education minister accusing these critics of 'peddling falsehoods'. Fellow Catholic Christopher Pyne joined in, uncharacteristically declaring that Catholic opponents of Gonski 2.0 were being 'dishonest'. At the same time, *The Australian* and Tony Abbott were keen to point out that there would be adverse political fallout for the Liberal party if

---

[25] This information, leaked to the media, was based on a confidential report to the Catholic bishops of NSW, a report which came out of a review by former Gonski panellist and Liberal Party notable Kathryn Greiner. See 'Catholic school system shifting funds from rural schools, report finds', *Guardian Australia*, 4 May 2017. Not all Catholic educators were against Gonski 2.0. Sydney's Archbishop Anthony Fisher, possibly reacting to the revelations about urban needs taking precedent over rural needs, said it was time to end special deals in favour of 'fairness'. See 'Budget 2017: PM's Gonski move may be too clever', 6 May 2017.

CHAPTER TWELVE

Turnbull and Birmingham continued to pursue their allegedly quasi-socialist, anti-Menzies and anti-Howard education agenda against the Catholic system.[26] By late May, the government was facing the threat of a national Catholic anti-government publicity campaign at the same time as the states and territories had combined to oppose the government's Gonski 2.0 proposal. By now the Catholic pressure tactics were well-rehearsed and involved demonstrations outside MPs' and Senators' constituency offices, phone calls and emails to MPs and Senators' Canberra offices, local leafleting campaigns, parents' protest meetings (televised of course) and robocalls to constituents and parishioners.

There was little to be done about the states and territories but behind the scenes, Turnbull and Birmingham moved into negotiations with the National Catholic Education Commission (NCEC), whose principal negotiator was Christian Zahra, a former ALP Victorian MP. As late as 21 June, however, and just before the Gonski 2.0 measure was due to be sent to a Senate vote (before it went back to the House of Representatives for final ratification) the NCEC was still dissatisfied with the progress of the negotiations.[27] In the end, Turnbull and Birmingham successfully bargained with the crossbenchers in the Senate, including the Nick Xenophon Team, offering them their desired six-year (instead of ten-year) implementation timetable for needy schools, an (originally-promised

---

[26] Abbott tweeted, 'Knowing a little about politics I suspect that the government will decide that it's on a loser if it does anything that looks like it's disadvantaging Catholic schools'. 'Catholic school system shifting funds from rural schools, report finds', *Guardian Australia*, 4 May 2017. *The Australian*'s attitude was summed up in 'Poking the sleeping serpent will come back to bite you', *The Australian*, 4 May 2017.

[27] 'Minister's tweaks fail to address concerns of Catholic schools' Media Release, NCEC 21 June 2017.

in 2013) National Schools Resourcing Board (NSRB) and tighter control of state spending of Commonwealth funding. Concessions were also made to Liberal senator Chris Back who, like Jackie Lambie, wanted needy Catholic schools to remain where they were in funding terms until reviewed by the NSRB, and to Pauline Hanson, who wanted additional funding for disabled students.[28]

At 2 am on the morning of 23 July 2017, the amended bill successfully passed its Senate hurdle and the Gonski 2.0 model was set for partial implementation at least in 2018. Not everybody was happy. Catholic education authorities were still displeased with the amended version, leaving Coalition politicians apprehensive about an anti-Coalition response among Catholics carrying into a late-2018 election campaign. If the government gave in to the Catholics by year's end, the ISCA sector would demand the same kind of treatment, leaving the Coalition vulnerable to charges of special deals for wealthy fee-paying schools in that election year.

When the Gonski 2.0 dust settled, the AEU promised to continue with its anti-Gonski 2.0 campaign, as did the ALP, who scheduled it for their next series of election campaigns due to start in late 2018. The ALP's new policy emphasis was on the threat to social cohesion and the economy posed by inequality. The war, it seems, was not quite over yet.

---

[28] Hanson had caused a national scandal over her crass call for autistic students to be taken out of mainstream classrooms and educated separately. See 'Children with autism are 'holding our kids back': Senator Pauline Hanson', *Sydney Morning Herald*, 21 June 2017.

CONCLUSION

Originally, the Commonwealth school-funding proposal had been envisaged by its architect, prime minister Menzies, as a seeding project for all schools. His scheme would be limited in time, restricted in expenditure and would have a slight bias to the Protestant non-government sector. After Menzies retired in 1966, the Liberal-Country Party coalition developed a clear idea of its future funding priority for schools, which was to increase Commonwealth financial support for the non-government sector. After 1966, a succession of conservative education ministers arranged and rearranged the scope and nature of Commonwealth school funding to suit their political beliefs and ends. They did this by bringing Commonwealth school funding into a partisan political arena where they consciously used their time in office to establish an increased basis of political support for Coalition education policy among socially secure and socially aspirational parents, who could be very helpful when elections were called.

Time was on the Coalition's side. Between late 1963 and 2017, Liberal-led Coalition governments were in power in federal parliament for just over thirty years, compared with the ALP's twenty-one years in government, giving conservative politics a time-in-office advantage when it came to laying a sustained policy platform and achieving its political objectives for the non-government school sector. On that basis alone, the national Liberal Party has dominated school-funding policy in Australia over the past half century. Not only did the Coalition have an arithmetical edge in years in power, they also had three important strategic advantages.

First, once sectarian politics had been all but laid to rest in the 1960s, Coalition education policy was almost invariably backed by a predominantly conservative press that favoured the educational, political and social role of non-government schools. For example, during the 1960s and on to the mid-1980s, the *Sydney Morning Herald*'s editorial line had been consistently anti-ALP. After a brief change of editorial policy in 1984, the *Herald* reverted to an anti-ALP line during the Keating prime ministership. Meanwhile, from the mid-1970s onwards, the nationally-influential Murdoch press (rebadged in 2013 as News Corp) had developed an increasingly pro-Coalition relationship with successive conservative governments, almost to the point of political symbiosis.[1]

The Coalition's second strategic advantage lay in the duration of its post-war governments, which included three lengthy periods in office. These were the Menzies-McMahon period (1963–72), the Fraser era (1975–83) and the Howard years (1996–2007), compared with the ALP's single long-term Hawke-Keating government (1983–96), during which time only Kim Beazley Jnr was properly on top of school education policy, but whose tenure in office lasted just under two years (1991–93). In a Commonwealth education funding system that needed a long lead-in period and a long phase-out period, time in office meant time to undo what had gone before and time to arrange and establish what was needed for the future. Bearing in

---

[1] From c. 2001 onwards, the major Sydney-based News Corp newspapers *The Australian* and *The Telegraph* seemed to have an uncanny ability to divine the intentions of successive Coalition governments. They also act as willing outlets for Coalition ministerial comment and opinion.

CONCLUSION

mind that a minister of large departments usually needs two years to settle into office, Coalition education ministers John Gorton, Nigel Bowen, John Carrick, David Kemp and Brendan Nelson averaged 3 years 243 days each in the job during the period 1963–2006.[2] ALP minister Kim Beazley Snr managed to stay in office for a productive 2 years 327 days. The other long serving Labor ministers were Susan Ryan, who was in office for a less productive 4 years 135 days, and Peter Garrett, who stayed in the job for a fraught 2 years 290 days. Of the other Labor education ministers, they were either short-timers or, as with John Dawkins and Simon Crean, not especially focused on school education.

Indeed, here are three illustrative indicators of the Coalition's success in implementing policies that favoured non-government schools. By the time Prime Minister McMahon lost power to Whitlam in 1972, Commonwealth financial support through capital grants for non-government schools under education ministers Gorton and Fraser had risen steeply by 1258 per cent since the first year of Commonwealth funding in 1965. By the time the Fraser government lost power in 1983, maximum Commonwealth recurrent per capita financial support for non-government schools under Carrick, Fife and Baume had risen 201 per cent compared with the immediate post-Whitlam carryover figure into the early Fraser years. If we factor into the equation funding for both major school sectors, by the time the Howard government had lost power in 2007, Commonwealth financial support for non-government schools 1995–2007 had risen 137.4 per cent compared with a 68

---

[2] Including Fraser's two periods in office.

per cent rise in Commonwealth funding for government schools during the same period.³

The prime movers of this accretionary rise in Commonwealth funding for non-government schools were Liberal Party education ministers Gorton, Fraser, Carrick, Fife and Kemp, who each contributed in different ways to this process of educational aggrandisement. If we adopt a variation of the criteria applied to Christopher Pyne as a measure of success or failure in the education portfolio, of the five Coalition ministers Carrick was the most successful of them all. It was Carrick who developed a strategy of turning the Coalition towards the Catholic vote to reach a broader electoral constituency; it was Carrick who best turned that strategy to his party's advantage, first in New South Wales and later in Canberra; and it was Carrick who served his party's present and future schools constituency at a national level by laying the funding groundwork for steadily improving their financial position and enduring status. To make this happen, Carrick and his predecessors and successors, normally the initiators of Coalition education policy and normally the kinds of parents who sent their children to non-government schools, developed a divided and divisive approach to schooling.

The first element in the Coalition's thinking was that the Protestant non-government school sector, meritocratic and exclusive in nature, was culturally and politically aligned with the conservative worldview. As such, this element of the non-government sector deserved special

---

3   Comparisons based on tables in G. Burke and A. Spaull, 'Australian Schools: Participation and Funding 1901 to 2000', *ABS Yearbook 2001*, http://www.abs.gov.au/Ausstats/abs@.nsf/0/A75909A2108CECAACA2569DE002539FB?.

See also M. Harrington, 'Australian Government funding for schools explained', Social Policy Section, Department of Parliamentary Services, Parliament of Australia, p.18. For Kemp-Howard era see above Chapter Nine.

CONCLUSION

treatment when it came to funding. Catholic schools, too, eventually came into the same consideration because, while not initially aligned with conservative thinking, they were anyway a constitutional necessity as part of the Commonwealth's justification for its funding arrangement. Over time, as far as the federal Liberal Party was concerned, the Catholic sector would become more culturally and politically aligned with Liberal Party values. This was especially apparent between 1996–2017. Summing it up, funding both kinds of non-government schools became, as former prime minister Tony Abbott famously remarked, part of the Coalition's DNA.[4]

The second factor in the federal Coalition's approach to school funding was a negative view of the government schools, which had to be part of the Commonwealth's funding arrangements for constitutional reasons. Government schools were increasingly seen by Coalition politicians in Canberra as a necessary but unwelcome burden that should be more of a state concern than a Commonwealth issue. The Coalition view was that, by indirectly absorbing taxpayers' money from the states and territories and taking additional funding from Canberra, the government school system was double dipping, hence accusations by Abbott others that public education diverted money away from non-government schools.

Moreover, since the 1990s, a not-too-hidden Coalition position has been a tendency to be critical of comprehensive government schools and their teachers as underperforming repositories of radical political thought and action, encouraged in these subversive activities by state education departments staffed by leftists who favour uniformity and 'levelling-down'. These alleged characteristics, part of a prolonged

---

[4]   Cit., 'O'Farrell takes axe to education', *Sydney Morning Herald*, 12 September 2012.

and ongoing culture wars agenda since the 1980s at least, are claimed to be responsible for Australia's declining academic and even moral standards.[5] Former prime minister John Howard best summed up this view in a January 2004 interview when he (paradoxically) accused government schools of being values-neutral and yet imbued with union-influenced political correctness.[6]

The third strategic advantage the Coalition had over that forty-year period was not of its own making: it was more to do with the ALP's dithering and internal disagreements about school funding policy and its failure to find a coherent and popular strategy until the Rudd era. In effect, during the post-war period, the ALP took too long to arrive at a realistic and elector-friendly position on funding for all schools.

The ALP's modern chronicle of internal divisions over the school funding issue began with the 1951 national conference adoption of state aid, a decision which was subsequently thrown out during the 1955 split. The national executive then remained opposed to state aid throughout the 1960s. The ALP in New South Wales, on the other hand, decided to move toward direct state aid, a stand which brought it into public and a politically debilitating conflict with the rest of the party. To resolve these internal tensions at the national level, Whitlam stepped in and persuaded the national executive to

---

[5] Probably best exemplified by education minister Julie Bishop's intended comment in late 2006 to a history teacher's national conference in Fremantle that government school history curricula was taken 'straight from Chairman Mao', a remark that horrified her department when they first saw the text in a pre-conference press release. The 'Mao' reference was deleted from the actual speech. See, 'Gloves off in culture wars', *Herald Sun*, 28 October 2006.

[6] 'PM queries values of state schools', *The Age*, 20 January 2004. Howard's point was that union values and 'political correctness' (fair wages, gender equity, diversity and inclusion) were the wrong values.

CONCLUSION

adopt a state-aid policy in 1969, preparing the way for a Karmel-engineered attempt at funding fairness and inclusion in the 1970s, only for the ALP to cut back on funding to non-government schools and stack the Schools Commission. After Whitlam's demise, the funding arguments continued within the ALP, with perhaps the most public of these being Lionel Murphy's 1981 dissenting High Court judgement in the DOGS case. While it is true that the subsequent 1980s Hawke approach was consensus-based, his education minister Susan Ryan, among other combative actions, sponsored an ALP national conference vote in 1984 for the abolition of non-government schools altogether.

After a relatively peaceful state-aid period from 1985 to 1996, the ALP was supplanted by an educationally opportunistic Howard government in 1996, and ALP attempts to draw up a winning education policy during the first two Howard governments (1996–2004) failed.[7] Eight years later, after witnessing the socially disruptive effects of the Kemp SES strategy, ALP opposition leader Mark Latham's response was to use his predecessor Simon Crean's draft policy and place that preparatory work and other policy programs under the aspirational image of a 'Ladder of Opportunity'. Latham also drew up a funding reform program that contained what was described by a hostile media as a 'hit list' of non-government schools to be targeted for cuts. This supposedly election-damaging policy allegedly contributed to a Howard-led Coalition victory in 2004.[8] Then came Kevin Rudd's 2007 borrowed slogan: an 'Education Revolution'.

---

[7] Kim Beazley (Jnr) was ALP leader 1996–2001 and 2005–06. His education slogan in 2001 was 'Knowledge Nation', an information technology strategy.

[8] Latham's funding policy has gone down in ALP mythology as one of the reasons why the ALP failed to win that 2004 general election but as it happened, Latham's policy was quite popular with the voters. The ALP actually lost the election more

Influenced by a political myth surrounding the 2004 election result, Julia Gillard had to haggle with the states and the non-government sector during the 2013 Gonski negotiations instead of just pushing her way through the barrier of interest group politics. Finally, in 2017, faced with a Turnbull government's needs-based Gonski 2.0 policy, a strategy that included funding cuts for non-government schools, the ALP opposition decided to react by supporting parental choice and agreeing with Catholic sector cries of foul play, seemingly just another ALP pirouette in a long history of twists and turns.

All in all, and flying in the face of the national ALP's reputation as the champion of public education, Labor's position on state aid from 1963 through to 2007 has been erratic and ineffective.[9] Based initially on firmly-held ideological obsessions that were then followed by sporadic outbursts of class hostility, the national ALP has more recently tended to focus more on money and slogans than on the quality of education in government schools. This is mainly because any campaign regarding 'quality' has quite rightly been seen by the ALP and by the teacher unions as a Liberal Party political attempt to undermine public education and drive up non-government student numbers. Caught between ideology and pragmatism, when attempting to be ideological the ALP overreached badly in the 1970s, with the Schools Commission. When attempting to be pragmatic, as was the case during the Hawke and the Gillard governments, the ALP took a wrong turn by negotiating itself into the funding

---

on the ALP's early 1990s record on interest rates. See Murray Goot and Ian Watson, 'Explaining Howard's Success: Social Structure, Issue Agendas and Party Support, 1993–2004', *Australian Journal of Political Science*, Vol. 42, No. 2, June 2012, pp.253–276.

[9] There is a strong argument that until the 2010 general acceptance of the national curriculum, the real initiators of progressive educational change in Australia have been the states and territories, notably New South Wales, Victoria, the ACT and Queensland (after the Bjelke-Petersen era ended in 1987).

CONCLUSION

corner of the 'not a dollar less' promise. One key indicator of the national ALP's educational policy inadequacies (and the Coalition's proficiencies) since the 1970s has been a 1977–2014 drift away from government schools towards non-government sector. In 1977, 79 per cent of all students attended government schools. By 2014 that proportion had dropped to 65 per cent.[10]

After 2007 the ALP did at last instigate a version of Commonwealth quality control when it brought in My School and NAPLAN and founded the statutory (and apolitical) Australian Curriculum and Assessment Authority, which was to design and implement the national curriculum. All three of these initiatives were retained by the Abbott-Turnbull governments, despite hostility from neo-conservative think tanks and the reactionary wing of the Liberal Party. As for the first Gonski scheme, an almost universally popular Gillard initiative, it failed because of political circumstances that were beyond Gillard's control. Gonski did at least establish the idea of equitable needs-based funding in Australian popular, media and political consciousness.

One of the key reasons for the Gonski scheme's failure was the Catholic Church's ability to pressure prime minister Gillard into acceding to their demands for separate treatment. This was a far cry from the church's political position in 1963, when Cardinal Gilroy was only able to make tentative suggestions to the New South Wales government and Archbishop Mannix had alienated his tribal community from the possibility of receiving any form of

---

[10] 'Government schools enrolment on the rise', *Media Release*, Australian Bureau of Statistics, 2 February 2017. There has been a 0.3 per cent drift in the opposite direction since 2014, probably a consequence of rising school fees. http://www.abs.gov.au/ausstats/abs@.nsf/Latestproducts/4221.0Media%20Release102016?opendocument&ref=story.

direct government support. The Church's constituency comprised 5.4 million parishioners, or 25 per cent of Australia's population, just 2.3 million people less than the population of New South Wales, Australia's most populous state. From 2003 to 2014 the Church had its own forceful and well-connected monarch in Cardinal Pell, who was supported by princes among the bishopric who often had close, even cosy connections with their secular counterparts at the state government level. The Catholic organisational structure too, with its grant-funded but internally-managed school systems, its own hospitals, its own universities, its own charitable organisations, had within its grasp the ability to hold governments to ransom by urging its congregations to vote for the politicians who promised the Catholics a better deal. This was unique in Australian politics and gave the impression that a non-elected Church leadership under Pell was, in some circumstances, more politically powerful than any state, territory or Commonwealth jurisdiction. This comfortable arrangement (for the Catholic hierarchy at least) was to come to an end in 2017 when a Catholic prime minister, a Catholic education minister, non-Catholic non-government schools and the states and territories and the ISCA schools combined to insist that, when it came to school funding, it was time for Catholic exceptionalism to come to an end.

When it comes to the Liberal Party's anti-public education stance, its approach to education funding since 1966 has been consistent: increasingly unconcealed, increasingly politicised, increasingly ambitious and increasingly effective. On only one occasion did the Coalition falter in meeting its objectives and this was during the Abbott ministry. Blinded by personal and partisan hostility, Pyne and Abbott outmanoeuvred themselves in a fashion that aroused a deep

CONCLUSION

level of popular, media and political revulsion. This, in part, became a Gillard success. Her negotiating skills and pragmatic approach – and hamstrung by ferocious media and political aggression – actually got things done.[11] According to Fairfax media analysis, the Gillard government passed 329 bills in both houses during its first 700 days compared with the Abbott government's 262 bills.

By acting in an ideologically belligerent way, the Abbott minority government, unable to negotiate with the Senate, provided the reaction that laid the foundations for the Birmingham needs-based reforms of Gonski 2.0, reforms that were, in Turnbull's words, a breakthrough attempt to 'bring the school funding wars to an end'.[12] In the short term, Birmingham's politically-motivated policy decision seemed to work. Gonski 2.0 gained an 86 per cent approval rating in a May 2017 poll, but the major polls showed that while there was approval of Gonski 2.0, the ALP continued to lead a faltering Turnbull government by a steady six points.[13] And in a July speech, ALP leader Bill Shorten outlined his long term economic and social policies for election year 2018 as his 'defining mission'.[14] Progressive commentators such as *The Guardian*'s Greg Jericho took a positive approach: 'Bill Shorten's inequality pitch has rustled the jimmies of

---

[11] See, '"Policy paralysis": Tony Abbott's government the slowest for nearly five decades', *The Guardian*, 24 August 2015. Three weeks after its publication, Abbott was forced out of office by his own party.

[12] 'Schools funding: Malcolm Turnbull dubs new $19b education policy Gonski 2.0', *Sydney Morning Herald*, 3 May 2017.

[13] See for example, 'Coalition MPs at risk on current polling', *The Australian*, 27 June 2017. It was at this stage in the Turnbull government that worldwide political commentary about the end of neo-liberalism increased.

[14] See, '"Inequality kills hope": Bill Shorten sets out defining mission if he wins government', *Sydney Morning Herald*, 21 July 2017.

conservatives'.¹⁵ Conservative commentators such as the *Herald Sun*'s Rita Prahani took a different and apprehensive approach, 'Why Bill Shorten simply needs to shut up'.¹⁶

An ALP government's priorities under Shorten would be reducing inequality by focusing on hot button inequality issues in education, taxation, wages, workplace relations, health, gender identity, home ownership and the accommodation rental market. Having slammed Gonski 2.0 as unfair to government schools and having learned from the progressive independent Democrat Bernie Sanders' 2016 US presidential nomination campaign and witnessed the unexpected success of leftist Labour Party leader Jeremy Corbyn in the UK's 2017 snap general election, Shorten seemed prepared to harness voter dissatisfaction with machine politics. After nearly a quarter of a century of ALP centrism, Shorten planned to move away from the politics of pragmatism towards a progressive left social justice agenda in education that would deal with natural and distributive justice issues. Turnbull's May 2017 declaration that the school funding wars were over now seemed premature. War looked likely to re-erupt all over again in 2018.

Having said that, I shall leave almost the last word to Van Davy, the redoubtable former Teachers' Federation activist and a former

---

15   *The Guardian*, 24 July, 2017. 'Rustling a Jimmy' is contemporary slang for causing discomfort.

16   *Herald Sun*, 24 July 2017. The article was a prelude to a standard News Corp 'class wars' rebuttal of ALP policy. Between September 1986 and July 2017 major News Corp outlets used the term 1173 times. During that time, *The Australian* led the 'class wars' charge with 591 references. Unsurprisingly, peak use of the term by News Corp media came during the period 2007-13. See 'Shorten's class war rhetoric a dire portent of poll campaign', *West Australian*, 26 July 2017, and 'Class war, a cheap shot', *Herald Sun*, 22 July 2017.

CONCLUSION

Schools Commissioner, who is still politically involved in social justice campaigning:

> Funding of schools is consequential ... not a focus, not a priority, not a driver of my thinking as the funding battle leaves unaddressed, even obscures, the major issues confronting us ... [A] less adversarial and more trusting political context is seen to be fertile ground for the replacement of Australia's fractured schooling system with a cohesive schooling system for the Australian public – an Australian schooling system – to be managed nationally.[17]

What, if anything, is clear about school-state relations in Australia is that partisan political interference in school education tends to disadvantage one sector and lead to educational division, not the kind of socially cohesive schooling valued by Van Davy. We saw that when the Coalition favoured non-government schools during the 1960s and when it tried the same approach in the 1990s. What is also clear is that such a partisan action provokes a politically and socially contentious reaction, and we saw that during the Whitlam years. What we also know is that when a Commonwealth Government comes up with a funding solution that purports to be sector-blind but which then attracts hostility from vested interests on almost all sides, we are back where we started. We saw that with Gonski 2.0. What is really needed is a national consensus that there should be a base funding level for each student, that Commonwealth school funding will be distributed over time on a fair and equitable basis and that Coalition governments at state, territory and Commonwealth

---

[17] Correspondence with the author, 11 February 2016, combined with an excerpt from the abstract of Van Davy's University of Newcastle PhD. The full dissertation can be accessed at: http://nova.newcastle.edu.au/vital/access/manager/Repository/uon:3545.

levels see government schools as an investment to be valued, not as a liability to be endured. And that is the job of Gonski 2.0's National School Resource Board, which will, as has generally been the case with the Australian Curriculum and Reporting Authority, need to keep itself at arm's length from government interference. Then, perhaps, the war really will be over.

BIBLIOGRAPHY

Unpublished Manuscripts and Dissertations

Jones, K., Transcript of an interview with Ken Henderson, 7 August 1985, National Library of Australia, NLA ID 1648415/TRC/1858/2/57.
Kenway, J., High Status Private Schooling and the Processes of an Educational Hegemony, Ph.D. dissertation, Perth, WA, Murdoch University, 1987.
Davy, Van, Australian Schools: Social Purposes, Social Justice, Social Cohesion, Ph.D. dissertation, Newcastle, University of Newcastle, 2008.

Major Government Reports

Report of the Committee on Australian Universities (The Murray report), 1957, Canberra, Government Press, 1957.
Tertiary education in Australia: report of the Committee on the Future of Tertiary Education in Australia to the Australian Universities Commission, (The Martin Report), Canberra, Government Press, 1964–65.
Schools in Australia: Report, (The Karmel Report), Canberra AGPS, 1973.
Girls, school and society: report by a study group to the Schools Commission, Schools Commission, Woden, A.C.T., 1975.
Final Report/Royal Commission on Human Relationships, Canberra, AGPS 1977.
Quality of Education in Australia: report of the Review Committee, (Karmel Report), Canberra, AGPS, 1985.
Review of Funding for Schools, (Gonski Report), Canberra, Department of Education, Employment and Workplace Relations, 2011 (published 2012).

Books and Chapters

Ayres P., *Malcolm Fraser: A Biography*, Richmond, VIC, William Heinemann Australia, 1987.
Bean, C., 'The Coalition and the Electorate 1983–1993', in Costar, B. (editor.), *For Better or For Worse: The Federal Coalition*, Melbourne, VIC, Melbourne University Press, 1994, pp.79–114.
Beazley, K.E., *Father of the House: The Memoirs of Kim E. Beazley*, North Fremantle, WA, Fremantle Press, 2009.
Bongiorno, F., *The Eighties: The Decade that Transformed Australia*, Collingwood, VIC, Black Inc., 2015.
Campbell, C., and Proctor, H., *A History of Australian Schooling*, Sydney, NSW, Allen & Unwin, 2014.

Cannon, J., editor, *A Dictionary of British History*, Oxford, UK, Oxford University Press, 2009.
Carrick, J.L., *The Liberal Way of Progress*, Sydney, NSW, Liberal Party of Australia (N.S.W. Division), 1949.
Carrick, J.L., *The Liberal Way: An Outline of Liberal Philosophy*, Sydney, NSW, Liberal Party of Australia, (N.S.W. Division), 1957.
Catholic Education Office, *Celebrating 40 Years of Government Financial Assistance to Catholic Schools in Sydney 1968–2008*, Sydney, NSW, Catholic Education Office, 2010.
Chalmers, R., *Inside the Canberra Press Gallery: Life in the Wedding Cake of Old Parliament House*, Canberra, ACT, ANU Press, 2011.
Cox, C.B & Dyson, A.E. (eds), *The Black Papers on Education*, London, Davis Poynter, 1971.
Fife, W., *Wal Fife: A Country Liberal*, Wagga Wagga, NSW, Peribo, 2009.
Fitzgerald, R., and Holt, S., *Alan "The Red Fox" Reid: Pressman Par Excellence*, Sydney, NSW, New South, 2010.
Foster, R.F., *The Irish Story: Telling Tales and Making It Up in Ireland*, London, Penguin Press, 2002.
Frame, T., *The Life and Death of Harold Holt*, Crows Nest, NSW, Allen & Unwin, 2005.
Freudenberg, G., *A Certain Grandeur: Gough Whitlam in Politics*, Melbourne, VIC, Macmillan, 1977.
Furphy, S. (editor.), *The Seven Dwarfs and the Age of the Mandarins: Australian Government Administration in the Post-War Reconstruction Era*, Canberra, ACT, ANU Press, 2015.
Gilchrist, M., *Wit and Wisdom: Daniel Mannix*, North Melbourne, VIC, Freedom Publishing, 1982.
Gillard, J., *My Story*, North Sydney, NSW, Random House, 2014.
Hancock, I., *John Gorton: He Did It His Way*, Sydney, NSW, Hodder, 2002.
Hawke, B., *The Hawke Memoirs*, Port Melbourne, VIC, William Heinemann, 1994.
Hocking, J., *Gough Whitlam: His Time*, Carlton VIC, The Miegunyah Press, 2014 edition.
Hogan, M., *Australian Catholics: The Social Justice Tradition*, North Blackburn, VIC, Collins Dove, 1993.
Hogan M., editor, *Justice Now! Social Justice Statements of the Australian Catholic Bishops First Series: 1940–1966*, Sydney, NSW, Department of Government and Public Administration, University of Sydney, 1990.
Hogg, J.W., *Our Proper Concerns: A History of the Headmasters' Conference of the Independent Schools of Australia*, Parramatta, NSW, Macarthur Press, 1986.
Howard, J., *Lazarus Rising: A Personal and Political Autobiography*, Sydney, NSW, HarperCollins, 2010.
Johnson, R., 'To Wish and to Will: Reflections on Policy Formation and Implementation in Australian Distance Education', in Evans T., and Nation, D. (eds), *Opening Education: Policies and Practices from Open and Distance Education*, London, Routledge, 1996, pp.90–102.
Little, G., *Speaking for Myself*, Melbourne, VIC, McPhee Gribble, 1989.

BIBLIOGRAPHY

Lloyd, C., 'Edward Gough Whitlam', *Australian Prime Ministers*, Sydney, New Holland, 2013.
Macintyre, S., *Australia's Boldest Experiment: War and Reconstruction in the 1940s*, Sydney, NSW, New South, 2015.
Marginson, S., *Markets in Education*, St Leonards, NSW, Allen & Unwin, 1997.
Marr, D., *The Prince: Faith, Abuse and George Pell*, Quarterly Essay 51, Carlton, VIC, 2013.
McMorrow, J., *Reviewing the Evidence: Issues in Commonwealth Funding of Government and Non-government Schools in the Howard and Rudd Years*, Sydney, NSW, Australian Education Union, 2008.
Menzies, R.G., *The Measure of the Years*, London, Cassell, 1970.
Mitchell, C., *Making Headlines*, Carlton, VIC, Melbourne University Press, 2016.
O'Brien, G. W., *The Color of the Law: Race, Violence, and Justice in the Post-World War II South*, Chapel Hill, University of North Carolina Press, 1999.
Pyne, C., *A Letter to My Children*, Carlton, VIC, Melbourne University Press, 2015.
Robb, A., *Black Dog Daze: Public Life, Private Demons*, Carlton, VIC, Melbourne University Press, 2011.
Ryan, S., *Catching the Waves*, Pymble, NSW, HarperCollins, 1999.
Shelledy, R.B., 'The Catholic Tradition and the State: Natural, Necessary and Nettlesome', in Joireman, S.F. editor, *Church, State, and Citizen: Christian Approaches to Political Engagement*, Oxford, Oxford University Press, 2009, pp.15–34.
Starr, G., *Carrick: Principles, Politics and Policy*, Ballan, VIC, Connor Court Publishing, 2012.
Taylor, T., 'Under Siege from Right and Left: A Tale of the Australian History Wars', in Taylor, T., and Guyver, R., (eds), *History Wars in the Classroom: Global Perspectives*, Charlotte, NC, Information Age Publishing, 2012, pp.25–50.
Taylor, T., 'Scarcely an Immaculate Conception: New Professionalism Encounters Old Politics in the Formation of the Australian National History Curriculum', *International Journal of Historical Learning, Teaching and Research* (UK) 11, 2013.
Walsh, K., *The Stalking of Julia Gillard*, Sydney, NSW, Allen & Unwin, 2013.
Wilkinson, I.R., Caldwell, B.J., Selleck, R.J.W., Harris J., and Dettman, P., *A History of State Aid to Non-Government Schools in Australia*, Brighton, VIC, Educational Transformations Pty Ltd., 2006.

Newspapers and Periodicals

The Advertiser
The Age
The Australian
Australian Associated Press
Australian Financial Review
Bulletin
Canberra Times
Catholic Weekly

The Courier Mail
Daily Telegraph
Goulburn Post
Herald Sun
The Independent
The Monthly
Quadrant
The Saturday Paper
The Scotch Collegian
The Sunday Age
Sunday Herald Sun
Sun Herald
Sydney Morning Herald

Journals

Australasian Catholic Record
Australian Journal of Political Science
The Australian Journal of Public Administration
Curriculum Journal
International Journal of Historical Learning, Teaching and Research

Other Sources (Specific Details in Footnotes)

ABC Lateline
ABC News
ABC PM
ABC Sunday Profile
Anne Summers: speeches
Australian Biography Online
Australian Bureau of Statistics Yearbooks 1962–2015
Australian Council for Educational Research
Australian Dictionary of Biography
Crikey.com
Current Issues Brief: Parliament of Australia.
Election Speeches, Museum of Australian Democracy
Hansard
Ministerial Media Centres
Obituaries Australia, National Centre of Biography, Australian National University
Obituaries Australia, National Centre of Biography, Australian National University
Parliamentary Business: Bills
Parliamentary Business: Senate Committees
Parliamentary Library
PM Transcripts, Department of the Prime Minister and Cabinet
United Nations Educational Scientific and Cultural Organization: Legal Instruments
Whitlam Institute

INDEX

A

Abbott Coalition government xxiv, 253–4, 263–6, 297
Abbott, Tony
    on election promises 252
    loss of leadership 255, 266
    misogynistic attacks on Gillard 223
    and needs-based school funding policy ix
    opposition to Gonski 2.0 283
    as prime minister 255
    relationship with George Pell 195
    response to Gonski report 242
    on schools funding 205, 243, 251, 253, 296
Accelerated Christian Education group 153
Achievement Reporting and Innovation System (ARIS) 225, 225n13
Albanese, Anthony 235
Albury North High School 117–18
Allard, Tom 268
ALP see Australian Labor Party (ALP)
Amis, Kingsley 123
Anderson, Chris 126
Anthony, Doug 106–7, 108, 152n36
Arnott, Felix 138
Askin government (NSW) 37
Askin, Robert 'Bob' 21n36, 64
Association of Heads of Independent Girls' Schools (AHISGS) 51n13, 52, 75
Association of Heads of Independent Schools of Australia (AHISA) 51n13

Association of Independent Schools 178
Australian Commission on Advanced Education 79
Australian Council of State School Organisations (ACSSO) 140, 154, 167
Australian Curriculum, Assessment and Reporting Authority (ACARA) 262, 295, 300
Australian Education Act 250n2
Australian Education Bill 244, 247
Australian Education Commission 71n20
Australian Education Union (AEU) 201, 20122, 225, 226, 231, 265, 282, 283, 286
Australian International School, Ryde 103
Australian Labor Party (ALP)
    defence policy 14–15
    Federal Conference 1963 15
    school funding policy 292–5
    Schools Commission policy 54–5, 55, 100–1
    social justice perspective xxiii–xxiv
    split in 1955 xi–xii, 12
    state aid ban 9, 18, 69
    see also NSW Labor Party; Victorian Labor Party
Australian Labor Party (Anti-Communist) xi
Australian (newspaper) 288n1
    on ALP leadership conflict 236n35
    anti-Gonski campaign 231n24
    attack on government schools 127
    attacks on Gillard 228, 228n22
    on SES system 217

Australian Parents' Council (APC) 10, 105, 154, 166, 170, 171, 176–7, 178
Australian Schools Lobby 205
Australian Teachers' Federation 133, 140–1, 155, 166, 171
Australian Universities Commission 79, 87
Average Government School Recurrent Costs scheme (AGSRC) 183, 208–9

B

Back, Chris 286
Balaklava High School, South Australia 120
Baldwin, Peter 205
Balfour Act 1902 xiv–xv
Barber, Michael 220
Barnard, Lance 83, 89–90, 122
Barnett, Colin 246
Baume, Peter 153–4, 179
Bean, Clive 192, 194, 216
Beazley, Kim, Jnr 183, 219, 219n1, 222
Beazley, Kim, Snr
    at HMC conference 1973 96
    on Calwell 17
    as education minister 84, 89, 96, 97, 101–2, 118, 289
    on need for Schools Commission 99–100
    as shadow education minister 75, 81
Bedford, Eric 140
Bennett, David 100, 101, 101n38, 113, 141
Berejiklian, Gladys 277
Berg, Shirley 177
Better Schools program 250–2, 253, 263
Birmingham, Simon 268, 269–70, 274–5, 276, 277, 279–80, 284–5
Bishop, Bronwyn 172, 292n5

Bishops' Central Committee 52
Bjelke-Petersen, Joh 88n3, 144
Black Papers series (Cox & Dyson) 123
Blackburn, Jean 88, 101, 136
Blair, Tony 219, 220
Block, Cathy 136
Blunkett, David 220
Bolt, Andrew 254
Bolte, Henry 56, 63n4
Bonnor, Chris 279
Boston, Ken 230, 266, 278–9
Bourke, Richard 29n50
Bowen, Lionel 105
Bowen, Nigel 66–7, 74n24, 98–9, 289
Boyson, Rhodes 123
Brown, Joan 170
Brumby, John 222
Building the Education Revolution (BER) program 228
Burrow, Sharan 201
Button, John 147

C

Cairns, Jim 122
Caldwell, Brian 220
Calwell, Arthur xi
    on 1963 election loss 27
    death 42
    election speech 1963 22, 23–4
    leadership of ALP 15
    life after politics 42
    memoirs 81–2
    relationship with Mannix 16–17, 22
    relationship with Whitlam 81
    on scholarships 40–1
    on science grants 40
    standing among Catholics 17, 189
Canavan, Kelvin 191–2
Canberra College of Advanced Education 48
capital grants 56, 71, 76, 77
Cappo, David 189

INDEX

Carrick, John Leslie
  background and character
    103n30, 129–33
  dispute with Teachers' Federation
    140–2
  as education minister 20n34, 129,
    130, 134, 135–6, 144, 145, 146,
    147–9, 152n36, 289, 290
  as General Secretary of NSW
    Liberal Party 20–2, 57, 129
  on the Liberal Party 132
  as National Development and
    Energy minister 149
  relationship with Jones 130,
    134–5
  and Schools Commission 134,
    135–6, 139, 140–2
  as Senator 103
  support for state aid 20–2
Carroll, James 52, 149n29, 162, 173
Casey, Andrew 154
Catholic Church
  conservative turn 194
  'Melbourne Line' 4
  Rerum Novarum 4, 4n6
  social justice xxiv, 1–8
  'Sydney Line' 4, 9
  Veritatas Splendor 194
Catholic community
  Menzies' status 32
  rise in social and political status
    xxiv
  targeting by Liberal Party 193,
    195–6
Catholic Education Commission 52,
90
Catholic education system
  exceptionalism 296
  FC grants under SES system
    209–10
  financial difficulties xii, xxi, 33,
    36–7, 71, 72, 99, 190–2
  over-funding 272–3, 284
  response to Gonski 2.0 282,
    284–5

response to Karmel Report 93–4
  state commissions 90, 93–4
Catholic schools
  alliance with Protestant schools
    58–9
  buildings and facilities xvii, 8, 37
  Commonwealth funding xi, xv,
    77, 94, 120n21, 143, 154, 190n4,
    191
  De La Salle secondary schools
    100
  enrolments xvi, 8, 157
  fees 37
  Goulburn school closures xvii,
    xix, xx, 1–3, 7–8, 9–10, 11
  non-diocesan schools 8n12
  number of 156, 157n42, 183–4,
    217
  in outer-suburban and regional
    areas 165
  secondary school expansion xvi, 8
  staff xvi, 37
  state aid debate xxii–xxiii, 65–73
Catholic vote
  1993 election 188, 189–90, 197
  1996 election 197
  2004 election 216
  church attenders vs non-attenders
    188
  prior to 1993 192
  size of constituency 296
Celestine, Mother 1
Census Collection Data districts
  (CCD) 207, 211
Chalmers, Rob 19
Chamberlain, Francis Edward 'Joe'
  10, 17, 18, 69
Chartwell Society 195
Chipman, Lachlan 126
Christian fundamentalist schools 153,
  165, 180, 200
civil rights movement 7
Clarke, DB 170
'class wars' 298n16
Cobbold, Trevor 232, 271

– 307 –

Cole, George 19
Colleges of Advanced Education 48, 63, 79
Commonwealth Grants Commission 112
Commonwealth Scientific and Industrial Research Office (CSIRO) 13
Commonwealth secondary scholarships 24–5, 37–8, 40–2, 54–5, 57, 77
Commonwealth Teaching Service 79
comprehensive education 123
Connors, Lyndsay 170
Constitution
    Section 96 13, 98
    Section 116 xii, xx, xxi, 12
Cooley, Alan 110, 111
Corbyn, Jeremy 298
corporal punishment 260, 260n23
Costello, Ray 102, 141
Council for the Defence of Government Schools (DOGS) 74, 84, 115–16, 116–17
Court, Charles 144
Cox, Brian 123
Cox, Eva 137
Cramer, John 12
Crean, Simon 189, 219, 222, 289, 293
Credlin, Peta 255
Crisp, LF 126, 126n30
Csapo, Laszlo 193
Cullinane, John 1–2, 9, 10
curriculum
    culture wars 127, 198, 292n5
    moral panic over 123–7
    see also national curriculum
Curriculum Development Corporation (CDC) 164–5

D

Daniels, Bill 231, 239–40
Davy, Van 141, 170, 174n24, 298–9
Dawkins, John 151, 153, 159, 163n8, 182, 185, 289

De La Salle secondary schools 100
Democratic Labour Party (DLP) xii, xxn8, 9, 10, 18, 21, 27, 40, 57, 82
denominational schools, DOGs case against state aid 115–16, 152
Department of Education, Employment, Training and Youth Affairs (DEETYA) 207
Deveson, Anne 138
disadvantaged schools program 113, 139n15, 147
Dixon, JM 76
Donnelly, Kevin 217, 260, 261
Drewe, Robert 83–4
Dyson, Anthony 123

E

Edgar, Don 114, 114n11
Education Council 262, 274, 276, 283
Education Resource Index (ERI) funding system 176, 182, 206, 206–7, 270
Education (Scotland) Act 1872 xiii–xiv
educational standards
    'dumbing down' controversy 127
    moral panic over 124–7
elections: by-elections
    Bass 1975 122
    Bendigo 1969 68
    Corio 1967 57
    Dawson 1967 57
    Gwydir 1969 68
    Higgins 1968 58
elections: federal
    1961 xi
    1963 xi, 22–7
    1966 45
    1969 57, 57n24, 74
    1972 82–3
    1974 116
    1975 128
    1983 155–6
    1984 178–9

INDEX

1993 186, 189, 197
1996 196–7
2001 213
2004 215–16, 293–4n8
2007 198, 218
2010 235
2013 244
2016 274
England, school system xiv–xv
Enrolment Benchmark Adjustment (EBA) scheme 200
Evans, Chris 235
Evans, Gareth 167
Evatt, Elizabeth 138, 139
Expenditure Review Committee 121, 163

F

Fairbairn, David 74n24
Family Court, establishment 138, 139
Farish, Stephen 207
Faulkner, Vincent 170
Ferrari, Justine 217, 231n24
Fife, Wal 21, 149–53, 149n29, 165
Fightback! 186, 187, 189, 192
Fitchett, Ian 68
Fitzgerald, Ross 12
Fraser Coalition government
    education agenda 133–4, 150
    education funding 140, 143–4, 154
    fiscal restraint 143, 144
    'New Federalism' 135
    rating of Cabinet 152n36
    Schools Commission's criticism of 145, 146–7
    social reform agenda 139–40
Fraser, Malcolm 20n34
    as army minister 59, 60
    character and background 62–3, 79–80, 102
    as defence minister 59, 74
    as education minister (1968—69) 47, 59, 63–4, 65–7, 70–3

as education minister (1971—72) 75, 76–7, 78–81
ideological position 62, 102
as interim prime minister 128
as Liberal leader 119
as Opposition education spokesman 104–5
as Opposition primary industry spokesman 102
as prime minister 129
relationship with Gorton 57n25, 59n1, 74
and Schools Commission bill 102–5
social justice arguments 73, 78
on state aid 63–4, 65–6, 70–3, 78
Free, Ross 183
Freudenberg, Graham 16

G

Garrett, Peter 233–4, 236, 236n34, 240, 246, 289
Gavrielatos, Angelo 231, 240
Geelong Grammar 38
gender inequality in schools 136–9
Gillard, Julia
    background and career 221–2
    challenges to her leadership 236
    as deputy prime minister 222
    as education minister 218, 223–9
    loss of leadership 247
    media attacks 228, 228n22
    meeting with Catholic bishops 234–5
    misogynistic attacks 222–3
    misogyny speech 223
    My School initiative 224–7
    national curriculum 227, 234
    as prime minister 223, 233–5, 271, 297
Gillard Labor government
    achievements 297
    Australian Education Bill 244, 247

Cabinet reshuffle 236
National Education Reform Agreement 245–6
response to Gonski report 240–1, 243–4
school funding policy 235, 243
Gilroy, Norman 9, 11–12, 295
Girls, Schools and Society report 136–9
Gonski 2.0 ix, 282–6, 294, 297–8, 300
Gonski, David ix, 230, 232, 264–5, 281, 282
Gonski no-loss system 271
Gonski panel, review of school funding system 229–32, 235
Gonski report
    findings 237–8
    Gillard government response 240, 243–4
    Opposition response 241–2, 243
    recommendations 238–9
    stakeholders' initial response 239–40
    submission 235–42
Gonski scheme
    compromises made 247–8, 250–1
    negotiations with stakeholders over 244–6
Gorton Coalition government 57n24, 74
Gorton, John
    background and character 46–7
    as education minister 32–3, 34, 34n3, 47, 289
    as education and science minister 42–3, 45–6, 47–50, 52–3, 57, 58–9
    'Gorton style' 47, 74
    as Prime Minister 57–8, 57n25, 59, 68
    relationship with Fraser 57n25, 59n1, 74
Goss, Peter 279
Gotto, Ainslie 46n3, 58
Goulburn incident xvii, xix, xx, 1–3, 7–8, 9–10, 11
government schools
    Coalition attitude towards 203, 291
    Commonwealth funding xxii, 34, 92, 117, 200n19, 212
    conservative attacks on 127, 133–4, 203, 291–2
    devolutionary initiatives 267n38
    enrolments 157, 181n32, 295
    funding cuts 140, 144, 147–8, 154
    number of 156, 217
    and parental choice 146
    in post-war era xvii–xviii
    secondary scholarships 37
Greens ix, 282
Greiner, Kathryn 230, 284n25
Guilfoyle, Margaret 127–8, 128n32, 129, 152n36

H

Halfpenny, John 115
Hamer, Rupert 'Dick' 115
Hancock, Greg 101
Hancock, Ian 58
Hanson, Pauline 286, 286n28
Harden, TJ 120
Harradine, Brian 172
Hart, Denis 215
Hartley, Bill 115
Hastings, Peter 11
Hawke, Bob 156, 163, 174–5, 179, 180–1, 182, 185
Hawke Labor government
    factions in Cabinet 162–3, 162–3n7, 163n8
    higher education policy 164
    inherited budget deficit 162
    legislative guarantee for school funding 175–6
    New Schools Policy 179–80, 190, 195, 196, 200, 202
    school funding policy 156, 163–4, 173–7, 181

INDEX

Hawkins, John 95
Hayden, Bill 121, 148, 160, 162
Headmasters' Conference (HMC) of Independent Schools of Australia
    in 1960s and 70s 51
    advice from Gorton re Commonwealth funding 52–3
    alignment with Liberal Party 53–4, 75
    concerns over Karmel Committee 89–90
    Public Relations Committee 51–2, 53
    response to Karmel Report 94–6
    science education 52
    science fund 14
Healey, Colin 53–4, 95
Heffernan, Bill 222–3
Heffron, Robert 9, 18
Hewson, John 186, 187, 189
Hockey, Joe 255
Hogg, J Wilson 76, 89–90, 90n7
Holt Coalition government 7, 56–7
Holt, Harold 19–20, 45, 46–7, 56–8
'Holt Jolt' xi, 14
Holy Family School, Doveton 120
Howard Coalition government
    residualisation approach to school education 204–5
    school chaplaincy program 199
    school funding arrangements 200, 207–15, 216–17
    and school history curriculum 198, 227
Howard, John Winston
    criticisms of government schools 127, 181, 203, 292
    and curriculum culture wars 127, 198
    election campaign speech 1996 196–7
    on proliferation of non-government schools 202
    state aid advocacy 21
    as treasurer 143, 152n36

'Howard's battlers' 197–8
Howe, Brian 163, 189
Hughes, Barry 117–18
Hughes, Paul 170
Hughes, Victoria 170

I

Independent Public Schools (IPS) education program 267
Independent Schools Council of Australia (ISCA) 51n13, 231, 239–40, 250, 271–2, 275, 283
Index of Community Socio-educational Advantage (ICSEA) 224–5
Industrial Fund for the Advancement of Scientific Education in Schools 14
innovations program 110, 113–14, 117–18, 120–1, 147
Institute of Public Affairs (IPA) 195, 260, 260n22
interest group politics 193, 195–6, 197
Interim Committee for the Australian Schools Commission (Karmel Committee) 84, 87–9
Ireland, National School system xii–xiii, 29
Irish Catholics, persecution 2, 2n2
Islamic schools 152

J

Jensen, Peter 194–5, 215
Jericho, Greg 297
John Paul II 194
Johnson, Richard (Dick) 177, 179, 179n30
Jones, Alby 102
Jones, Ken
    career and influence 26n45, 32
    on Peter Baume 154
    relationship with Carrick 130, 134–5

relationship with Gorton 32–3, 58
sacking of 166–8, 169
on secondary scholarships 25
survey of non-government schools (1960) 71, 71n20
on Wal Fife 149–50
war service 130
the 'Junta' 10, 100

K

Karmel Committee (Interim Committee for the Australian Schools Commission) 84, 87–9
Karmel, Peter 84, 85, 87, 88, 89, 177, 178
Karmel Report
    Catholic response 93–4
    HMC response 95–6
    non-government schools' response 94–6
    political response 96–100
    recommendations 91–2
Keane, Bernard 263, 263n29, 267
Keating, Brian 2, 7–8, 9
Keating Labor government 183
Keating, Paul 162, 163, 186, 196
Kemp, David 186, 188
    background and career 199
    as Employment, Education, Training and Youth Affairs minister 199n18, 207, 208, 209, 214, 271
    as Opposition education spokesman 196
    as Schools, Vocational Education and Training minister 199–206
Kennedy, J.F. 26–7
Keogh, Francis 2
Kerr, John 128
Kirner, Joan 102, 115–16, 115n13, 140, 148
Kitney, Geoff 197
Klein, Joel 225, 225n13

Kogarah Marist Brothers High School 120–1
Kramer, Leonie 122, 123, 125–6, 125n28

L

Labor Party see Australian Labor Party (ALP)
Lamb, Barry 120, 121n22
Lambie, Jackie 286
Laming, Andrew 280
Latham, Mark 215, 216, 219, 235, 293
Lawler, Peter 58
Lawrence, Carmen 230–1
liberal education 49
Liberal Party
    attitude towards Catholics 188–9
    domination of school funding policy 287–92
    duration of Coalition governments 288–9
    sectarian divisions 20n34
    social justice rationales for school funding xxiii, 21, 50, 73, 205
libraries
    NSW ALP proposal for state aid 12
    in primary schools 8, 55n20
    secondary school funding scheme 47, 77
Library Association of Australia (LAA) 55n20
Liverpool Girls' High School 120

M

McAllister, Ian 216
McAuley, James 122–4, 124n25, 124n26, 126
McCarthy, Wendy 137
McGraw, Barry 114, 114n11, 227
McGregor, Craig 41

INDEX

McKinnon, Alison 137
McKinnon, Ken
    as chair of Schools Commission 101
    as de facto junior minister 134
    defence of change in educational practice 124–5
    on education funding 118
    gender inequality in schools study group 136
    on operations of Schools Commission 114–15
    on organisational problem 112
    on public service obstructionism 110–11
    recruitment of staff 101–2, 105
    relationship with Carrick 133
    sacking by Fife 151
    on three-tier funding category system 142
Macklin, Jenny 256
McMahon Coalition government 82
McMahon, William 'Billy' 48, 75, 80, 82, 255
McNamara, Tony 102
Mannix, Daniel 16–17, 16–17n25, 22–3, 295–6
Marriage, Alan 141
Martin, Francis Michael 88, 93
Martin, Jean 136
Martin Report 48
Matheson, Louis 113
Mathews, Race 100, 101n28
Menzies Coalition government 6–7
    Catholics in ministry 12
    direct state aid 24, 25, 27
    Education White Paper 11
    national science education policy 39
    secondary school scholarships 24–5, 37–8
    secondary school science grants 24, 33–7, 38–9
    university funding 11, 13
    US naval base at Exmouth 14–15

Menzies, Robert
    death 42
    election speech 1963 22, 23, 24
    preference for non-government schools 28
    retirement 42
    state-aid decision xix–xxi, 13–14, 19–22, 28, 31–2
    status among Catholics 32
Merlino, James 276n12
Minogue, Danny 17
Mitchell, Chris 217, 217n42, 228n21, 231n24
Morrison, Scott 274
Morrow, Ann 201–2
Morrow, Jim 212
Moyes, Peter 101
Muldoon, Thomas 31
Mulock, Ron 155, 172
Murdoch, Iris 123
Murdoch press 127, 177, 288
Murkin, DP 118
Murphy, Lionel 116, 152, 293
My School initiative 224–7, 295

N

NAPLAN (National Assessment Program — Literacy and Numeracy) 224, 295
National Board of Education, Employment and Training (NBEET) 182
National Catholic Education Commission (NCEC) 90, 250, 285
National Council of Independent Schools 76
national curriculum
    ACARA recommendations 262
    development 227
    Donnelly-Wiltshire review 259–61
    history curriculum 160, 198, 227
National Curriculum Board 227

National Disability Insurance Scheme (NDIS) 246–7
National Schools Resource Board (NSRB) 286, 300
'The Need to Succeed' 278
needs-based school funding 270
Nelson, Brendan 198, 210, 210n31, 214, 289
New Schools Policy 179–80, 190, 195, 196, 200, 202
New South Wales Board of Studies 124
New South Wales Teachers' Federation 67
Newman, Campbell 246
News Corp 283, 283–4, 288, 288n1, 298n16
non-government schools
    in 1950s and 60s xviii–xix
    Coalition policies favouring 289–92
    Coalition preference for 201, 204–6, 214
    enrolments 156–7
    favoured under SES funding system 208–9, 211–12
    fees 38, 81, 214, 281
    funding at expense of government schools 204
    funding by states 37, 55n19, 63n4, 200
    funding of new schools 153, 200, 202
    needs-based funding 176
    number of 156–7, 179, 183–4, 217
    over-funding 270, 271–2, 272n6, 275
    reaction to Karmel Report 94–6
    three-tier funding classification 142, 151, 151n32, 165–6
Northern Ireland, school system xiii
NSW Labor Party: Conference 1963
    state aid for science blocks and libraries 12
    student allowances 18–19

O

O'Brien, Eris 2, 10
O'Connor, Brendan 236, 236n34
O'Farrell, Barry 245–6
Office of Education 32
O'Reilly, Neil 152, 152n36
O'Sullivan, Neil 12, 19
Our Lady of Lourdes Catholic Primary School, Prahran 272
Our Lady of Mercy Preparatory School, Goulburn xvii, 1

P

parental choice 146, 146n22
Parfitt, Carolyn 147
Pell, George 194–5, 210, 215, 234, 234–5n32, 235, 296
Piccoli, Adrian 261, 269n1, 276n12, 277, 277n13
Plibersek, Tanya ix, 275–6
Prahani, Rita 298
Preston, Barbara 204
Prime Minister's Department, Education Division 32
Profumo scandal 16, 16n22
progressive education 123
Pusey, Michael 114, 114n11
Pyne, Christopher
    attacks on Gillard government 241–2n43
    character 257–8
    on Coalition school funding policy 251–2, 253
    as education minister 253, 255, 256, 257, 258–60, 261, 262–3, 265–7, 268, 296–7
    on Gonski 2.0 284
    higher education announcements 258–9
    as manager of opposition business in lower house 256, 267–8
    progressive politics 257
    response to Gonski report 241–2

INDEX

review of Gonski model 262–4
review of national curriculum 259–61
on SES funding model 232–3, 241
as shadow education spokesman 210n31, 232, 241–2, 251–2, 255–6, 256n13

Q

Quality of Education Review (Karmel) 178

R

Rae, Peter 104
Rainbow Public School, Randwick 118
recurrent grants 56, 56n22, 71, 76, 77, 94
Reece, Eric 88n3
Reid, Alan 5, 12, 15
Reid, Elizabeth 136
residualisation 204–5
Rhiannon, Lee 282
Robb, Andrew
    background 193
    Catholicism 194
    and interest group politics 193, 195–6, 197
    review of 1993 election campaign 187–90
    social and political philosophy 193–4
    targeting of Catholic community 193, 195–6
Robson, Leonard Charles 14, 50
Ross, Ken 207, 213, 217
Ross-Farish Index 211
Royal Commission on Human Relationships 138
Royce, Jon 102
Rudd, Kevin 217–18, 217n42, 219–20, 222, 229, 247, 250, 279
Rudd Labor government (2007–2010)
    Building the Education Revolution (BER) program 228
    Education Revolution 220–1
    election win 198
    Home Insulation Program 233, 233n28
    My School initiative 224–7
    Teach for Australia program 226
Rudd Labor government (2013)
    Better Schools program 250–2, 253
    funding of ACT Catholic schools 273
Ryan, Susan
    background and career 136, 159–61, 173
    conciliation meeting with Catholic bishops 173–4, 174n23
    as education and youth affairs minister 159, 161, 161–2, 164–7, 169–75, 178, 182, 184–6, 289
    factional alignment 163
    Murdoch press campaign against 177
    restructuring of Schools Commission 169–70
    sacking of Ken Jones 166–8, 169
    as Special Minister of State 182
    and state aid debate 170–4

S

St Brigid's School, Midland 120
Sanders, Bernie 298
Santamaria, B.A. 'Bob' 5, 6, 17n25, 19–20, 20n32, 105n32
Scales, Bill 230, 231
school chaplaincy program 199
school funding
    AGSRC needs-based system 183, 208–9
    capital grants 33–5, 56, 71, 76, 77, 117, 139n15, 144, 147
    class-based approach to 39–42

disadvantaged schools program 139n15
EBA scheme 200
ERI needs-based model 176, 182, 206–7
innovations program 117–18
needs-based school funding 270, 281–2
per capita funding 71–3, 85, 106–7
recurrent grants 56, 56n22, 71, 76, 77, 94, 139n15, 144
SES system 207–15, 216–18, 229
state: Commonwealth ratio xxii
symbolic political power xxvi
three-tier funding categories 142, 151, 151n32, 165–6
school funding wars ix
school league tables 226–7, 227n17
school retention rates 164, 170
Schooling Resource Standard 238, 239, 244, 245, 250, 272
Schools Commission
 abolition 182
 as advisory body 146
 attacks by conservatives 124–7
 autonomony 134, 140, 146
 branches 110
 calls for establishment 55, 64–5, 100–1
 criticism of Fraser government education policy 145
 disadvantaged schools program 113, 147
 dispute over curriculum 122–7
 educational priorities 121–2
 first annual report 121–2
 funding 121, 127, 139, 139n15, 140, 143, 144, 147, 148
 on gender inequality in schools 136
 Hawke government concerns over 166
 innovations program 110, 113–14, 117–18, 120–1, 147
 operational practice 114–15
 relationship with education department 134, 166
 relationship with Grants Commission 112
 restructure under Ryan 169–70
 review of role 145
 staff 101, 103, 105, 110, 141, 142, 142n18, 146
 State Planning and Finance Committees 112–13
 teacher centres 119–20
Schools Commission bill 102–7, 103
Schools Council 182, 202
science education
 in HMC schools 52
 secondary school Commonwealth grants 24, 33–7, 38–9, 77–8
scientific capability, concerns over 12–13
Scotch College, Melbourne 95, 95n15, 96n20
Scotland, school system xiii–xiv
Shorten, Bill 249, 249n1, 259, 265, 279, 297–8
Slattery, Margaret 176–7, 178
Smith, Stephen 218n43
Snedden, Bill 102, 106–7, 107, 116, 118, 119
social justice rationales for school funding
 ALP perspective xxiii
 Catholic position xxiv, 2–3
 Liberal Party versions xiii, 21, 50, 73, 205
socio-economic status (SES) funding system 207–15, 216–18, 229, 233
South East Asia, fears of instability in 26–7
South Vietnam, overthrow of government 26, 27
South Yarra Primary 272
Spurr, Barry 261
state aid debate xxii–xxiii
 in 1983—84 166, 170–4, 179

INDEX

DOGs case 115–16, 152, 293
    prior to 1969 election 65–73
state schools
    buildings and maintenance xviii
    enrolments xvii–xviii
    staff xvii
    states' funding of xxi
States Grants bill 1973 102, 103
States Grants bill 1996 205–6
States Grants (Science Laboratories) Act 1971 77n28
States Grants (Secondary School Libraries) Act 1968 77n28
Steel, Peter 120
Stoward, J 120
Summers, Anne 137
Sun Herald 107, 109n1, 150
Sydney Church of England Grammar School 14, 50, 76
Sydney Morning Herald 18–19, 64, 66, 70, 81, 89, 118, 124, 138, 147–8, 150, 172, 288

T

Tannock, Peter 101, 151–2, 170, 230
Teach for Australia program 226, 226n16
teacher training 48–9, 79
Technical Teachers Union of Victoria 141
Telegraph 288n1
Thiele, Bill 136
Thompson, Lindsey 95, 97
three-tier funding system 142, 151, 151n32, 165–6
Torsh, Daniela 136
Travers, Basil 'Jika' 75–6, 89, 94–5, 126
Turnbull Coalition government
    Gonski 2.0 ix, 282–6, 297–8
    needs-based school funding ix
    Quality Schools program 281
    school funding arrangements 273–4, 281

school funding policy 269–71, 274, 276, 280, 281–2
Turnbull, Malcolm 255, 266, 274, 280, 281, 297
Turner, Monica 172, 178

U

UN Convention against Discrimination in Education 6
Uren, Tom 132n4

V

Vanstone, Amanda 199, 199n18, 200, 207
Victorian Labor Party 69–70
Vietnam War 57, 59, 74

W

Wales, school system xiv–xv
Walsh, Max 107
Walsh, Peter 163, 163n8
Warhurst, John 216
Watson, Peter 215
Watt, Chris 240
West, Stewart 162
Westacott, Jennifer 240
Wetherell, Ern 9
Wheeler, Frederick 110, 111, 111n8
Whitlam, Gough
    address to HMC 89–90
    at ALP Federal Conference 1963 15
    on blocking behaviour of Opposition 106
    calls for education inquiry 40, 55
    on McMahon 75
    as Opposition leader 65, 66, 69–70, 74, 82
    on premiers' conferences 98
    as prime minister 83
    and Schools Commission 55

  on state aid 66, 67–8, 69–70,
   292–3
Whitlam Labor government
 achievements in 1973 107–8n37
 crises 119
 dismissal 128
 duumvirate 83–4
 education funding 117–18
 Expenditure Review Committee
  121
 loss of support 109, 109n1
 Overseas Loans Affair 122
Whitley, Alice 88
Widdup, David 136
Wilenski, Peter 166–7, 168–9, 177
Williams, Helen 169, 182
Williams, John 169, 174n24
Willis, Eric 21, 97
Wilson, Ronald 112
Wiltshire, Ken 260, 261
Women's Electoral Lobby (WEL)
 160
Wood, Desmond 101
Wyndham, Harold 8–9
Wyndham Scheme 8, 9

X

Xavier College, Kew 95
Xenophon, Nick 285

Y

Young, Mick 161
Young, Sally 255

Z

Zahra, Christian 285